STAMPEDE OF THE NATIVES

LINGUISTIC TRACKS UNVEILING THE LOSS OF THE MYSTICAL KUNDALINI

BARBARA M. REDZISZ

the Peppertree Press
Sarasota, Florida

For information regarding permission,
call 941-922-2662 or contact us at our website:
www.peppertreepublishing.com or write to:
the Peppertree Press, LLC.
Attention: Publisher
1269 First Street, Suite 7
Sarasota, Florida 34236

ISBN: 978-1-61493-152-2

Library of Congress Number: 2013903856

Printed in the U.S.A.

Printed September 2013

I would like to dedicate
STAMPEDE OF THE NATIVES to;
Ma Jaya Sati Bhagavati,
Werner Erhard of EST,
Hilda Charlton,
and
Professor Steedman
of Hunter College of New York City.

GANGA PRIYA ARRIVING AT THE KASHI ASHRAM

PREFACE

S TAMPEDE OF THE NATIVES is part memoir of a personal Kundalini experience and part historical research into the confusing if mystical, source of the often maligned and little understood Kundalini experience. It is a narrative that uses the actual source of prehistoric female centered human language to rediscover the suppressed mother based roots of what has been called mysticism.

It also deals with two massive historical developments that have fused at the present time to create the perfect storm of chaos. One deals with climate change, the other deals with the OVER EVOLUTION of the left hemisphere of the human brain.

The title of my book STAMPEDE OF THE NATIVES emerged out of my dual quest of how women have been so universally abused, exploited, treated as slaves and as second class citizens, and how the body of Mother Earth shares in the same destructive debasement.

The feminist movement of the fifties exposed some of our ancient mother based heritage out of female centrality. How was that mother based centrality lost? How has the singularly worshipped physical body of Mother Earth as the ultimate source of creation been forced to succumb to a similar fate?

At about the same time in the fifties, humanitys African origins were becoming accepted as a firm reality.

It became apparent that geologic catastrophes of drought, famine, volcanic eruptions, an ice age and floods, followed one after another across that stricken African continent. Except for a few bone fragments that still remain, there are a few artifacts that surface out of that prehistoric time.

When the recurrent catastrophes enveloped our ancient

ancestors they may not have had the time to carry off their belongings. Only their infants, tattoos and stories accompanied
them on their periodic dispersals.

It was to those ancient stories that they carried with them
that I had to turn. But how? Somehow I had to find the roots of
that ancient human language. How and from where it may have
emerged? Who gave birth to it?

I realized that it was in the actual prehistoric sounds of human
communication that I would find the answers to how female centrality and the singular worship of Mother Earth had been lost
and how we evolved into the planetary madness that exists today.
Most creatures use the extended vowel sounds to communicate.
Birds also use chirping and cooing sounds. Dolphins click their
way through life. The moan of whales echoes across the deep
oceans. Human beings evolved sounds that came to be associated
with consonants. The consonant sounds that existed at the beginning of human language are still with us. Most were made by the
organs on the mothers face. The mothers face was the same two
hundred thousand years ago as it is today.

To decipher the roots of language I somehow had to rediscover
those consonants that existed at the beginning of human communication. To that end the SOUND and SHAPE of the capital
letters of the Western Alphabet came to my aid. All the other
alphabets are in code. Only the capital letters of the Western
Alphabet are related to the SHAPES and SOUNDS that created
them out of the organs on the mothers face. I had to establish
rules how to classify and interpret their origins.

It also became apparent that most of the letters emerged not
only out of the specific individual mothers face but also out of
the body of Mother Earth. My book, THE SHAPE OF SOUND
expands on the story of that search.

Then I had to deal with the roots of the OVER EVOLUTION
of the left hemisphere of the human brain and how it fed into
the stampede into a stricken flight into oblivion. Along the way I
had to trace the unveiling of human madness, shift into fantasy,
female orgasm, establishment of habit through a filter of infantile

fear, male ignorance of their role in paternity, lack of paternal protection, rape, eunuch uncles, gangs of brothers, shift from left handedness of the mothers to the right handedness of the fathers, the larger shift from the worship of the physical body of Mother Earth to the male deification of the sun and then to the 'rational' hidden mind of the Father God in the sky.

The left hemisphere of the human brain working in a tunnel based singular focus is where male violence is stored. Human male sexuality is based on the eye of seeing. The eye driven images follow each other in a straight line, one after another. When fear strikes a human being, it becomes associated with the image. The image leads to imagination, then into fantasy and then into the definition of reality based on that fear driven fantasy.

The left hemisphere of the human brain does not deal with relationships, compassion and love. It deals with selfishness, repetitive behavior, detachment, secrecy, greed, individualism, competition, violence and war.

Along the way through the evolution of linear language and linear writing a shift occurred in the human being. The left hemisphere began its journey of primacy into the future, suppressing and obliterating the circular activity of the female right hemisphere of the brain. It is in the right hemisphere of the human brain that the female essence of compassion, cooperation, creativity, mother love and bonding resides.

The loss of female centrality and the worship of Mother Earth is based on the over evolution of the male essence locked in the left hemisphere of the human brain. To discover the clues to that ancient construct I use the examples out of my life, the Tantric chacras, the Kundalini energy symbolized by the snake, the evolution of the ubiquitous number seven, human violent prehistoric heritage, the shift of writing from the left hand to the right hand, male ignorance of paternity, rape, castration of first born son to act as the protective eunuch uncle.

I also discovered that the Kundalini experience is native to bipedal women who in the last stages of labor activate the birthing breath to push the large head of the baby out of their narrow hipped bodies. The birthing high paced breath working like a bellows fans the Kundalini energy lying coiled like a snake at the base of the spine. As it rises it fills the laboring mother with orgasmic ecstasy and a bonding with the new infant. It also brings with it a capacity for healing, prophecy, ruling and wisdom. It is what has been called as a religious or a mystical experience. As the high panting breath, it is also shared by long distance runners.

The trials of ancient mythological heroes were based on trying to experience the birthing breath of the ancient mothers. To that end they sped off on trials of discovery, of fear diffusion, of fighting everything in sight. To help defuse their panic, eunuch based shamans used trance, drugs and rituals. The death knell to the Kundalini experience during birth at the time of the shift into male centrality came with clitoridectomies used as a removal of the birthing ecstasy of the mothers and the power inherent in that experience. Religion has its physical basis in the mystical Kundalini. With the movement into the left hemisphere of the brain, religion became a rational expression searching for meaning in the closed ratio of the human mind.

FROM MA AFTER READING THE FOLLOWING TEXT

That is this high potent mine, the death' as mind of purity. It is that mind, Ganga Priya, that you work from, write from, go to publishers from. It is that mind that you are writing what is, not what others want you to do. Do you understand me? It's from something inside of you, you don't turn back, you don't look back, you don't look at pain behind you, you walk toward a light. Do what you have to do, let the flowers fall. Do you understand me? And you walk straight.

MA

TABLE OF
CONTENTS

AVIS

I sat up in bed, fully awake, trying to catch the tall end of a dream as it disappeared just past the point of its crystallization, into some obscure level of its origin, when through the darkness a phrase filtered itself back to me.

"Your name is Avis", it said, not exactly a voice, there was no physical texture to it, just a phrase hanging in space repeating itself without any sound, a phrase more experienced than heard, a shimmering in the darkness somewhere in front of me, just above my head.

"Your name is Avis." I repeated to myself turning on the light and writing the phrase in my notebook. Avis. My name is Avis? What does Avis mean? Looking it up, I found nothing in my dictionary that defined it exactly. The closest thing had to do with birds and maybe sheep. Rara Avis flashed before me, rare bird, perhaps that's what I am, a rare bird. Birds can see from great heights. Avis, one who sees, that's maybe what I am, one who sees. Or maybe it's because I make a greater effort, as they say in the Avis rental automobile commercials. 'Avis , we try harder'. Because the phrase had awakened me, I knew that it was probably important.

"Your name is Avis", well, it's also Barbara. In Catholic Poland where I was born, we were named after the saints closest to our birthdays. So all the girls born around December fourth were named after Saint Barbara and celebrated their name days together. My mother called me Basia, or Basienka. When she got angry she yelled out Baska. My sister usually spat out Basioryzda. My father when he wanted something, crooned Basiunia. Friends in American schools called me Babs, Barbie or Bobbie, I disliked the sound of all of them. My last name is Redzisz and there are so many variations on that theme that I used Regis to Americanize it.

Many of us immigrants followed that same tradition in the early fifties. Starting my showbiz career as a Copa girl with the Mickey Mouse name of Basha Regis, the owner of the Copacabana nightclub gleefully informed me that my name sounded like a stripper. At the age of eighteen with my dignity compromised I didn't much enjoy his demeaning comment.

Dorothy Hammerstein, my mother in law, and wife of Oscar Hammerstein II, called me Bawrsha (Boer-shah). One of the last times I remember hearing the strange sound pass her lips was when she stood at the foot of my hospital bed. After taking her linen duster and draping it across the hospital bed at my feet, she peeled off her long brown French leather gloves, finger by finger, saying;

"Bawrsha, we can't help you with your miscarriage. I spoke to our lawyers and Howard told me that if we were to pay your hospital bill it would implicate us in a commitment for your support. It's not the $200.00 for the hospital bill you see. That's not the issue. It's the fact that it would set a precedent and make us responsible for you. Jimmy (their son and my husband) must somehow raise the money and pay for the miscarriage. After all you are his wife. Ockie (Oscar Hammerstein II) did say to me that if you or Andy" (Oscar Hammerstein III), my son and her grandson, "ever needed a coat or something like that, you could let us know and we'd see what we could do. I'm sure you understand our position, dear." She added to soften the blow.

I lay there, already shaking from the six month miscarriage, free from the fetus that I carried as dead tissue for the last six weeks of the pregnancy. The blood pulsed out of me spreading like a warm and comforting pool under my body, accompanied only by silver tadpoles dancing behind my eyes as the darkness enveloped me. The day before, my husband, James Hammerstein, stood at the foot of that same hospital bed, and after I asked him to pay for the hospital bill and take me home, answered;

"I agreed to pay for the birth of a baby and not for a miscarriage." Then he turned on his sneakered heel and joined his buddies at the athletic club for a game of squash.

A transfusion was needed to replace the blood that poured out, leaving me in total peaceful darkness. Even the swimming tadpoles behind the bottomless chasm of darkness surrounding my eyes, became quite still.

In spite of all that had happened I used the name Hammerstein because it was more impressive and easier to spell than Redzisz. Then in time guru Baba Muktananda flicked me with a peacock feather across my forehead and named me Chan-dan (fragrant wood). What's in a name?

The original Barbara Maria Redzisz was very good to me. My luck seemed to change when I adopted Basha Regis and then completely ran out when I became Basia Hammerstein. Could it be that I changed my name? Or did the name change me?

I couldn't go back to sleep. The litany of names brought me back to my youth in Poland, the death of my mother, the nightmare of my marriage, the loss of my voice following the second miscarriage and the chaos that I experienced in my relationships with most men. I longed to get away from the reality that my life had become. It's not the way it was supposed to be, I told the silent darkness. How many times must I try and fail?

In my real life I am alone. My dreams, on the other hand, teem with people like the sub-continent of India. I live a parallel life there and return night after night, picking up images, revisiting people, reliving lives. I long for sleep to get away from being awake and alone. But now as I pondered over the new name of Avis that had been given me, even sleep was denied me.

I may be Avis, the one who sees but certainly not the one who speaks or sings. As an immigrant child I fought to be understood for all those wrenching early years. How did my despair as a transplant translate itself into the loss of my voice? What happened at the time of the miscarriage and divorce that left me so paralyzed that the effort to push through the paralysis left me hoarse and speechless. Why couldn't I be the only thing I have ever wanted to be, a singer? The last time I sang in public still fills me with helpless frustration.

I spent six months with a coach getting a program together,

paid hundreds of dollars for rehearsals, arrangements, copying of scores, and when I felt I was ready, I auditioned for a show-case in a restaurant called the Gypsy, in Hollywood. Usually I'd gotten hoarse after the audition, or after the performance. This time I'd gotten past the audition, even past the first show. During the second show, in the middle of a word, a tiny little light, not unlike a star burst, exploded on the left side in the back of my throat. I started to choke. One moment I was singing. The next moment nothing came out but a choking, raspy sound followed by a terrible itching. Tears filled my eyes and rolled down my cheeks. I tried to hold back the coughing. People looked up at me concerned, their faces reflecting the spotlight off me. I gasped out an apology, gulped down some water, and retreated off the stage.

The demon that sabotaged my singing didn't even wait till the next day. It put me out of commission right there on stage, in the middle of a note. I backed off into the dark, and into the despair of my voicelessness.

What is my name? What is Avis supposed to mean? Will it give me a clue as what I'm supposed to do with my life? What's more to the point, what is the part I'm supposed to play? If I knew my real name maybe I'd find out. All those other endless, repetitive dreams of not knowing where the theatre is, where the director is, or the stage manager, where my lines are, where do I stand, what do I say? Nobody told me what part to play and where to play it. There is never enough time to find out.

In a dream, I open a book and the script is unintelligible, or I don't have my glasses, or it is in some language I don't under-stand, or the dark letters seem to be swimming around on the white page, or they exist in some kind of obscure pictographs. In most dreams I am running looking for something that I lost. I think that I left it in my pocketbook somewhere in another house, in another theatre, in front of a cathedral, perhaps in an-other dream. At any moment the curtain is going up. I have to face the audience. The lights are upon me. I stand there in a panic immobilized by my inability to find the part I'm supposed to play. With my heart pounding and my palms sweating I wake up, write down the dream and keep looking for the answer. Why can't I simply be myself? Why do I have to play some kind of part?

I had tried everything; philosophy, anthropology, analysis, group therapy, est, sex, Actualizations, exorcism, Rolfing, hypnotism, Yoga, Sandstone, nutrition, psychodrama, regression. I even sat at the feet of the guru Baba Muktananda and watched him swat the keening, heavily breathing people, with his peacock feathers, and Krishna Murti the Indian mystic, under the oaks in Ojai, who kept telling his eager adepts "watch the way your mind works", that's all that you have to do "watch the way your mind works" and the Karmapa, the Dalai Lama of Tibet, with his orange robes and his bare muscular sunburned arms, tying an orange string around my neck, and Werner Erhart, brilliant impenetrable Werner. All of them offering something but giving no real answers.

The longing for some kind of an answer persisted and swelled in me and I carried it to the laps of my lovers, dropping it on them in the form of my passion. Most of them felt that passion was not a necessity in sex. No matter what I did, I felt like a displaced person.

Where do I go from here? Peering into the darkness of Los Angeles, the ribbons of late night traffic snaked up to the hills behind me, and down to Santa Monica and the sea in front of me. On my way back to bed I noticed that someone has stuffed a flyer under my door. Absentmindedly I opened it. The face of a beautiful black haired woman looked back at me. A female guru giving a retreat in Topanga, it informed me.

Why not a female guru? I tried all the disciplines men had to offer and none of them worked for me. I couldn't sing without sabotaging my voice. I really didn't want to act. Why not a female guru?

The woman's name was Joya Santanya. Her face stared back at me from the flyer with a slight look of defiance. Not as excruciatingly beautiful as Elizabeth Taylor but close, more of a Joan Collins look-alike. The smoldering dark eyes seemed vacant, with no allure to them. Her jaw appeared a bit slack. The black

hair and smooth dark skin might have established her origins as
Indian. She was giving a retreat at Topanga Canyon, and I decided I'd go.

I had an interview with a potential new agent that Friday
morning, so I'd have to be late for the weekend retreat, but I was
curious to go and see what the female guru had to say. With that
decision tucked away, I went back to bed and fell asleep.

EXPENDABLE

That Friday I dressed carefully, making myself up to appear as young as possible. After keeping me waiting in his ante-room which was filled with pictures of stars that he handled, the agent finally had me ushered in. There was no way to get a job in Hollywood without an agent. They held and still hold great power. It's not like New York City where you had been able to go to an open call for the stage, or a cattle call for a commercial. In Los Angeles, agents were the bottom part of the funnel that you had to pop up through to get to auditions and readings. He seemed furtive after he saw me, impatient that I was wasting his time, pacing back and forth across the room, never alighting too long on anything.

"Hammerstein huh", he glanced at the smiling picture and resume I handed him along with my hopes. "You related to Oscar?" The inevitable question.

"Only through my son, Oscar was my father-in-law."

"You knew him?" He looked incredulously at me.

"Yes, as well as it's possible to know a father-in-law, I mean, I was married to his son, James Hammerstein when Oscar was still alive. I'm divorced now." For some reason I wanted to clarify my position.

"What kind of man was he?"

"Talented, productive, I would say a man's man." What else can one say when one knows too much.

"Great guy wasn't he? Boy he and Rogers wrote some great shows! Why are you looking for work? You must have gotten away with some, ah…a lot of loot."

"No I didn't, I'm looking for work." The rage was lifting in me, preceded by the pounding of my heart.

"Why couldn't he help you while he was still alive and you were still young?" I flinched as he scrutinized me. Although assured by well meaning friends that I still looked young, my five decades betrayed me.

"He didn't work that way, at least not within the family." And it's none of your fucking business, I wanted to add.

"What'sa matter, you got no talent? Ha ha." I flushed as I sat there with my heart pounding and laid out my credits. While I relayed my credits to him, I impaled myself on the spokes of time.

"I've worked on Broadway. I've done stock. I did leads in dinner theatres all around the country. I did the Milliken Show for four consecutive seasons. I even did Maria in 'Sound of Music' three years ago at the Adobe Horseshow Dinner Theatre in El Paso." He looked at me quizzically. I realized that I looked a bit past nineteen which was supposed to be Maria's age in "Sound of Music".

"I used lifts," and to show him, I pulled the skin of my face up by the hair in front my ears. "I'm sure you know what lifts are, those little pieces of clear adhesive that you glue in front of your ears and attach rubber bands to them. They go over the top of your head, to give you an instant face lift. Barbara Cook taught me how to use them when I was in 'Music Man.'"

"They must have worked magic." He wedged himself past me so that our bodies touched. "What part did you play in 'Music Man?" He stood back and surveyed me, as I squirmed. Was the casting couch next?

In the past I had lied that I had understudied Barbara Cook, but all I did in the show was to play one of the Pick-a-little Ladies. Who cared, why bother to keep lying. The images flashed back. I also lost a baby in the sixth month of pregnancy, it died in me. I walked around with a dead fetus until I was disoriented and almost died, I wanted to add.

"Chorus, ha!" He wasn't much impressed. "You got any film on you?"

"No, just live theatre."

"That don't matter here. I need film on you." I knew that he would ask me for a film clip. Clips were very expensive, but I was hoping that my credits from the "Great White Way" would impress him. They didn't.

"Don't you handle people for the theatre at all?"

"L.A. is not a theatre town, lady. This is the capitol of the movie industry you know. Anyway, I have some women your type... your general age." He looked me over. "And you'd be in conflict with them, you know what I mean, you know how women are. I can't even keep them in jobs. There's not much call for women your age. I mean, even old <u>stars</u> can't get jobs. Do you have some kind of gimmick?"

"Like what?"

"Like, you know, Tiny Tim with his banjo and Frank Zappa with his pile of..."

"No", interrupted him, "I have no gimmick." I tried again. "I can act and I can sing." My last singing effort at the Gypsy flooded me with frustration and despair. He doesn't have to know that I lost my voice. If I get the job I'll use Cortizone, like I did in the El Paso Dinner Theatre to get through the 'Sound of Music."

The phone rang. He answered it and proceeded to have a long whispered conversation into the mouthpiece, giving me the benefit of his back. Hammerstein name or not, he figured that I wasn't important enough, not to be rude to.

I picked up my resume, backed up by my smiling youthful picture, and left the office. By the time I got back to my car I felt as if some part of me had shrunk. Its shrinking left a lump in my throat that no amount of swallowing could dislodge.

It was a beautiful day in May with the sun sparkling over the ocean in the distance, filtering through the ochre smog of L.A, leaving the hills soft and violet behind me. The air cleared somewhat as I drove north along the Pacific Highway and then up into the hills along the Canyon named Topanga, where the artists and hippies still lived and where retreats were held.

How I loved California, with the hills surrounding Los Angeles cupping it on the edge of the ocean, with Venice and its smelly canals and the ducks paddling around, upending in the murky waters, with the health food restaurants, fresh fruits and vegetables overflowing in crowded markets, they were all there. But even California didn't seem to be enough.

What do I do with a life that's left over? My son was off to college, I had rented my house in Rockland County, New York and here I was again, trying to figure out what to do with myself. I had become a middle aged single woman, expendable.

Carefully navigating the close turns of the canyon and trying to maintain the speed limit, I had gotten a ticket there once before for going too slow. Only in California could that have happened. Checking the directions on the flyer, near the Northern end of the canyon, high up in the hills, I made a sharp left turn and the car crunched its way down a gravel filled driveway into a grove of massive towering oak trees.

THE RETREAT

Somewhere behind the buzzing insects and chirping birds I heard the magic sound of Hindu chanting. Following the music to a series of stone buildings which sat up against the side of the hill, I spotted an entrance where a pile of shoes carpeted the ground. As Joey Faye from 'Top Banana', my first Broadway show, would have said, "Dis must be da place." I dropped my fee into a bowl at the entrance and quietly crept through the haze of incense to a spot on a narrow ledge that ran around the room and perched myself up against the back wall.

In front of me stretched a long room crammed wall to wall with people sitting cross-legged on the floor. In front of the room on a raised platform sat the beautiful woman whose face I had recognized from the flyer. Wedged up against her, on the floor at her feet, sat a group of musicians who swayed and with their eyes closed, lead the chanting. Most of the other members of the congregation were silent. There were no places left to sit on the floor. Chairs were provided for older members and those who couldn't sit in the lotus position. They were all taken. I backed up against a narrow perch against the wall and made myself as comfortable and as unobtrusive as I could.

The presence up on the platform was a very imposing woman with thick long black hair which fell forward covering the sides of her face. Her deep color came from a sun tan, not from the sub-continent of Asia. Indian skin color has more taupe and less gold to it. I knew from the flyer that she was thirty-seven, twelve years younger than I. She looked some indeterminate age, sitting ensconced on her purple pillows, glistening as she moved her arms. Dozens of gold bracelets jangled, as did the chains around her neck. As she slowly moved her head a row of diamonds glistened in each ear. On the stone wall behind her hung many pictures of Hindu saints, and one picture of Jesus. He looked rather lonely.

Flowers were everywhere as were her closest followers who clung like mussels to every possible outcropping around her. All were in deep meditation, stiff in their lotus positions with their eyes closed, except for the musicians who lead the chanting. A dark haired young man sang a song about a woman who 'was weaving a basket of gold'.

As I breathed the incense, scenes of our church in Poland mingled with the music. The memory of Christ hanging, bleeding on the cross and the ducks paddling in the shallow stream inder the bridge and the Jews in their long black hassocks scurrying between their houses in the distance and... I was sharply brought back as I noticed that the chanting had stopped.

Suddenly through thick dry lips, with her eyes closed, the guru on the platform, Joya Santanya, with a strong and pronounced nasal Brooklynese accent took us through a meditation. As she started to speak a buzzing started to hum in my body. A kind of heady feeling of pleasure enveloped me. I settled in, as she began.

"I will now give you, yourself...

Next few days you will experience yourself...

What you do... what you receive... is totally up to you.

You can waste it... but you can never lose it.

You may forget it...You will be reminded by life itself...

We begin each morning...

By giving up that which we don't need to Kali...

The black mother who sucks out impurities...

If you do not know Kali, or are not familiar with her...

Just give up what you don't need to Mary, to Christ, to Vishnu, to Brahma, to anyone...

But give it up...

She will not take from you what you do not give up freely...

Close your eyes, feel your own being...

Feel the breath coming in and out...

Feel the Shakti pouring through...

Learn to listen to your own mind...

And see what it's willing to give up..."

The sound of a sitar broke through the air and a male voice started a hypnotic Hindu chant. Another male voice joined the first baritone and then a low female alto wove her way through them. More singers gathered up the chant and sent it floating gently above us, stretching outward like banks of low lying clouds spreading out from the center.

"Straighten up..." A change in tone, an order from Joya Santanya, the guru.

Repeated over and over, by the blend of female and male singers, the chant spun its way through the room and through my body. The guru continued,

"You will be given a breath, an exercise to open up your chakras and indeed they will open. There are many in this room

Ma Jaya Sati Bhagavati

who have touched the feet of the guru, though many of you do not understand what that means."

She gazed straight ahead, her eyes apparently focused on some inner middle distance inside her head.

You'll be introduced, some of you for the first time to Hanuman... The God of humility...

For no matter what you do, there is no way you can make it to liberation unless you have humility, Hanuman will guide you...

Once you find the value of humility you will find out that you were born perfect...

That you have already been liberated...

So, it is only a matter of a moment of acute awareness to acknowledge your perfection...

You have the right, the birth right to find happiness...

This life, complete happiness...

You have no right to your sorrow... it is not yours...

You are only loaned this body... this body that will decay...

Your soul is your own, and even that belongs to God." She flicked her arms forward and the gold bracelets jangled.

"You are alone upon this earth...

Don't let anyone kid you. Don't care how much money you have...

How many friends you have...

How close you are to your family, how many kids you have your husband, your wife...

You are alone, completely, utterly alone, you and your Maker. Once you acknowledge your Maker, through the guru, through the teacher...

Then you will find you are your own guru, your own teacher...

You will connect like you've never connected before and that means happiness...

Happiness that comes from fulfillment in this life...

Keep your eyes closed. To touch the face of the formless is the essence of this whole teaching...

If there are any problems concerning Shakti, too bad...Just breathe in and out of your heart..."

She opened her eyes and looked around.

"I usually get up and get out now, as fast as I can, especially when it's lunch time, but there is a woman who walked in here, a woman who wanted something desperately."

I sat there up against the wall on my small ledge in the back of the room and at first meditated then listened with utter disbelief, at this apparition up in the front, this female guru, called Joya Santanya who had a highly pitched Brooklynese accent and who was going to take us to God. All I really wanted was to sing without losing my voice and maybe get some help with my aching hip. Some of what she said I had heard before at est, at Baba Muktananda's, with Krishna Murti, even in church. The part about going to God through the teacher sounded too Catholic for me with the priest as mediator. I listened and barely understood some of the other things she said. What was Shakti? I vaguely remembered Kali, the Hindu Goddess with blood dripping from her fingers, wearing a necklace of skulls around her neck with her foot planted on the neck of an apparently unhappy small male person.

All of a sudden I realized that the lecture part was over. She was focusing on the people around her. I was the only person who had entered late. My heart started to pound. Her eyes swept around the room and fixed themselves on me.

"What is your name? Get up!" An undisputed order.

A second before all that I saw before me were the backs of many hairy heads. Now, faces were looking at me, faces with eyes, eyes that wondered why their Ma was asking me to stand up. I didn't want her or them to know who I was, so I came up with the name Baba Muktananda had given me the summer before at his ashram in the Catskills.

"Chan Dan" I mumbled, as I stumbled to my feet.

"Why are you here?" I didn't have time to answer. "Who named you?"

"Baba Muktananda."

At that she nodded,

"I have been in close contact with him in the last few weeks and the children of his ashram. Come." She held out her hands to me. I plowed through the sea of knees to get to her.

"You are filled with Shakti, but it's blocked. Do you have a guru?"

"No." I shook my head.

"Yes you do, his name is Nim Charoli Baba." She pointed to one of the pictures on the wall behind her of an older man, draped in a loin cloth, smiling a toothless smile, reclining on a plaid blanket. "He is Ram Das' guru and mine. Do you know Ram Das?" I had heard of Ram Das when I was on staff with est.

"Yes."

"Nim Charoli Baba is your guru, you are bursting with Shakti, with a well of Shakti, a well of love. It must come out. You are what they call here a MA. Are you married?"

"No."

"Good, your name is Ganga Priya. My girls, gather around her and sing to her."

She flicked her hand at them, her bracelets jangled. The diamond earrings sparkled as young women in Indian dresses scurried around making room for me to sit on the floor in front of her. A space was cleared where only packed bodies existed before. I climbed over some more knees and watched with utter disbelief as about half a dozen women began to chant, clap their hands and dance around me. After she gave the order, her arms fell heavily at her sides. Two tall, young blond men in white tunics rushed from both sides of her and as they grabbed her arms she seemed to swagger back and forth and to reawaken.

Gently as if tiptoeing across a still glass surface of a lake, one of the musicians began to chant,

"Hey MA, Hey MA, Hey MA Durga
Hey MA, Hey MA, Hey MA Durga."

As I had gotten closer to her, plowing through the bodies on the floor, tears started rolling down my face, tears over which I had no control. A strange heady sensation of intense pleasure spread itself through my body. It felt like being stoned. The buzzing grew louder in my ears. The soft palate in my mouth seemed to rise upward, pushing up inside, against the inner bridge of my nose. The closer I got to her the greater was the feeling of sadness, of pleasure, and of being stoned. I thought, it must be the incense that is doing this to me. She leaned over and threw me a necklace of wooden beads.

"Here's a mala for you. Sing to her my virgins, sing to her. For she is a MA, I want all of you to become MA's. All of my girls will become MA's and all my men will become BABA's. You will go out into the world and share the love that is God. You are the God, remember that. Open your hearts and experience yourself."

I couldn't believe what was happening to me, women were clapping and singing, like the Hari-Krishna's at the airports, except this group was doing it around me, in a very cramped space. A beautiful female guru who had a Brooklynese accent just told me that I was a MA, gave me another name; Ganga Priya, and said that I was not only a MA, but a teacher. I was becoming more and more stoned. Tears were pouring down my face and my neck itched from where they were drying. The string of brads, similar to a rosary, rested in my lap where she had thrown them.

As Joya finished her last statement, through the incense, the chanting and the jumping bodies, I could see that her eyes rolled up into her head, only the whites showed. She seemed to stiffen and tilt back. The two tall young blond men raised her by her elbows and half walked and half carried her out of the room. As the door closed behind them I heard one turn to the other and with a German accent inquire through his blond beard.

"Did you skveez her oranchjoos?" I never got the answer for the door banged shut behind them.

As if on cue, the dancing stopped, the singing stopped, and people pushed toward the exits. Few remained sitting on the floor stiff in their lotus positions. Like a jilted bride left alone on the church steps, I remained in the center of the room abandoned by all. Filing past me, some of the people surveyed me with vague curiosity. I joined them outside for a lunch of fruit and yogurt. As I ate my yogurt under the oaks of Topanga Canyon, the stoned feeling, the sadness and the rush of pleasure left me. I became myself again, more or less, the same person who arrived a few hours earlier.

She called me a MA. What does that mean? Anyway what do I

do with it? What an immensely powerful presence, what does she know? Obviously, something more than I do. I looked around. All these people came to see her, along with all those others who are with her all the time. I looked down at my hands. They were no longer tingling like they had been inside. Strange sensation, not exactly like being stoned, more intense, but something like it. Was it the incense? I bought some of it to try at home.

That night, back in my apartment in Hollywood, I burned some of the incense that I had gotten at the retreat. Although I liked the smell of it, I didn't get high at all. I also looked up the word Shakti in one of my books and it said that Shakti was the name of the female principle of the Godhead in Hindi. The Hindu Pantheon was based on a male trinity 'Shades of Catholicism'. Each male aspect of that trinity had a female principle from which it derived its power. That female principle is called Shakti. The Shekinah of the Hebrew Caballah as the female aspect of the Godhead flashed through my mind. It is also the name of the power, or the force that moves through all of life and through human beings. I didn't know what they were talking about but I liked the fact that the female principle was part and parcel of the male aspect. I found that interesting and comforting because the female principle has been left out completely in the Christian trinity. You might say it was the Holy Ghost but since the Holy Ghost as often as not was called a He, then women as participants in deity didn't exist in Christianity.

Saturday came and went with little incident except that I couldn't find a chair to sit on. The ledge against the back wall was taken, so I had to sit on the floor. I ached my way through meditations. My knees were killing me and my left hip was throbbing.

When I was pregnant with my son many years before I had thrown my hip out of joint and it bothered me from time to time. Now, sitting in the yoga position on the floor, the old pulling ache kept returning. My back ached and my legs fell asleep. I began to understand why yoga evolved as a stretching exercise. With all that sitting, the body fell asleep through lack of circulation, not necessarily through complete relaxation. My left leg seemed to be locked in an upright position at the hip and no amount of pushing could get it down. I felt like a trussed supermarket chicken as I sat there with my body screaming in pain.

Sunday morning I decided, the hell with it, I was going to be comfortable. I had tried being authentic without props. The pain interfered with my concentration. I brought with me four pillows and got to the retreat early. Finding a place in one of the corners up against the back wall, I sat on one pillow, put another behind my back and propped up each knee with the other two. For the first time since the retreat began, I was not in constant agony.

The place setting up the retreat was like backstage at the theatre before a show. People argued about who was responsible for what, had anything been left out. Unplugged cables and microphones lay scattered around the floor. Boxes of flyers, flowers and incense were emptied and distributed. The musicians were already in place. After the room filled up with the other participants, Joya slid in and ensconced herself on her purple pillows. She folded her legs easily into the double lotus and without further ado, gave us an order.

"I want you to sit still and not move.
Aha, close your eyes,
No one in this world can do it for you...
You're alone, damn it, <u>you're alone with your breath</u>...
You have no husbands, no wives, no children...
You're dying to have yourself...
Nothing exists except the force of the true I...
Keep your eyes closed, you do not open them for anything...
There's nothing to see outside yourself...
There's nothing to bear witness to, outside yourself...
At the base of the spine she rests, the most disastrous,
The most complete force of the universe, Kundalini
Behind the third eye, the place called awareness,
which you, as a human being rule...
No one can rule your awareness, no guru, no teacher...
No one outside yourself has control of your awareness.
They can play with it. They can tamper with it.
But they cannot control it...

Keep your back very straight, for you are above the beasts,
You are above the animals.
You were given the opportunity to walk with a straight spine.
To sit with a straight back...
Now bring your awareness to the base of the spine...
If your mind keeps wandering away, bring
it to the base of the spine anyway...
No movement now for you are Yogis...all that means is union...
Yogi means union of mind, body and soul...
At the base of the spine she begins to rise,
slowly with force...the Mother... God...
She rises to the second chakra, the sexual organ...
Now concentrate more upon her virtues...
She pierces the tightness of your being...
As She touches the fear of your lust
As She Tantrically opens you,
just concentrate on the second chakra...
Now, the third chakra the solar plexus, with the navel,
the great feeling of power, so many of us cannot handle...
Concentrate your awareness, She begins to rise to the heart...
Bring full awareness to that chakra...which holds your world
welcoming the Shakti in your heart...the Christ center...
She touches your heart...
You are ready for Her when you desire the fullness of life...
She rises to your throat, creativity...communication...
To the third eye, between the eyebrows... inner vision...
Bring your awareness there, receive the Mother...
To the top of the head, Siva-Shakti...the dance of the heart...
She is gentle, for you are gentle...
She is complete, because you yearn for completeness...
She dances with her Lord,
in a thousand petal lotus on top of your head...
She reigns over your being and you are Her subject...
She takes you into yourself...Deeper, go deeper...
Let yourself return from where that comes,
No movement...stillness, peace, oneness, silence....

Formless… Beyond all form…The vastness, beyond the vast
No guru, no teacher, no nothing……..Formless…
Gently let Her take you and have no fear…..
Become light and firm, become nothing…..
Lighter, keep Her, keep Her…let go….
Be yourself, in a quiet way…touching a quiet God….
Begin to bring your awareness to your heart…
Begin to breathe slowly, gently, in and out of the heart…
Touching the true I, the I, that has no ego….
Gently begin to fill upon yourself…
Feel the Mother inside of your heart
and know this peace is yours."

She stopped. Into the awesome silence broken only by the
buzzing of insects outside of the window, a male voice accompanied by a sitar began to gently chant, as she continued.

"Breathe into your Heart." She led us. Female voices and
cymbals joined softly in the swelling sound.

"Go deeper." She directed through the chanting.

Nim Charoli Baba

AMBUSHED BY DEITY

May 22, 1977

In the past while meditating and telling myself to go deeper, I felt a small drop and sometimes experienced a fuller relaxation. Now after hearing the command from Joya to 'go deeper', I felt as if I had stepped into an elevator and plunged from the top of the Empire State Building down to the center of the Earth. I catapulted deep into myself and felt as if the wind that whistled past my body was leaving my aches and pains behind. As she gave directions to breathe deeply into the heart, with the haunting music behind her, I felt as if I were being pulled gently back, as if some unseen force, a magnet, drew me straight up and back, forcing me to sit very tall. I found myself as stiff as a ram-rod, and then my breathing started to accelerate becoming faster and faster, louder and louder. The hair on my body, on my arms and my legs, stood up and my clothes moved imperceptibly as I became completely still and waves of goose pimples swept over me. The sensation started somewhere in back of my knees, moved up and around in waves around my body, around my spine. They came closer and closer together, until my body became a pulsation. Then all of a sudden an explosion of heat, light and ecstasy, again in expanding, ever widening circles, occurred somewhere near the base of my spine and rose like a volcanic eruption of great pleasure up through my body. I began to rock back and forth. A roaring filled my ears. Heat and ecstasy rose and cascaded upward, intermingling with light that seemed to spark on and off inside my head, reflecting fragments of multi-colored crystals. I had the momentary image from some great height of watching an atomic bomb explosion, a pushing up from the center and then rising, gathering heat, light, and with a great roaring sound exploding in its own center somewhere below me.

Then at a point, I realized that my breathing accelerating louder and faster was breathing me! I had no control over it. The waves of goose pimples were coming in an expanding spiral. As the ecstasy poured through me I felt as if I were sitting in the center of a great flaming pyre. I could almost see the flames going straight above me, and wondered if it was visible to others. Over the roaring that filled my ears I could hear the frantic pace of my own breath and felt no desire to stop it. Some part of me was like a bystander, a witness to the ecstasy that racked my body. My palate arched up high inside of my mouth. Popping noises filled my nasal cavity and lights splintered in my head behind my eyes, as a roaring filled my ears.

Through all this churning and the eruption of pleasure that was using my body as a vehicle, I heard Joya's voice above the music yell out as if to me.

"Rise above the breath, rise above the breath." With great effort and with only the image of her voice to guide me, I rose above the breath. The heat and light that pulsed in my brain subsided. Only the goose pimples continued to erupt across my body. Then a spasm wrenched me forward, and I was sobbing uncontrollably. Except I wasn't sobbing. It was sobbing me. There was a part of me that stood aside and watched another part of me that I had been aware of before, but only in my dreams.

Somewhere in all of that activity, the something in me became aware that I had stopped breathing. I had not taken a breath since the last sob. The group was still chanting. Many verses later, a long space of time barely felt through the fog of my ecstasy, I took my first breath, more out fear than of need. When my breathing returned I became aware that splinters of light still pulsed in my brain. Along with the rapture, a throbbing ache was spreading at the base of my spine. As I opened my eyes, I also realized that I was drenched, my body was wet and my blouse clung to me. Looking up I realized that Joya was staring at me.

"Are there any questions?" She looked straight at me. I was speechless. Blissed out, I was later to learn.

"Ganga Priya stand up." That was me, my new name, she was

ordering me to stand.

I sat there in my soft pillows fumbling to make a move. The others around me pushed me up into a standing position. I reeled as I held on to their shoulders.

"Tell them what happened to you Ganga Priya."

Mixed emotions careened inside of me. One side of me felt a great desire to remain anonymous with my new found joy, cradle it in my arms. Another part of me was jumping up and down like a demented child, screaming, I did it! I did it! I touched it! I touched something fantastic!

I looked around me. The outside world was the same. Backs of heads were turning to look at me revealing inquisitive eyes. The room was the same. The sun shone outside. Musicians were strumming their guitars. My body subsiding and gathering strength was becoming a bit more settled and limp. Inside of me a great upheaval had taken place.

"Tell them." Joya's voice coaxed me.

I didn't know what to say, how to explain it. If I said too much, would it go away and never come back? I looked around again feeling that something was expected of me.

"Teach them, teach them, Ganga Priya."

"I…I, just had this experience that I can't describe," I stumbled through the words, my tongue heavy, my mouth dry.

"You don't have to describe it, everyone look at her, look at her face. You are looking at someone who has just been raped by God."

I swayed and reached out for the shoulders around me to steady myself. Raped by God? So much for under statements. Should I tell them that it seemed to me that my skin had exploded, not that God touched me. My skin attached me to the universe. The ecstasy of the universe became mine. It sounded silly, flippant, nothing 'spiritual' about it, so I went into a story about it, not of it. Raped by God? How about a reattachment to something greater than myself? How about a reattachment to the universe?

"I just had this unbelievable experience. I knew that something was out there. I sensed it through the joy that rose in me when I listened to music, sang Italian arias and when I fell in love. I've been looking for a key to where its source was, to open the door to that source. I've had many dreams where there were many doors that I wanted to open. I either had the wrong set of keys or the door led to another door. When I finally got through, a large obstruction got in the way. Something always got in the way. I think that today I opened the door, the door that wouldn't open for me before." I continued, blown by ecstasy.

"When I was very small and went to sleep I had dreams of sparkling diamonds and rubies and mounds of precious glistening jewels. I tucked them into my clothes, stuffing my pockets, trying to bring them back into my waking state. The awesome sense of loss I felt when I woke up and found that all those precious stones had been left behind in some other world, where dreams are made. For the first time in my life I feel as if I brought the precious stones back with me." I looked over to Joya and she nodded, as if she understood what I was saying. When I told the dream to my mostly male analysts in the past they judiciously explained to me that I was looking for orgasmic sex. I doubted it, so I plunged on, trying to find some more pertinent answers.

"In 1975 I took the est training and it opened up a lot of dreams that I had stopped dreaming. One was that I was climbing a mountain and I was looking for a river, then I realized I was sitting on a rock with the river running under it. I've been trying to roll that rock away for many years. When Krishna Murti was in L.A., I went to Ojai to hear him. He spoke of watching the mind. I was dealing with my emotions, emotions that would not be stilled. I couldn't get past them to look at the working of my mind.

Then I spent some time with Baba Muktananda at his ashram in the Catskills. He touched my forehead with his thumb and swatted me with a peacock feather, gave me a name, but nothing happened.

I liked the chanting and the food, so I went back and bought a bus from him, which he used as an office and in which I trundled 3,000 pounds of furniture back across the country to Hollywood. It was a white school bus, 31 feet long. After I got back to Hollywood I put an AD in the Movement newspaper to sell it.

BABA MUKTANANDA

SIDDA YOGA DHAM ASHRAM IN THE CATSKILLS

Ralph Graber read the AD and he told me that he had a dream that he bought Baba's bus and was the bus white? I said "yes", and we had a deal. It was that man who gave me the original information about the retreat. It was he who stuffed a flyer under my door. It all seemed to dove-tail in a strange way, and here I am." I stopped and looked around, that was it. I didn't have any more to say. Joya came in and saved me.

"This is your last life, Ganga Priya, your last life if you want to make it so. That is your choice. Don't take me for a fool. I know everything about you. You don't know who you are, but I do".

This was my last life? I wouldn't have to come back again? That was the best news I had in a long time. How to get through this life was the immediate problem. The feeling of "What's the use, I had done it all before" might be explained by this new piece of information. Maybe this last trip was patience, and acceptance for me. How do you do that? Whatever it was, I was willing to give it a try. Here was a woman that I could follow, and she demanded celibacy. I wouldn't have to make any more excuses not to have passionless sex. With her I got a glimpse that women could have some kind of experience on a 'spiritual level' without 'directing their semen upwards or retaining it.' When I asked questions about my lack of semen to direct upwards, the male gurus told me to do the best I could and not think so much. The implication remained that because women didn't have semen to ferry upwards we were somehow 'spiritually' inferior.

I had an overwhelming feeling that for the first time in my life I was on the right track. There must be somewhere that this energy, this current, this river, this Shakti, or Holy Ghost had not been deflected, suppressed, ignored, but flowed on through as female energy and nurtured women along with men.

Near the end of her last sentence Joya's speech again became slurred. Her jaw slackened. Her back stiffened. As if on cue the chanting was picked up by the musicians. The two tall blond Germans, half guided, half carried her out of the room. Just before the door closed behind her she looked back at me and, with her eyes rolling in and out of focus, dumped into my lap:

"You will run a house for me. Ganga Priya, take care of my children."

I sat down again. The chanting continued. This time the people were not eager to leave. The retreat was over, yet no one seemed to want to go home. When Joya left the room, the feeling of being stoned subsided. I sat there shaken, but myself again. What happened to me? <u>Raped by God?</u> What was all that heavy breathing and then not breathing for all that time. What was the ecstasy that encased my body in a flood of goose pimples, the heat, the lights flashing in my head, and now, the throbbing ache at the base of my spine? Could this have been a 'religious' experience? I don't even believe all that. What happened to me? It was in my body, not any place else. It was as if my skin touched the ecstasy of the universe and filled me with passion. The ecstasy of St. Theresa? The Passion of St. Thomas? Was that what it was all about? Women were burned at the stake to keep this from being experienced? Questions tumbled through my newly awakened brain. One of the women who had been at Joyas side came and sat next to me.

"How do you feel? Are you all right?"

"What happened to me?" I was grateful that someone spoke to me. "I feel like a limp rag."

"My name is Ishwari, and the Mother rose in you, you had a Kundalini experience."

"What's the Kundalini?"

"She has chosen you because she sees that you are a MA."

"What are you talking about, chosen me for what? What is the Kundalini?"

"You've been called."

"Wait a minute, I heard no voices." I knew that I was being flippant and smart-assed. "What's the Kundalini?" I insisted.

"It's female energy. It's the Mother and it rose in you as God."

"You mean that God is really a woman, the Mother?" It started to make brilliant sense to me, at least chauvinistically. "But my body felt as if it was on fire, and these waves of goose pimples washed over me. I know that I stopped breathing for a few minutes. Is that what God is all about?"

"MA saw that you were ready and she caused your energy to move."

"So God is an energy, not the Mother?"

"God is the Mother who expresses Herself in us, through the movement of the energy. You think too much. Leave your head alone. I can't explain it. Just accept the fact that MA saw that you were ready and caused the Mother to rise in you."

"But what for?" I insisted.

She looked at me as if I were crazy. "To be at one with God. Isn't that what you want?"

"I'm not quite sure that I know what you're talking about. I came here because I'm at the end of my rope with my life. I thought that a female guru might give me some clues, show me something that none of the male gurus have been able to. You know, how to get through my life."

"Would you accept it if she did?"

"Touché!"

"She has given you the gift of yourself, all you have to do is accept it."

"But all I wanted is a direction and some purpose to my life. I don't even know that I believe in God."

"What do you think happened to you?"

"I don't know what happened to me, that's what I'm asking you."

"God moved in you." She was getting impatient at my obtuseness.

"You're kidding, all that heat, light and pleasure? That was God moving in me? I thought that God lived up in the sky." I smiled and gave her a knowing look.

"God moved in you, as you." She knew the litany.

"What do I do with it?"

"Nothing, from now on you will be guided."

"Come on. Who's going to guide me? Did this happen to you too?"

"Yes, but not in the same way. It's all different with everyone, and it's all the same. MA got me off drugs with her love, her energy. You'll find out."

"Listen. Speaking of drugs, I have this sensation of being stoned when I'm around her. What's that?"

"It's her love, her Shakti. You're blessed enough to resonate with her Shakti. She is a saint, she is with God all the time. When you are open enough you can feel it. It comes alive in you."

"I don't experience love. I have this feeling as if I were on a trip, you know, high. I feel stoned when she's in the room. Who's gonna guide me anyway?"

"The you, that is the divine you. The you that came to MA in search of God."

"I was hoping to find someone who could help me with my voice and to heal my hip, and maybe find some purpose to my life, that's all I wanted."

"There are no accidents. You were led here to experience the God in yourself. Don't think so much, you don't know how blessed you are." I couldn't let go of it.

"The experience happened in my body, not any place else. I heard no voices, had no visions, none of the trappings that I associated with the church of my youth. All I experienced was this awesome outpouring of pleasure."

"What do you think that God is about?"

"Pleasure? You'd better explain that to the Calvinists. All I experienced was heat, light, goose pimples and my breath stopped." As I spoke about it the movement stirred in me again and the heat spread upward.

"You must have faith."

"Shades of Roman-Catholicism. In what?"

"In MA. She recognized something in you. Now it's up to you. You can ask questions, or you can accept it and get off the wheel in this life. You've been around long enough."

"That's how I feel. I've been around long enough. You mean I can stop spinning if I believe that Joya is God?"

"Something like that. She is the guru and she can lead you to yourself. That's where God is, that is why you must have faith in her."

"How about if I accept her as a teacher or a guide? But God?

Come on. It's all well and good for you to believe, but I find faith hard to come by. I still want to understand what happened to me in there. The base of my spine is still throbbing. Whether God raped me or not is a moot question, but it certainly was a physical experience. What does the spirit have to do with it?"

"I'm not talking about the spirit. But you can't have the spirit without the body, it needs a vehicle, a temple. Your body is the vehicle through which you as yourself, or your God rises. God is only you awakened. There is nothing outside, it is all within. You are now the awakened God within, you have been called. All you need is faith and patience."

"I'm short on both. I've been an agnostic, maybe even an atheist for most of my life."

"Just believe in MA. You will realize that religion came out of the kind of experience you had. What you have been given is an opportunity to experience the content before it became form and dogma. What you had in there and what will grow more and more in you is what used to be called a religious experience."

"But it's in my <u>body</u>." I insisted. "I feel shaky, is it dangerous?" The implications were starting to dawn on me.

"It can be."

"How?"

"Some are not ready. But you were chosen by MA and she knows. You don't know how lucky you are. People meditate for years, fast, isolate themselves in the desert, dance themselves into trance, take drugs, to go through what you just did. Leave it alone. If you go home and read up on it, your mind will go bananas and you'll try to understand. You can't understand it, get it? There is no way for your mind to understand it. The energy is called Shakti. We have the name for it from the Hindus. It can also be activated under other physical circumstances like great grief and despair. There is a symbol for it, a snake, because, as it rises, it uncoils like a snake up your spine. As it rises it purifies you, burns out the accumulated garbage. It brings with it bliss and ultimately Samadhi."

Another new word, Samadhi. But, during the experience I remember the spiral of light swirling around me, like a snake unwinding. It was getting a bit too much for me.

"How did it happen to her? I read in the flyer that she had been married and had some kids, that she comes from Brooklyn and that her background is Jewish. So, what happened to her?"

"She studied Hatha-Yoga to lose weight. They showed her one of the breathing exercises and she went into a trance, into Samadhi. When she realized what happened to her, she got into a tub of water and did one of the breathing exercises for sixteen hours until she had a vision of Christ."

"You're kidding, she saw Christ?" The tub of water and the breathing exercises went by the boards as the news hit me.

"He even spoke to her. He came four times." Ishwari nodded her head sagely.

"What did He say?"

"When the time is right you will know." The carrot on a stick, I thought.

"How did it happen to you, Is wary?"

"Ishwari." She corrected me. "It was more gradual. I saw a white light floating in the corner of the room one night and when I touched it, it was cool and almost solid, like a cool solid brick. I knew enough that it was a sign and that I had to get on the spiritual path. It was difficult for me for I lived in Berkeley and was strung out on drugs most of the time. That's okay with me now, but the celibacy, you know, no fucking, isn't easy. It's only MA's love that keeps me pure."

"Well, then it's not sexual frustration that causes this."

"Who knows? Not in me now anyway."

"What do I do now? Will I have that experience again?" Oh God, I hoped that it wasn't a one shot deal.

"Probably, there is no way of telling."

"You said that it might be dangerous." I could feel the insistent ache at the base of my spine.

"I wouldn't worry about it. You may need more sleep for the next few days but that's all."

"You said that the feminine energy's at the base of the spine. Where's the masculine energy?" I had images of erect penises.

"It's in the brain. The third eye part of the brain, where the pituitary gland is. When the feminine energy rises up your back and goes up to your brain, it joins Siva, the masculine energy, and when they join, enlightenment occurs."

"What is Siva?"

"Siva, the dancing god Siva, the keeper of masculine energy." She looked at me with guarded contempt.

Shakti and Siva coupling in the mind and creating ecstasy and enlightenment. What a wonderful way of dealing with it. Hindus certainly had it figured out. Not only did they include the female energy on the way to enlightenment, but they gave her a consort and ecstasy to boot. I really liked all that. As I was thanking Ishwari for all the information she gave me, I was riveted to the spot. Goose pimples and heat rushed through me again, but this time on a much smaller rollercoaster as I realized that Siva was the mirror image of the mind watching itself. SIVA was AVIS spelled backward.

MALIBU CLIFFS
Ishwari was orchestrating future events.

"**M**A would like you to come to our house tonight. It's her birthday in a few days and we're having a party for her. Do you have a car?" I nodded.

"Do you have room for some people?"

"Sure."

We walked outside. She called a group together. In a few minutes eight people piled into my four seater convertible. We headed north to Mullholland Drive and then to one of the other canyons further west. Most of my passengers were younger than I, in their twenties and thirties, but behaving much younger, like little children. The distance between us seemed greater than only of age. I was treated with great care, someone who had been newly found, newly awakened, the focus of MA's grace.

"Why did she ask me if I were married?" I asked the crowd around me as I drove the heavily-laden car through the curving, darkened road of the canyon.

"Because it would cause you no hang-ups with your husband to be celibate." Obvious answer.

"Are all of you celibate?" I looked at the tightly packed young ingenuous faces around me. "Have all of you given up sex?"

"Yes." The voices around me answered. It was hard to believe.

"But, who is she?" I wondered what the rest of them would say.

"She is the Mother." One voice replied. "She is Kali, she is Durga." Another voice interjected. A girl's voice with a small edge to it answered. "She is MA, that's all."

The residents of one of the houses in L.A. were throwing Joya a birthday party and great preparations had been under way while the retreat was still in progress. As we came to the top of one of the hills, the canyon road peeled off to a dusty mountain path.

Before us on the crest of another hill, backlit by the setting sun, an enormous modern house came into view. A large field spread before it ending in the distance on the shores of Malibu. Against the vermillion sky, the glass of the sprawling building glowed as if on fire. Through the two storey open windows I could see candles flickering in the gentle wind. Once inside the door, pictures of saints of all religions hung on the cavernous walls. Most were Hindi, but Christ and the Virgin Mary hung comfortably among them. There were altars in nooks and crannies holding banks of flowers and burning incense. Mattresses and pallets covered the floors. Sleeping bags were everywhere.

Immediately upon arriving, the musicians collected around an empty throne like chair in one corner of the room and began chanting. More incense was burned. More flowers were stuck in vases, more people filed in; including many who could not attend the retreat. Sitting on the floor, on the chairs, on the staircase and on the landing above, they filled the space until there was no room to move.

The headlights of cars followed one another up the hill and flashed by the windows as they found places to park in the fields around the house. It was almost dark when Joya arrived in a large van. The nearness of her presence sent a wave of excitement through the assembled worshippers. They started to wail her theme song.

"Hey MA, Hey MA, Hey MA Durga..."

As she swept laughing into the room, the sensation of being stoned spread through me, as did also a small edge of fear. Presents appeared around her chair. Pushing her way through the bodies on the floor, her white teeth flashing in her brown tanned face, she plowed her way to the empty seat in the corner.

"Make room for MA, Make room for MA." She flung herself into the chair and pulled herself up, only to sigh and sink back down again. I had the sensation of tingling in my hands and feet as it expanded to fill the rest of my body. The area in the back of my throat started to lift. My sinuses started to pop. The top of my hair felt as if it were being lifted upward. I began to grow very stoned again. I was one of many who seemed as stoned as I, but I saw no drugs being passed, no joints being smoked.

The ache at the base of my spine grew more pronounced. Then it happened again, just as it did earlier in the day, the movement inside of me, the heat, the gooseflesh, and sound of other people breathing fast and loud in the darkness around me. As I stiffened and sat straight up, the excruciating pleasure spilled in accelerating waves over my body. Joya's voice filled the darkness.

"Wandering wanderer, Begins to find his way home...
Let the silence touch you...
Let this moment fill you...
You are eternal...
Where you have come from...
A man and his God...
There are no words to describe the presence of God...
You are the presence...
You are filling this moment, as it is filling you...
Let it happen. Let it take you and sustain you...
There is nothing for me to give you...
All your answers are in yourselves...
All of you have been touched quietly in your own being...
Within yourselves the lost love begins to grow...
You are born free...
Each and every one of you was born free...
The mind steals your freedom from you...
You look outside of yourself trying to find it again...
Close your eyes and sit straight...
Bring your awareness to the top of your head...
Let the mind slow down....
Do not try to stop it, but bear witness to it...
Become as a child...
Simple awareness to the top of the head...
Simple like a child..."

Her voice trailed away and I lost track of time or place, or even awareness. I don't know how long I sat there in that blissful bottomless haze. When after the passage of some undetermined time

I came back, the room had grown completely dark. The stubs of a few spent candles still flickered in the darkness. People were sleeping on the floor all around me. Joya was gone. The corner chair was empty. The presence had departed. Except for the gentle breathing of people sleeping on the floor around me, a great silence hung in the May night.

PA... RA... ME... DICS

I had stumbled into something I did not understand. Something I had read about, dismissed as fancy, and now had to deal with. Whatever it was, it had found a home in my body.

That night, I slept as if drugged. The next day I tried to explain to my show biz friends what had happened to me. They thought I had gone crazy.

"What are you going to do, join a cult? Around a woman guru no less?"

"All that is well and good but something happened to me around this woman and I can't explain it. I've never had that sensation before. I felt that I had touched the hem of some great mystery, a mystery that words could only barely describe."

"It sounds like you had an orgasm."

"Listen, I've had orgasms, and this wasn't one of them. It seemed to happen to my skin, my whole body, not, you know, to my private parts."

"How about a cosmic orgasm?"

"I don't know what that is."

"How about menopausal flashes?"

"Nope, had one hot flash in the garden three years ago and that was it. This was different."

"You sure they didn't spike your yogurt?"

"No, I'm sure, but that wasn't it."

"Then what is it?"

"I don't know, but I'm going to find out. They do an awful lot of singing and some of those people are very good. Maybe I'll be able to sing without sabotaging my voice. It might be worth the effort. Anyway, where's your sense of adventure?"

The next day I called the L.A. house and spoke to Ishwari who told me;

"MA would like you to come to her house in New York and then go to Florida with her."

I was set to go. While in New York I could get my taxes done, see my son, clean up my emotional house while expanding my 'spiritual' horizons.

I had no money to make the trip, but I had all the furniture which I had schlepped across the country in Baba Muktananda's bus. On Tuesday morning I called an antique dealer who said he would stop over on his way to his shop in Beverly Hills. When he arrived he began itemizing the things I wanted to sell. As he peered around the treasures that I had accumulated over the past twenty years, estimating prices and writing down items, I began to sneeze. I sneezed once, he said.

"Gezund-heit."

I said, "Thank you" and, sneezed again.

He answered with another "Gezund-heit."

I said "Thank you," again and sneezed three more times in rapid succession. At this point I waved my hand for him to stop blessing me. I thought that the objects he was picking up and moving around might have stirred up some dust. Then I proceeded to sneeze about thirty times in rapid succession and, as I sneezed I could feel my nose solidifying and becoming completely stuffed. Breathing through my mouth, I ran to the bathroom for a Kleenex. On the way I became so nauseous that I barely made it to the john. A spasm doubled me up, and I threw up the dinner I had the night before. Then the diarrhea hit me and I barely had time to position myself strategically over the john. Vomiting and diarrhea vied for precedence in my body. Within a few minutes nothing remained in me, my stomach flattened down like on a cadaver, as the dry heaves rocked me. All of a sudden a cramp clutched me right under the breast bone and churned its way down past my uterus and into the base of my spine. I didn't know what to go after first.

After pulling up some clothes, I fell on the bathroom floor as sweat poured out of every pore in my body. With my legs buckling under me, my arms also ceased to work. The only thing that

I could do was to slither my way out into the foyer sideways like a sidewinder and pray that the antique dealer would find me there.

He did, the look on his face betrayed his utter disbelief. One moment he was blessing me because I was sneezing. A few minutes later I was inching my way across the floor like a snake, my body covered with sweat. He peered down at me, aghast.

"Is there anything I can do for you?"

Barely able to get enough sound behind my words I mouthed "Pa..ra..me..dics."

He ran to the phone and dialed information. After a short conversation which came to me as if through an echo chamber, he came back to comfort me. Spasms were now wracking my body, they seemed to start at the center and go in both directions; some up to my throat, the others down to my uterus. My nose was so solid that I could barely breathe. I feared that I might choke if I started to vomit again.

The poor man looked stunned as he covered me with a blanket he found lying on the couch. Within a few minutes, (they must have been stationed around the corner), the paramedics arrived and almost knocked the door down trying to get in. I lay in the foyer, my arms and legs completely useless, there was no feeling in them, no response from my brain. They lay there at strange angles like the limp appendages of a rag doll. My hair was wet and plastered to my head. The clothes stuck to my body.

Pictures of wounded men in combat as they tried to drag their shattered limbs flashed through my mind. Naively thinking that all they had to do was to force their legs to respond and they would. No way, there was no message from my brain to my legs or to my arms.

"What happened to you?"

One of the paramedics looked down at me and asked. I could barely shake my head. They looked at the antique dealer. He spread his hands and shrugged his shoulders.

"Did you take any drugs?" I shook my head. "Did you have anything to eat?" I shook my head again.

They busied themselves around me, taking my blood pressure

and listening to my heart, while commenting that I was barely alive. They had to keep pumping the cuff on my arm to find any pressure at all. As for my heartbeat, all they did was to exchange glances and, with one movement, hoisted me onto the stretcher and, very gently, but wasting no time, trundled me out to the waiting ambulance and with sirens screaming sped me through the early morning Los Angeles traffic.

As they wheeled me into the Emergency Room, all I could think of as the ceiling lights flashed above me was, they should paint the hospital corridor ceiling with flowers, because most patients are on their backs, only able to see above them as they are wheeled through the hospital corridors.

Through the blinding lights glaring down on me a form loomed into view. As it was asking me some questions, I could feel my arms and legs returning to normal. Then the form turned away, spoke to the paramedics and checked my chart, at which point I started to move and then sat up.

They all looked at me in utter amazement. A moment before I was a limp rag and now I realized that whatever I had gone through, it was over. I was returning to my normal state.The doctor wasn't all that sure.

"Do you take any drugs?"

"No." I answered, grateful that I could speak again.

"What have you eaten?"

"Nothing" My nose began to clear and I took a deep breath.

"It looks to me like you've had an allergy attack."

The paramedic looked doubtful.

"Lady, if I hadn't seen you soaking wet back there on the floor, I wouldn't believe that you were the same person sitting here talking to me." He brushed some of the wet hair off my face and his young blond face flushed. He then shook his head. The doctor gave me an antihistamine shot.

"You have amazing recuperative powers. If I hadn't seen the guys wheel you in and read this report" He waved the papers on the clipboard,

"I'd never have believed what happened to you."

"Do you have any idea what could've caused it?" I inquired hopefully.

He shrugged his shoulders, "Some kind of allergy attack."

"Could it be the flu?" I asked him.

"I don't think so. You had no fever". He checked the chart. "It happened too quickly. All of it this morning, wasn't it?"

"All within one hour. Have you ever seen anyone meditate themselves into that state?" I inquired.

"No, is that what you think happened to you? More like withdrawal symptoms, spasms, sweating and all. You said you didn't take any drugs?"

He didn't quite believe me. We were both shaking our heads as I got up off the table, limp but now focused and signed for the bill, silently thanking Actors Equity for my medical coverage. With only a blanket around me, and in my bare feet I walked outside and found myself in the brilliant sunshine of another California day. I hailed a cab for the ride home and spent the next two days asleep.

After I assured the antique dealer that all I had was an allergy attack, he came back and bought enough junk so that I had some money to fly to New York.

In the few days after the Kundalini experience, along with ending up in the hospital with all that vomiting, diarrhea and losing the use of my limbs, I had noticed another strange intrusion on my body. The toe nail on the big toe of my left foot was slowly turning a misty lavender. As the days went by it became purple and then it turned a solid black. I didn't know what to think about it. I feared if the progression didn't stop, I might lose the toe nail on my left foot.

Then with some research another insight flooded my questing brain. It seems that in Hinduism the River Ganges (GANGA) emerged from the great toe of God Vishnus left foot. The River Ganga as the water on the body of Mother Earth was a conductor of the energy flow that was identified as the Kundalini, the Mother energy out of the Earth.

It seems that there was a 'mystical' connection between the

Kundalini having been awakened in an individual, with one of the Gods of the Hindu triad and some of the changes that were happening to me. Joya had called me Ganga Priya, the beloved of the Ganges. I was in good company. I wonderd if Vishnus nail on his big toe on his left foot also turned black and fell off, or did it return to its original state. Since there was no further information on this issue in any of the books that I had been reading, then I assumed that things would be all right and I would not lose my big toe.

It explained to me why some of the gurus nail polished the big toe nail on their left foot and left their other toe nails bare. Since it was the left foot, then it is related to the left handed path of the ancient mother's and their mysticsl birthing breath that surfaces in the mythology of the big toe of Vishnu. He, of the sacred Hindu triad seems like the Christian Holy Ghost. Both deal with the uncharted fields of a 'mystery'. As I packed my belongings I wondered what else was going to happen to me and who would give me some answers.

On the way to the airport the cab stopped for a red light. In the distance I could see a bank of red roses and the next moment their smell filled my nose and my whole body. I had lost my sense of smell during my marriage more than twenty years before, and here I was in Los Angeles, smelling roses a block away. I settled back in the seat and wondered what kind of miracle had happened to me. And that was just the beginning.

QUEENS

When my plane landed at the Idlewild Airport I was picked up by one of Joya's followers. She was a small, pale faced woman with a bushy Afro which she kept under control with combs and rubber bands. After welcoming me warmly, she drove me to one of Joya's houses in Forest Hills. As we drove through Queens where I spent so many struggling years as a teenager, I became aware that it held no emotional links to the past for me. There were no tugs at my heart, no areas of sentiment left. Queens, was Queens, and that was that.

After we left the sprawling Idlewild Airport , that subsequently became JFK, we began passing familiar landmarks. The little neighborhood park I had walked through every day to Schimer Junior High Scvhool was gone, covered over by Van Wyck Boulevard. Somewhere under all that expanse of concrete there may still remain a broken foundation and traces of the tall iron fence that kept us kids out of the park after dark. Only curious archeologists in the future might find some traces of it at some distant date. For now it was gone, obliterated by asphalt and the crush of whizzing cars.

The seedy bars along Liberty Avenue were now even more decrepit with lurid pictures of topless go-go dancers and darkened massage parlors. We sped along Woodhaven Boulevard which wasn't as familiar to me as Sutphin Boulevard which had been my route home from the subway, a spot flashed by where I had my first flat tire on my first car, so many years before.

We turned to Queens Boulevard. It had changed a great deal. There were no more weed filled lots flanking its potholes. New apartments filled all the once empty spaces. It had become a true boulevard with wide lanes on which traffic moved more briskly than in the past when I bumped my way along going to the Copacabana at night or later home to Farmingdale from 'Fiorello' to care for my dying mother.

The Tudor Houses in Forest Hills had been as inaccessible to me in my youth as the mansions of the North Shore of Long Island. They had been the enclave of the rich, flanked by tennis courts with padlocked iron gates. Now the sprawl of the city had caught up with them. Minorities squeezed in and the rich had fled.

The Tudor buildings with their ivy covered facades hidden by towering trees, always left me wondering how the people who occupied them, lived their lives. All I could do, as I sped by on the Long Island Rail Road with my nose pressed against the window pane, was to imagine the stories that were played out behind those neatly framed beige walls.

Then after I married Jimmy Hammerstein, who in many ways with his privileged background was as lost as I was, having a singular talent as a tennis player, was derailed by his father, Oscar, into becoming an assistant stage manager in one of the old man's shows, leaving his love of tennis and his singular talent behind. During endless tournaments we spent many a sweltering hot summer day at those elegant tennis courts in Forest Hills, watching the 'pros' battling it out.

What seemed left was only the echo of much more prestigious encounters of sweating, swearing players, with the pop of tennis balls on the now empty and padlocked tennis courts. Ironic that Joya and her caravan touched down on those hallowed athletic environs, isolated places, where I had spent the early years of my marriage, wondering what I had gotten myself into then and here I was again, asking the same question. On one distant level, during my marriage, I had stepped into an alien and different class of people. On a more recent level, I was catapulted into an equally alien realm of 'spirituality.'

Much had changed in the years between, for some of the elegant houses were now occupied by devotees of Joya. The rich professionals were gone, the poor couldn't afford them. There were several ivy covered buildings within walking distance of each other creating a close knit 'spiritual' community.

When Joya came to Forest Hills she stayed at one called Shiam's house, named after a little boy whom she loved. Her followers converged there to meditate, chant and "hang out with her" as Ishwari had informed me. A mass of true believers had found her and each other. They all seemed to have a great deal of faith. They considered her to be God, or if not God, at least a saint.

There was no faith in me. I wasn't even all that sure I believed in God. My closest hook on the infinite was the Virgin Mary, to whom I mumbled my prayers more out of habit than belief. Who were saints anyway? Martyrs dying for their God, clutching their faith to their bosoms, taking it with them to their often fiery graves? All that bloody violence that surrounded my youth, as nuns with great relish recounted gory details of burnings at the stake, torture, crucifixion, and beheading, all in the name of faith, all in the name of a belief in the true God, in the name of the same God who represented love and peace through His only son Jesus Christ. Then why all the blood and gore? Why all the suffering?

If they called Joya a saint then who was she really? What was her future? Would she too have to face eternity through a wall of flames or by hanging spread-eagled on a cross? I couldn't picture it, not that powerful presence with all those clanking gold bracelets and all those sparkling diamonds in her ears. She had something else she was offering and it had more to do with pleasure than suffering. Would she be allowed to survive if this were the Middle Ages? Was it pleasure that was left out of the equation that was the Christian Trinity? Was the suppression of the female, through the rejection of pleasure, which the Reformation through Calvinism took to such cruel barren ends, the real basis of Christianity? But why? And I knew the answer before I even voiced it. Because nothing rational, nothing coming out of the mind could be as all consuming and obsessive as the feelings of stoned pleasure that Joya, as the MA, evoked in people. Whatever her message was, it used pleasure as its vehicle.

I never wanted an intellectual faith, as I plodded through my Bachelors Degree in Philosophy at Hunter College. I wanted something that gathered all of me, including my passions, into itself. Here she was, the clue that might save the planet from all that rationalized left hemispheric, right handed brain, the evolutionary thrust into all that destruction and violence. She housed in herself the beginning of an inkling into another possibility, another direction, that if allowed to flower might save the despairing over-sensitized tormented human animal and make its survival as a species possible.

A small light flashed on and off in my brain, an undefined potential had taken root there. The spark was so insistent, so demanding of my attention, that there was no question in my mind I would pursue it until WORDS would define and concretize its now sporadic manifestations.

The experience had to do with a kind of stoned pleasure, not necessarily the sex act. The sexual energy may be its underpinning, may be part of it. Psychologists and psychiatrists would call it repressed sexuality. All of her followers claimed to be celibate. They rejected the rational mind calling it the ego and the enemy. I hadn't gone that far with it. I liked my mind. My mind worked very well for me. Something else held me captive. It held my voice captive. It held my left hip captive. It held my joy captive. I wanted to find out what it was, so I could free myself of it. Relationships with men did not release me. Talking it out with analysts did not release me. Talking it out down to the nub, down to the nitty-gritty, down to the place where I thought it all began did not release me.

Even after I got my Bachelor's Degree in Philosophy from Hunter College I thrashed about hoping to find something else. The male philosophers all dealt with reason, not with those other areas of human experience, emotion, intuition and trance. Here was another possibility, not through single focused linear thought, but through physically expressed pleasure. It was pleasure activated from some other level but expressed through the body. "Raped by God" she called it, a level where, whatever it was she called God, existed. What if I were "raped by God"? What would I give birth to, since there would be no physical child that would use my body to pop itself through. At that time words like self-realization and enlightenment were only words that my new companions threw about with pedantic sagacious alacrity. They held no meaning for me.

Could this woman from Brooklyn with her nasal accent and all that clanking gold jewelry be a saint? I had never felt stoned around anyone before. Is being stoned with pleasure part of religious ecstasy? I've been in love most of my life but this was a different feeling than being in love.

It was a long standing joke in my family that when spring came, I would fall in love. I always considered it a blessing, the expression of my joy, but my family mocked me and my passions.

Along with my left-handedness, which they tried to stamp out in Poland and partially succeeded by tying my left hand in a sock, forcing me to use my right hand, calling my frustrated left arm, the hand of Satan. They considered me a bit strange.

I've also had sex, both good and bad, but this was something very different. What about the brush I had with the hospital right after it and my black toenail? Was that all part of it? What happened to my body after the brush with divinity?

It seemed I've lived a life of repeated reawakened passion. Reawakened but not too fully realized. The same feeling, but not as all consuming, also awoke in me when I sang. The sounds pouring out of me so moved me that I couldn't breathe, and often had to stop singing to catch my breath and quiet the cascading goose pimples before I could continue.

Maybe Joya can help me find a way out of the dead-end my life had become. Having come across the continent to Forest Hills, I knew that although I had vague misgivings about what I was doing, I would give the situation every possibility for success. The only thing she demanded was celibacy and that was no problem. I had slowly eased myself away from having sex, wondering what it was in American men that changed when they reached the age of twenty. They seemed to leave the possibility of passion behind them and settled for the calisthenics of sex and being serviced by women. God, how tired I got of all that banging. There must be more to it. You come, then I'll come, or I'll come and then you come. Or, we'll both come together, which wasn't all that easy and ultimately not as satisfying as it was cracked up to be.

The wells of my passion would lie dormant in me as far as men were concerned. Women moved me to affection but not to passion. Singing didn't work for me, due to the panic and the hoarseness. This new overwhelming thing that happened to me in Topanga and as I thought about it, the heat and the pleasure built up in me, this new thing, maybe through it I'll find my way back to the joys, to the wonder that I had lost, to the hope that had been alive in me when I was still a child. Where had that little girl gone to who had been so joyful and so alive?

Maybe surrender wouldn't be that terrible either, I wondered what Joya meant by surrender. If we were celibate then it wasn't sexual surrender, so that wasn't it. I had some misgivings about it but looked forward to finding out. The questions which dogged my heels all of my life now took on the dimensions of an avalanche which I was following downhill at a full gallop.

When I reached Forest Hills with my matched brown luggage and my high heeled brown boots, it was as if I had stepped through a time warp. The gap was greater than just generational. The occupants looked at me, as they passed me, with no acknowledgement. One long haired Indian-shirted devotee with one finger lifted the string pearls which hung around my neck, and inquired.

"Real?"

"I don't know." I answered defensively.

"You know they stick a piece of sand in the shell to get that pearl?" Guilt trip time. I lifted the beads from the contemptuous digit.

"That should give the oyster a great deal of opportunity to work out through pain whatever problems he has to face in this life." I gave her some est jargon. Not to be outdone she continued.

"I don't eat meat and I don't wear leather or fur or anything made from animals. I have a reverence for all life. All life is holy."

I looked at her grubby sneakers and the cotton shirt that not only needed ironing but a good washing. Wonderful.

"You don't look like you belong here." She continued.

"Joya told me to come here to this particular house and then join her in Florida." I threw out my trump.

"MA asked you to Florida?" She looked at me incredulously.

"Yes." Her whole attitude changed.

"Then come on, you can sleep on the mattress in the living room. Durga Das is in Europe and he won't be back for a while. What's your name?" She asked me.

"Ganga Priya." I gave her my new moniker.

"O my, Ma must love you, you're the Beloved of the Ganges." She looked impressed.

Now that I had a spot of my own on the floor, I felt a little less at sea. In one of the corners of the room, which was, once when the rich had occupied it, a large oak lined dining hall, an inhabitant of the house was playing a guitar and softly chanting. His eyes were closed and he seemed out of it. People moved through the house and joined in the singing as they passed. An argument was going on in the kitchen about who was responsible for the shopping and why some of the tofu was missing. What the hell was tofu?

The children arrived from the nursery school and the place disintegrated into bedlam. Women slammed their way through the house doing chores, taking care of the children, while the men lolled around in the corners chanting and meditating.

Every inch of space was taken up by sleeping bags rolled out next to makeshift altars. Some of the altars were knocked together from orange crates and covered with bright pieces of embroidered cotton cloth. Others were made of teak and walnut with brass candle holders and silver frames featuring pictures of Hindu saints and of Joya. Some of them contained pictures of Nim Charoli Baba, the patron saint of Joya and of the rest of the group. Others sported pictures of Hanuman, the monkey god and Ganesh, the one with the elephant head. Pictures of a blue faced male god and one with an indeterminate face under a half moon who was called Siva, the mirror image of Avis. A shudder found its home in me.

All of the people had Indian names given to them by Joya, further separating them from an identity with their former lives.; Mukti Ram, Durga Das, Lakshman Das, Devaki, Ragu, Gunga Das, Gunga Ma, Durga Ma, Kali Ma, Yamuna Ma. They were universally admonished to stand alone before their God. Attachments were to be shed, like an unnecessary outer garment, leaving only the self, the real God within. Rather than the loss of attachments, not unlike what I had experienced at est, I saw a great deal of indifference. Who was to take care of the children if everybody severed their ties of initial bonding? Indifference called universal love seemed to be the ideal. Non involvement to an ultimate degree, seemed to be the desired goal. Great for men. Who will take of the children? I had the same problem before, when I was on staff with est. If we all become detached and self absorbed, who will take care of the children?

Those thoughts were pushed away by the singing of the newly organized group in the corner, and by the freedom with which they allowed the sound to flow through them. Nothing seemed to stand in their way. They opened their mouths and the sound just poured out. I marveled at their freedom. If along with this awesome experience that I had in Topanga I could sing without all the problems that I had with my voice, maybe it would be worth the surrender.

The houses in Forest Hills were planning for Joya to be with them. She usually visited them once a month. Being from Brooklyn herself, while in New York, she visited her natural children. New York was her second base of operations after Florida.

SO HO

T he next night was Saturday and everyone gleefully piled into various beat up cars and dilapidated vans and headed to as yet to be discovered downtown industrial area in New York, soon to be called So Ho (South Houston Street). The deserted industrial factories had been discovered by the creative community and converted into open airy lofts. One of Joyas artistic followers was letting us use his studio for her service.

Another irony, my former husband also occupied a loft in So Ho, around the corner from where we were assembling. After the tennis courts in Forest Hills, there seemed to be other spiral circles than just the Kundalini that were spinning around me.

I had not seen our female guru since my experience in Topanga, the weekend before, and was growing more and more in awe of her. The awe was heightened by the adoration of her devotees. It was difficult not to be sucked into it.

A contribution of a few dollars was collected at the door. We proceeded up a flight of dark stairs with broken banisters and swinging light fixtures, into a large airy room filled with enormous plants which faced the windows and hung suspended from metal ceilings, which I hadn't seen since we landed, in Jersey City from Poland almost forty years before.

More pictures of Hindu Gods plastered the walls and Indian rugs were thrown over broken and quickly assembled couches. People were everywhere, bunched up at the door, on the stairway and sitting on the floor in lotus positions, wedged up against other bodies, being trampled by late arrivals attempting to find room for themselves, slightly edgy at the crush, not unlike the penguins at the South Pole. The people I had already met ignored me when I smiled at them. There was a rudeness about them that I found to be a common characteristic. Courtesy was a 'drag' they explained to me, an unnecessary social prop, a burden to be jettisoned, an 'attachment' to be discarded.

It was murky in that loft with candles burning on ledges and the smoke of incense weaving its way to the ceiling from flower pots, with the musicians wailing and chanting;

"...Kali bolo, Kali bolo, bolo, bolo MA..."

Then excitement stirred through the group, the musicians changed their chant, as Joya came up the stairs, her song pre-ceeding her.

"Hey MA, hey MA, Hey MA Durga..."

This time she was even more deeply tanned so that her eyeballs flashed white and her brown eyes seemed lost in the darkness of her face. The white lace dress she wore glowed in the murky incense-filled twilight of the loft. Like a bride, I thought, as once again she pushed people aside to get to a couch hidden under a mountain of silk throws and purple pillows on the other side of the room.

"How many times does Ma have to tell you to leave a path for her?"

The nasal Brooklynese voice rang out. She stopped, hugged some people, pushed others away and laughed hysterically at something one of her followers said as she settled herself into her cushions. I could feel the gooseflesh start at the back of my legs and swim upwards. The sensation of being more and more stoned enveloped me as waves of pleasure swept over my body.

It was easy to sit there and do nothing because just the state of sitting was pure bliss. Thoughts chased each other across the moving picture screen of my brain. I didn't need to stop to look at them or even try to deal with them. They just floated by. Joya looked around the packed loft with its clouds of incense and plants swaying from the ceiling and saw me, at which point she introduced me to the group.

"This is my beloved Ganga Priya, stand up Ganga Priya, let them all see you! She is a MA, look at her, she is a MA."

Then as I sat down, she went in to an extended harangue, charging that some of her followers were not devoted to her.

"You don't love MA enough, she's taking you to God and you don't love her." She yelled that their hearts were not open. She threw some of them out. People wailed and trampled on each other trying to get close to her, as close as the crush of bodies allowed. The meeting went pretty much as the retreat. She spoke about God and about complete devotion to the guru and about complete surrender. She chose some people to come to Florida. Then she ordered the chanting to begin. With the chanting began the deepest meditation I had experienced since the Topanga Canyon retreat. Again the movement exploded somewhere near the base of my spine, and as the goose pimples coursed over me, the heat this time spread upward and across my back between the shoulder blades. My breathing accelerated and was almost out of control when she said directly to me.

"Regain control of your breath Ganga Priya, get hold of yourself."

This time there was a sharpness to her tone. As I came down and became more and more part of the room, the sharpness in her voice made me feel slightly uncomfortable.

FOREST HILLS

A fter the meeting in So Ho, everyone who was allowed or in-vited back to Forest Hills piled back into their beat-up cars and their dilapidated vans. We sped East across the 59th Street Bridge to the house in Queens where I was staying, and where I was to learn, a marathon session was to take place.

After Joya arrived, she settled herself into more of her pur-ple, lavender and red pillows and being handed some peeled grapes by one of her followers, popped them into her mouth while other followers braided her black hair and inserted flowers into the coils. Someone handed her a rose which she refused to take.

"It has thorns on it. You have to take the thorns off when you give a rose to the guru. If the guru gets pricked, you will get kar-ma, a lot of karma if the guru is pricked by a thorn."

The person obediently peeled the stem and handed the rose to her again. She smiled, smelled it and threw it down on the pil-lows before her.

She spoke of God and how God was already in us. All we had to do to know God was to open our hearts and listen to her. In the middle of the conversation she yelled over to one of the men to get someone on the telephone in California. She had a cross-country hook-up connecting all of the houses. When they got on the line she yelled into the mouthpiece as if they were across the street. Screaming into the phone she told them how much she loved them and demanded to hear them profess their love for her. All the while she popped peeled grapes into her mouth and spit the pits into her hands while some of the men wove flowers through her toes.

"Touch my feet, my children…the guru's feet are holy."

People crowded around her, some apparently in pain since they were uncomfortable in the lotus position which was not fa-miliar to their bodies.

That night she had brought with her one of her favorite followers, a young man she had picked up at the beach a few years before and who had become her disciple and friend. She had been
attracted to his two piece bathing suit and the two of them hit it
off immediately. He sat next to her on the voluminous mountains
of pillows, decked out in magenta feathers and a tight black satin slit skirt. His big toes stuck out from between the show-hose
stretched over his long muscular hairy legs. They seemed to have
many private jokes between them, for everything he said doubled
her up with laughter.

She had invited a young, very straight and very proper lawyer
from the loft in So Ho to the house in Queens and was now ha-
ranguing him.

"Why are you resisting me? You think that you are better than
him?" She pointed to the bobbing magenta feathers next to her.
"You think that he is not God's child? God loves all of us, even
you. There are no throw away people. God is a kind Mother, but
God is also without pity because you have an ego. You don't love
yourself, you must surrender to me and the Mother will be kind
to you. I am the best thing that happened to the planet since
Christ. You think I'm crazy don't you?"

She pierced him with her eyes. The lawyer looked at the floor
and then away, his initial curiosity was getting him more than he
bargained for. He raised his hands in a reluctant gesture.

"You will surrender, you'll see. You're here because you know
that I am the only one who can help you. Give in, it's your only
way." She picked up the rose and smelled it while the transvestite
squealed.

"I wish he'd give in to me. I'd save him. He'd never know how
close to God I'd bring him. Give him to me."

Joya rocked back and forth and screeched with laughter. I
looked around and wondered what I had gotten myself into. This
is like a lunatic asylum. At the moment the thought went through
my mind, Joya jerked herself upright and stared at me.

"Ganga Priya open your heart and don't take me for a fool. I
told you not to take me for a fool. You are stuck in what's right and

what's wrong. It's not for you to make judgments, give your righ-
teousness to MA, she'll 'eat it' for you this time, but next time you'll
have to 'eat it' yourself." It was as if she read my mind. I sat stunned
as she threw out.

"Charley, dance for us."

As Charley wobbled to his feet, I was aware that although she
yelled at me, and usually I would have felt humiliation and rage, I
felt nothing, just the intense feeling of being stoned. What did she
mean about 'eating' it?

The feather boa in the black satin dress strutted back and forth
over the pillows, stumbling and falling on his spiked high-heels
screeching with laughter, flirting over his shoulder and wiggling
his hips at the embarassed young lawyer.

MA JAYA SATI BHAGAVATI (MA JAYA)

"Oh do you think that this is terrible, how MA is talking to our lawyer. Well, you don't know what I know and what that pretty young lawyer also knows. He has to confront my dancing queen, there are things in that closed heart he has to face. Don't you my dear?"

The lawyer cringed and turned red. The girl next to him looked as if she was on the verge of tears, while the dancer threw his head back and shrieked with laughter.

"And you thought that I would never amount to anything?" He yelled out to the back of the room addressing a tiny grey haired woman who looked as if she hoped the wall would absorb her. She kept a wan smile on her face which seemed to stay there in spite of the way she felt.

"I want all of you to meet my mother. She wanted to meet Joya. Isn't it wonderful? I have two mothers. Both of them have a male daughter. Darling, even Solomon couldn't figure that one out."

He flapped his wrist into the air, screeching with laughter and collapsing into the pillows. Joya smiled benignly at the woman in the back of the room.

"Your son is a very high being, and you have been chosen as his mother because your heart is open and you are filled with love." The woman's face softened and her eyes filled with tears of gratitude. She nodded her head a few times but didn't say anything. As Joya spoke, her last few words slurred into each other and she grew stiff. Her eyes rolled back. Her two tall blond German assistants leapt up and again half walked, half carried her into a smaller closet-like windowless room.

Pressure in the room lifted as she was carried out. People jostled their way down the stairs, some went to gather up their sleeping children in preparation for leaving, others regrouped around the musicians and begun the Hanuman Chalesa, a beautifully haunting Hindu chant. I remained seated, still in my state of euphoria.

The chanting continued until dawn when word came from Joya for everyone to leave the house and go to watch the sunrise at Rockaway Beach. They again piled into their assorted vehicles and we drove through the deserted streets of Queens to the beach where I had spent every possible summer weekend of my teenage youth. It had gotten chilly and damp during the night, but we continued on and parked in an area behind the now darkened amusement park, in the process disturbing some skinny spotted dogs who were busy sniffing around looking for scraps to eat.

The riders jumped from their cars and ran down to the edge of the beach, acting, but not too well, like children. They seemed more like demented adults, aware of playing at being children. Across the Rockaway Inlet the now rising sun lit up the sky transforming the darkness into soft shades of pale gold.

As I followed them down to the edge of the ocean itchy eyed from lack of sleep, I wondered why do all of these gurus stay up all night? Werner Erhard never slept, Baba Muktananda never slept, neither does Joya. I like my eight hours and spend my life planning to get them, fretting that one hour less at night would have to be made up in the morning. Here I was, not unlike when I was on staff with est, awake all the time and exhausted.

I didn't want the frolicking congregation to feel uncomfortable around me because I was older, so I ran along with the crowd down to the water's edge, not fully believing their sincerity at experiencing the feeling of the beach at dawn. It seems odd that they had to have it pointed out to them that sunrise at the beach was a very moving and extremely beautiful experience. It seemed more to the point that Joya wanted to get rid of the whole crowd and have some time to herself.

I sat on one of the rocks, cold and damp from the sea spray, and peered northward to where I had spent so many summers, so many golden days of my youth, roasting my skin in the sun and catching up on my sleep. I looked down at the waves brushing the sand and wondered, if I were to write about the sea as it leaves the land what would the image be that I would evoke in words.

It looked like faces. The sea leaves profiles on the sand as it moves back into itself, profiles made of water and foam, profiles which disappear only to reappear as the waves return. It's a recurring process repeating the cycle of profiles, like the profiles of people. Only the profiles of people are more filled out, having more body to them, but they are just as transient, just as much at the mercy of time, as the profiles that the waves leave behind on the sand.

Leaving Joya's frolicking followers behind, I began to walk from Rockaway to Far Rockaway and marveled at the changes. Gone were the ethnic neighborhoods and their familiar, if segregated spots on the beach. The deep expanse of sand lay before me littered with garbage. Spots in the wooden boardwalk were caved in, leaving holes which threatened the lives of all who walked upon them. Large stretches of burned out buildings leaned upon each other, some with walls missing, showing interiors decorated with traces of gaily flowered wallpaper. In the distance, behind gated walls, with their tops barely tipped by the first rays of the sun, new gray concrete buildings loomed against the sky. Everywhere close to me there spread, like a miasma, a sense of destruction, loss and danger. It wasn't safe to be walking here at dawn.

One year, when I was still teenager, we had an awesome heat wave and some of us slept overnight at the beach, complaining only of the heavy morning fog which left us and the blankets soggy and wet at dawn. It would not be wise to do that now. Even with the warmth of the sun's rays full upon me, I felt uneasy. I hurried along the deserted boardwalk, looking not only over my shoulder, but all around me, all the while sensing possible danger.

The deep blue ocean and the white beach were still there. The turbulent water carried by the swiftly moving current was still there. The army base on the other side of the inlet, silhouetted by the sun, like a cardboard cut-out, was still there; but the broken, neglected boardwalk, surrounding burned out houses, hungry foraging dogs picking through the rubble, and an occasional poor woman hanging out her wash on a line from some half gutted building, made the scene look like the edges of Rome after the Second World War.

The house in Forest Hills was quiet when I got back and the front door was unlocked. I don't know what happened to the other beach goers but no one stirred as I curled my weary body in the corner of the room on the mattress belonging to the absent Durga Das. Within a few hours the children awoke and with them the rest of the house. Dogs sniffed at the edges of the mattress and licked my face. Dishes clattered in the kitchen. Fresh orange juice was being squeezed for Joya who was somewhere upstairs in one of the small rooms in the eaves. Incense and some candles were lit and the chanting began again. Meditating seekers after God, filled the corners of the room and the areas before the altars. The house was once again an ashram.

I lay there wondering what to do. What was the protocol, should I get up and join the chanters, can I meditate lying down? Some of the meditators who were lying down were snoring. I had slept in my clothes so dressing wasn't a problem, but doing the thing with a modicum of grace certainly was difficult. I shouldn't have worried about it, they were oblivious of me. With their eyes closed and their backs straight they were lost to this world, living for their meditations and their chants.

Kali Maha kneeled by my mattress and again informed me that Joya wanted me to come to Florida to 'hang out' with her.

"How long is she staying down there?" I asked a dumb question.

"She's leaving today, but you can join her as soon as you can."

"What do people do down there?"

I wondered if I should schlep all of my clothes with me.

"They hang out with her. What else do you need?"

"I have some things to do in Manhattan, then I'll come to Florida. Can I sleep here tonight?"

I looked at the mattress. It had become my friend and the only island of security I felt.

"Yes, Durga Das won't be here till next week."

"Can I leave some of my stuff here?"

I surveyed my matched brown luggage apologetically.

"Yes," she nodded her head, "just push it out of the way."

I changed my clothes and took the IND into Manhattan and spent much of my remaining time on the lawn in Sheep's Meadow in Central Park. At the ashram I felt I was in everybody's way. If any place was my home to me it was New York City, but having been away for the last few years without an apartment of my own, made me feel like a stranger. The mainstream flowed past me. I had stepped out of its current and stood looking at it from the sidelines. In the past I never thought I would be able to live away from New York, even thoughts of leaving filled me with panic, so I stayed on, filling my life with classes and friends, allowing my son to finish his schooling there. Now that too was all gone. My friends had all moved away seeking TV jobs in California when the theatre dried up. When my son left for college I had no reason to remain by myself in New York City. Until then I had stayed put, never really trying my wings in the distant places of stock and regional theatre that would have honed whatever ability I might have had as an actress.

When people asked me what I did, I usually answered, I was an actress, but that wasn't really true. Although I had studied with most of the good teachers along the way, I never stretched myself to experience my own possibilities and my own limits in acting.

Strange. Here I am in New York after these few years and I have no sense of having returned. I feel like a stranger in a familiar land. All of my dreams, at least if not born here, were aborted in this town. Here I am sleeping on the floor in Queens. Queens, where I grew up. Queens, where you escaped from….not to.

I made a list of people I would visit while in town, and Dorothy Hammerstein, my former mother-in-law kept popping into my mind. I guess I should see her, she might know where my son was at that moment. His college term had ended and I didn't know where he might alight next. My house in Rockland County was rented, so neither of us had a home base.

While lying on the grass in Sheep's Meadow, I looked over to the East Side where Dorothy Hammerstein lived; somewhere behind the buildings on Fifth Avenue in the canyons of Park Avenue. She sold the townhouse on Sixty-Third Street right off Fifth Avenue where she and Oscar had lived before his death. Surviving alone, surrounded only by servants in a lavish apartment on Park Avenue, she lived a life of opulent luxury.

I wondered what to do with myself. Maybe I'll stop over at Hunter College and see if Professor Steedman is still there. She was probably the most influential teacher I had in my life. The tiny, white-haired woman who wore a fresh flower everyday attached to a pin that said SMILE, created the Anthropology Department at Hunter. It was she who introduced me to vegetarianism as a way of life and into natural foods and vitamin supplements. This was in 1952 when we were called health nuts and faddists. It took thirty years for the rest of the country to catch up to what Professor Steedman taught us those many years before.

I had little resistance to what she shared with us because in Poland we ate nothing but health foods, nothing was packaged or preserved. My physical well-being changed and deteriorated when we landed in this country. With her prodding, not only my health changed but my attitude also underwent a transformation. Anthropology exposed me to the possibility of evolution and the relativity of human customs and values. Up to that point, I vehemently defended the concepts which came with my rather narrow provincial Polish Catholicism, but during her classes I saw other possibilities and other truths that gave me a broader perspective and freed me from the intellectual narrowness I had dragged with me up to that time.

I became aware that tribes all over the world had different belief systems and they were not necessarily centered round a male father God up in the heavens.

Hints of Matriarchy percolated through the heavily laden prose about male superiority. With each glimpse I realized that what I had been taught and so deeply questioned was not all that there was. Philosophy was a male game and here I was trying to understand it, arguing desperately that most of the philosophers missed the point.

I realized early in the game that there were no major women philosophers, and it took many years and the detours from many main roads to finally find out and to understand why.

What answers would flower in me and what fruit would I bear. Something unknown, unexplored had gripped me in its coils and I vowed to understand it. I vowed to be able to express it in WORDS, but how. Along with healing my voice and hip I would find a way to plummet the depths of what had happened to me. Along the way maybe I would also find the answer to why women were so universally abused and why men were in charge. What happened along the way that created the massive shift from female to male centrality, from cooperation to competition, from left handedness to right handedness, from peace to violence and unceasing war? Tall order, but on a deep philosophical and realistic level, living in a man's world, defined by men, for men, the question hung before me like a dark endlessly menacing thunder cloud.

<u>THUM</u> tum, tum, tum

Having put my domestic house in order, checking on my tenants in Rockland County, locating my son with his father on his school break and having my taxes done, I busied myself for my trip to Florida to 'hang out' with Joya.

Some of my stuff, my clothing and my matched luggage, was in Queens, in one of the homes in Forest Hills. I would pick it up on the way to Idlewild Airport. I wandered around New York enjoying the shop windows and found myself on Madison Avenue and Fifty-Third Street. As I passed a store front that displayed wall to wall television sets in its window, a Western movie was thundering across all of the screens. It was accompanied by the <u>THUM</u>, tum tum tum, <u>THUM</u>, tum, tum, tum of Indian drums. As I became aware of the drumming, I also became aware that it was having an effect on my body. As the intertnal movement of pleasure began to course through me, I started to rock gently back and forth. Then as I stood listening to the repetitive Indian drumming, the rocking became more and more violent. I had to grab a telephone pole and wrap myself around it to keep from falling down. People looked vaguely at my apparently bizarre behavior, but this was New York City and anything was possible. As the violent rocking and the flashing of fire and light rose inside of me, holding on to garbage cans and to a post office box, I eased myself down the street away from the sound of the drumming.

So it wasn't only around Joya that this movement inside of me became activated. She unlocked the door that had been closed to this experience and the sound of Indian drumming, in a specific repetitive pattern also activated the flow.

There was no way that I would schlep to Forest Hills after such a violent upheaval, so I rented a room in a local hotel and carefully positioned my still shaking body down to rest and hopefully to take a nap. It was still early in the afternoon and when it got dark, I planned to go down the street to Hamburger Heaven and have some dinner.

A while later, I opened my eyes, while still lying on the hotel bed feeling more peaceful. Somewhere in the Western sky the sun was slipping down into the Palisades on the Jersey side of the Hudson River, preparing the city for nightfall. It felt so good to be lying there relaxed and filled with such pleasant anticipation, that I was reluctant to get up. But the thought of a salad at the Hamburger Heaven spurred me to sit up and to make the first move. Stretching my arms above my head and arching my back, I chanced to look down toward my pillow and lo and behold.

There I was still lying there.

Part of me was lying there and part of me was sitting up looking down at my body quietly sleeping. The part of me that was sitting up was doing the thinking. The part of me that was still sleeping seemed almost alien to me. But I knew that I had to somehow re-engage it, or I would be in real trouble. Without a second thought, the thinking part of me plunged back into the sleeping part of me. I lay there, apparently of a piece, wondering what to do, scared to death that if I sat up again, I would leave my body behind. What then. What would happen to my body if I didn't occupy it?

The image of John Glenn the astronaut, looking down at the physical body of Mother Earth from his circling satellite, left me wondering at the mixed feelings that he must have felt, at being apart from the support system of his planetary nest. Here I was, also having looked down at my sleeping form on the bed. I lay there wondering. It got dark outside. I feared getting up and turning on the light. But I had no choice and with great almost numbing panic, I sat up again. This time I sat up in one piece. Good God, what has been happening to me. First Joya and the Kundalini, then the violent rocking from the drumming, and now, the separation from my body. What else was in store for me? I dreaded the thought as the memory of the trip to the hospital in Los Angeles filled me with growing concern. The black toe was the least of it. There was no turning back, even if I wanted to. The snow ball was rolling down the hill and I was destined to go along for the ride.

THE RANCH

Some of the people that I had met at the retreat in Topanga were already at the ranch in Florida, as was Joya. What was to become an ashram was still a ranch with horses that the Mother with her male devotees rode every day. Large wooden buildings surrounded a small body of water shaded by swaying palm trees and dense palmetto groves. Huddled among the palm trees were Indian temples. Her followers lived in large buildings around the pond and waited for her to alight in Florida. In the large structure that I was assigned to, every space that was available was taken up by mattresses, blankets, personal belongings, in corners, on staircases, even under tables. I was given a small space under a staircase and wondered what I was to do. Being ever helpful, I headed for the kitchen and offered to stir the reluctant soya beans into edible fare. No one was aware of the fact that the reluctant beans had to soak overnight in order to be palatable.

The pond at the center of the compound was fed by a natural spring. On the far side of the pond Joya came out surrounded by a covey of young men. She splashed her toes in the sparkling

MA

waters and they began to chant around her. Echoes of the outside world with the women cooking and the males chanting around the Mother, filled me with familiar resentment.

I decided that it would be polite for me to make my presence known to my hostess. So I presented her with a magnificent stand of orchids that I had picked up at the airport.

When my mother was silent with her own grief, I headed to the wheat fields around our house in Poland and often presented her with a drooping bouquet of poppies and bachelors buttons.

Joya surveyed the orchids that I had presented her with and informed me, as she shoved them aside, that something more substantial would have been better. Then she introduced me to the chanting assemblage. I was her beloved Ganga Priya, and that I was a MA. No one seemed impressed, as I joined them in the chanting. A woman named Durga wailed with such freedom and such awesome beauty, that I felt impelled to stay and find out how she could sing with such open joy.

The middle of the afternoon in Florida, in those days of July 1977, always brought a thunderstorm. You could set your clock by it. Dark, ominous clouds were beginning to gather overhead above the rocking chanters. Thunder and lightning was growing closer and closer as the newly risen wind thrashed through the palm trees. Joya was sitting up to her waist in the cool pond water. I thought that we should run for safety into one of the temples around the lake. She said no, and asked one of her male followers to get her an umbrella. Ramana galloped into the house and when he returned with a large black parasol, loud raindrops were already beginning to pelt down on us and were puckering up the waters of the lake. Joya opened the parasol while treading the water, and swam into the center of the lake with the thunder and lightning crashing around her. She handed the dripping parasol to Ramana, who was swimming beside her and with his free arm resumed holding the umbrella over her head to keep her hair from getting wet.

"MA will protect you, thunder and lightning won't hurt you. Get your asses into the water." She yelled out to us.

My upbringing dealt with being safe and to stay out of the water when there was thunder and lightning around. Since the whole assemblage plunged in after her without a second thought, I thought that I better do it too. She was right. The crashing thunderbolts stayed clear of us splashing around in the lake.

That night awakened around three o'clock, we were ordered to wash all the bathrooms and the kitchens in the houses that we were occupying. Dragging our weary bodies around, with our testy minds we scrubbed the bathtubs, sinks and johns, until they were sparkling clean and until they shone with the same ferocity as the Florida morning sun.

The next evening the same group assembled again at the edge of the lake. I joined them. Joya not only ignored me but turned her back to me, as I positioned myself on the grass at the far edge of the group. Hurt at being rejected so perfunctoraly, the bile rose in my throat and the pain planted itself above my stomach. I wondered what the others thought at the 'beloved Ganga

Priya' being so obviously ignored. No one seemed to notice, as with their eyes closed they continued with their chanting. Did I do something wrong? Had I in some way offended the Mother. I wandered around wondering what to do with myself. Trying to strike up a conversation with some of the others, I had questions that I wanted to have answered but there seemed to be no answers as I was told to stop thinking so much, open my heart and get rid of my ego. Easier said than done and anyway how do you do all that. I was shaken by the rejection and by my obvious inability to understand.

On my last day at the ranch, I cautiously slinked in behind some of the chanters surrounding Joya, again at the side of the lake, and hoped for the best. But the best was not forthcoming. She looked around and fixing me with her forbidding gaze, told me that I didn't belong there. That I should leave, if I wanted to. Covered with embarrassment I didn't know what brought that on. Maybe asking questions of what had happened to me and what was it that kept them there was not allowed. I didn't know. Questions were all that I had, so I knew that I would persist.

The next day one of her male adepts informed me that I was blessed, that MA was working on me, that what had been happening to me, all of it, was part of the teaching. I was being drawn in and then summarily rejected, that was part of the process. I didn't know if I could deal with that. She had 'eaten' my anguish before. Now I had to 'eat it' myself.

I thought that an ashram, like a monastery would have something like hooded chanting monks with their fingertips touching, weaving their peaceful ways through neatly manicured gardens. This whole picture seemed closer to what est was about but with a larger carrot on a stick, a massive dopple of ecstasy. Confused and not knowing what to do with myself and not wanting to impose on where I was not wanted, I left the ranch, cum ashram trying to save myself from further humiliating self deprication. Always looking for answers, it became one of my many coming and going over the years. In time I came to the realization that here were no answers. There were only stories.

Not only the singing of sad songs but my whole life was defined by a sadness that I dragged in my wake. I often wondered where had that joyful little person that I had been, gone to. When I sat at the feet of Baba Muktananda, I bawled. The same thing happened when I sat at the feet of Joya Ma. Tears rolled down my face, tears over which I had no control.

One day while sitting at her feet, for some reason I laughed out loud at something that she had said. She looked at me with mocked wonderment and remarked in her high pitched voice. 'Ganga Priya, I didn't know that you had teeth'.

So much for my joyful disposition. Then, in her own way she worked her magic on me.

THE BETRAYAL

My singing career may have been aborted by hoarseness. My acting career may have been stillborn by panic. My boundless energy may have been compromised by my calcifying hip. What remained in full force was my sadness and my enduring anguish. Where did that come from? As I lay on all those psychiatric couches staring up at all those cracked ceilings, I thought that I had plummed the depths of my psyche. There was nothing else to say. I had said it all. Or so I thought.

The only music that elicited a response in me was anything written in a minor key. I wallowed in the sadness and moaned along with anything that filled me with melancholy. The seeds of a massive depression were waiting to sprout at any minute and I didn't know how to keep them at bay. Everything I tried came to a dead end. Much of my life had been filled with a sadness that I carried in the area around my heart and the upper part of my stomach. It wasn't an 'idea' that I had a pain. It wasn't psychosomatic as doctors dismissed it while prescribing tranquilizers. It was an actual ache in the center of my body that gave me no rest. As I grew up it intensified. There was no way that I could get away from it.

At my sisters suggestion I even tried exorcism thinking that someone had put a curse on me. The exorcism didn't work as I sprinkled water in all the corners of my house and then on all the rocks bordering my property and plowed on hoping for an answer. I even asked Joya Ma if I was stuck in the Hindu 'bardo', the Christian 'limbo'. Suppressing a smile, she advised me that I was not and that I just should live and enjoy my life.

Then during one of my returns and longer stays at the ashram an experience unraveled with such pain, clarity and intensity that I began to get a glimpse at the process of grief defusion. It dealt with a situation in my distant past that I didn't even know was pertinent to the problems of my enduring sadness.

Joya Ma had made me the mother of the Lakshman house at the ashram. I was to keep it organized, clean, distribute the responsibilities for washing, sweeping, dusting and generally keeping it in spanking order. I also had to assign people to do the vegetable scraping and pulverizing that was going on with the Doctor Cursio detoxifying diet. Easier said then done. This was during the tail end of the hippie era and keeping things together was not part of the ethic.

Wednesday house meetings often found me understaffed and raging at the lack of responsibility from my house mates. I began to do much of the stuff alone. Not only the inside of the house became a recipient of my scrubbing but also the outside reeled from the onslaught of planting, landscaping and clearing that becme my endless obsession.

There was no path between the Lakshman house and the main building where our darshans, (meetings with the guru), were held. So I, with my trusted machete hacked my way through the stilleto like palmetto undergrowth until we had a clear access to the lake and houses on the other side.

One day, as I was whacking away at the prickly, resistant palmettos Joya rode by on her horse joined by the covey of young male devotees and pointed out with her whip,

"Look at my beloved Ganga Priya. See how hard she's working. You should learn something from her".

She rode off flicking her whip above the horse's rump. Any acknowledgement of my efforts from the 'mother', were greatly appreciated. That's all I really wanted, was some acknowledgement for all the work that I was doing.

One day Joya Ma was taken to the hospital. We were assured that she would come home soon, to keep our hearts open and to meditate for her. No one knew what her problem was. Those who were close to her kept it a great secret and the gossip only intensified the fear that was gripping the ashram. Some whispered that it had something to do with epilepsy. We could nly guess.

If the Wednesday house meetings had been sparse before, with Joya Ma gone to the hospital, no one showed up and the maintenance of the house suffered. The fact that I was not that great at delegating responsibility and secretly believed that I could do most things better, didn't help the situation.

I had come off the staff with est and we were admonished to 'take responsibility for all of it', no matter what it was. That is what I thought I was doing, as my housemates hid in their closets.

One day with the frustrated resentment of being so put upon, high in my throat, I sat in the back of a local garage station with the mechanic servicing my car and gave vent to my rage into a tape recorder. Then I sent the cassette to my 'friend' Ruth in Los Angeles. A short time later Joya Ma came home from the hospital. The house jobs were being done and everything settled down into a more or less normal pattern. I accepted my role as the house mother and began to enjoy the position as the house sparkled inside and the flowers outside began to bloom.

Then Joya Ma was taken to the hospital again. We meditated and chanted for her safe return. One day while standing over the blender that was emulcifying the carrots into orange goo, Billy, Joya Ma's major domo, nonchalantly asked me if I had written an article about the ashram. I answered no, I had not.

"Are you sure? He pressed me. It seems that a few months before an article had appeared in a supermarket tabloid about an ashram in Florida and how a female guru was running a cult, and how she was working the members into the ground like slaves and on and on.

I grew stiff wih panic as the cassette that I had sent to Ruth my 'friend' flashed through my mind. I shared the information with Billy and he advised me to get in touch with her. Shaking at the mess that I must have created with our neighbors in Sebastian the Fundamentalist Christians community and Jim Jones, the real cultist, massacring all of his followers in Guiana scream-ing across the nations headlines, I called my dear 'friend' in Los Angeles. After I asked her if she had given the cassette to anyone, she casually informed me that she had sold it for fifty dollars to a supermarket tabloid. With the Jim Jones massacre monopolizing headlines, she felt, without asking me that what I had been expe-riencing was news. She had no idea what a mess she had created for me. Cheerful as ever, under my facade of charm, we said our goodbys and I swore vengence.

That evening I related the news to Billy and asked him what I could do to make it up to MA. He advised me to write her a letter explaining what had happened. The worse thing was that she was in the hospital again and I was causing her extra stress. I didn't know where to turn as the current misery spun itself through my mind and body. It was getting late. Everyone had gone to sleep. The ashram was as quiet as a crypt.

Whenever in the past I had gotten upset I would get into my car and ride around until my aching heart settled down. I did the same thing that night, riding up and down US 1, crossing the causeway at Wabasso, continuing on my solitaty trek up and down A1A, as the hours passed.

Slowly I began to settle down and realized that I needed some paper to write Ma a letter asking her for her forgiveness. How I found an all night gas station that sold stationary I'll never know. I got some paper and with tears streaming down my face, staining the crinkly paper, I begged her forgiveness telling her how much I loved her and how greatful I was for her many kindnesses to me.

Riding up to the darkened hospital with only the sprinklers raining down on the parched grass, I slipped the note under the massive glass doors and headed through the darkness back to the ashram.

I couldn't go back to sleep in my anguished state that I had betrayed my mentor and hostess, I found a place before the Durga temple and rocking back and forth sobbed my way through the night until the sun spread its promise of dawn around my aching shoulders.

It was my day to make the gooey mush that as the Cursio diet we all had to detoxify with. With my face swollen from the crying and my eyes barely visible, I stood over the sink blubbering and scraping the endless carrots. People came by and asked me if I was all right concerned that the 'mother' of the house was in such a distraught condition.

Then over the loudspeaker came an admonition for me to pick up the phone. The female voice on the other end informed me that MA got my note, that she loved me, her Ganga Priya, more than ever and that I was to take a shower and go to bed. I would have skipped to the waiting mattress with joy after I doused myself in the shower.

I lay unconscious on that mattress, as if in a coma, for three days. The only conscious moments came when I opened my eyes for a split second and saw a glass of fresh squeezed orange juice on the floor next to the mattress and when a loud deep growling moaning sound occasionally spread itself through me.

At the end of three days, I had lost seven pounds and woke with a feeling of lightness that would grow until in time some of the sadness began to leave me.

Joya Ma may have forgiven me for my betrayal of her and my massive indiscretion but the ashram was less flexible in their judgment. I may still have been her beloved Ganga Priya but to the rest of the assemblage I was Ganga Pariah. Doing my 'outsider' number I left the ashram when the 'mother' came home from the hospital feeling that I was healed and ready to face my life on the outside.

GANGA PRIYA AND MA JAYA SATI BHAGAVATI

DREAM
RIDING THE HORSE BACKWARDS
**'Him who is willing, the fates guide.
The unwilling they drag.' —Seneca**

T he jouney that the Kundalini fuelled in me with MA's help
often yelling and screaming against its pull, digging my
heels into the dirt thrashing, screaming, cursing my fate, took
me where I needed to go in spite of myself.

After I took the est training in 1975 and joined the staff, I remember Werner Erhart, the founder of est, telling us at one of the
seminars, to ride the horse in the direction that it was going. That
night I had a dream. In the dream I was galloping through a dark
night on an enormous dark brown horse. (The fact that my car,
luggage, boots and clothing were mostly dark brown seemed like
a coincidence.) Branches whipped across my face. We seemed
to be on a a very narrow lane with barely enough room to thrash
our way through. So much stuff had grown up on either side and
over the top of the road that I couldn't see where we were going.
Facing the horse's shiny dark brown rump and bouncing along at
a very fast clip, I held on to the horse's tail for dear life. So much
for riding the horse in the direction that it was going.

Not only had I taken 'the road less travelled by' through an
uncleared dark wood, but as I barreled through and created my
own path, I gave myself an added buden. I was rtiding the horse
backwards. The horse seeming to have a mind of ts own sped in
the direction it needed to go. I could either join it, face forward,
or I could bounce along backwards and hold on to its tail.

How do you ride the horse in the right direction? How do you
change that inner life of facing in the wrong direction and of
wasted effort that the dream had forced me to face?

Dreams are where we really live. We deny the validity of their insistant messages when they wake us up in the middle of the night as night MARES. It was no accident that Werner used the image of the horse galloping in the right direction. One of the most ancient dream symbols of the life force is the galloping female horse, the MARE. When our lives are out of control we have night MARES.

The galloping giant within tries to awaken us to the fact that things weren't working, that we were facing our lives backwards, in the wrong direction.

The AHA moment took its time in coming. Then I realized that Joya Ma had created the first turning for me to face forward on the horse that I had chosen as my life. I beat my chest for having betrayed her.

The shame was so great that I didn't know how to face her. She had forgiven me. Could I forgive myself for such a blunder, for betraying her? As the word betrayal spun itself through my brain an ancient memory started to slip through my resistant consciousness. With a rush I realized that I had in some mysterious way created the whole scenario. I also came to realize the process of fear defusion and the way that anguish can be lifted, can be burned out, can be released. It has to be faced and re-experienced in full force. The former fear locked in the image has to be faced head on. It has to be fully re-experienced for it to find a way to dissolve and in time for it to disappear.

I had to travel very far back in time. The original betrayal had sunk its roots in me at the time when I was seven years old. This was in 1935 and we were living in Minsk Mazowiecki, the arm pit of Poland and my fathers choice of heaven. Being isolated from the civilized world of Warsaw was not bad enough but having no electricity and using an outhouse even in the winter, only added to the primitive conditions. My mother hated the place having been whisked out of Warsaw by my father after I was born, without having anything to say about it. She hated the isolation and dressed in her silk stockings and high heeled shoes even when we stumbled along together through the rough terrain of the woods.

It was a time before the Second World War when fear was etching its way onto the faces of our neighbors. The Aurora Borealis of the Northern Lights usually flashed their way through the Northern reaches of the planet. Around that time, in the middle nineteen thirties, the flashing red flaming streams of the Aurora Borealis flashed their way South, as far down as Warsaw. We saw people around us staring at the sky and clutching their faces in panic. Momma said that terrible times were coming. A terrible and bloody war was on its way, as people around her wailed.

We painted our houses olive green to camouflage them from possible future air strikes and glued strips of paper across the windows to deter any flying glass that might be blasted into the house. My father was beginning to make plans to return to the United States to renew his citizenship papers.

There was one consolation living in Minsk Mazowiecki. At the other end of a wide expanse of a golden wheat field there were barracks for the ulani, or Polish cavalry men who had been the pride of the Polish army. It was the young ulani on their besutifully groomed horses who were mowed down by Hitler's tanks in 1939.

In 1935 they sang their beautiful songs at twilight as they brushed their horses and the mist fell over the fields. The dogs began their echoing telegraph across the swaying wheat fields. To this day I remember the words to those sad songs of loss, longing, pride and patriotism.

Most Sundays we dressed up and went to the barracks and watched those handsome young men in their spiffy uniforms perform dressage. They showed off jumping through flaming hoops, and played games galloping to the center where there was one less chair than there were horses and men. A lot of scrambling went on as they hit the coveted chairs. The sole winner clutching the last chair was rewarded with wreaths of flowers that the champion horse nibbled at with shared joy.

My father went because he liked to talk about politics and the possibility of war and how Poland was being betrayed and sold out.

My mother went for another reason. She was very unhappy with Poppa. All those early dreams of a blissful marriage remained behind her in Warsaw. Poppa mocked her and us. We didn't much like him.

Her venture out to the barracks every Sunday in a new dress that she had sewn a week before, was for another reason. She had met someone and possibly fell in love with him. It was during the time when a whole contingent of young Russian officers were competing at the barracks with the Polish ulani. As they mingled after the dressage she met one of the handsome young Russian officers and began to spend time with him. I remember taking long walks with her through the woods surrounding the barracks. She and her officer would walk in front of us and I had to stumble along behind them with his adjutant, resenting the fact that I had to tag along behind them while the young officer monopolized my mother. I was immensely jealous when anyone came close or even looked at my mother. When we rode the tramways I used to hit people who brushed up against her. It used to elicit a great deal of laughter but I wasn't kidding. My mother was mine. She belonged to me. Woe to anyone who tried to separate us.

One day my mother dressed beautifully and smelling of her favorite perfume told me that she was going into town, to the coffee house and I was not to tell Poppa. Make sure that you don't tell Poppa. I assured her with my seven year old understanding that wouldn't tell Poppa. Even at my age I knew that she was going to meet the Russian officer and the jealousey consumed me like a flood of bile that blasted its way through my skinny frame.

When Poppa came home, the first thing that he asked me was. 'Where is Mamusia?

For a while I held on to the promise that I had made to my mother but at Poppas insistence I told him that she went into town and was at the coffee house. He blasted his way out of the house, even leaving behind the hat that he always wore, and a short time later returned dragging my humiliated mother behind him. He plopped down on the couch, buried his face in his hands and sobbed that his first wife left him and now my mother would leave him too. I didn't know that he had a first wife and what did that mean. Was my mother married to him? Even at that age my Polish Catholic mind could not grasp two wives at the same time.

My mother looked at me and without raising her voice, with great sadness rebuked me,

"How could you do this to me? How could you betray me so? How could you tell Poppa where I was when I asked you not to"? I stood there shaking and blubbering

'I'm sorry Mamusiu but he made me do it.'

Then my mother turned around and disappeared into the veranda. I ran behind her but I could hear the door slam behind her. She disappeared into the darkness that surrounded our house and I stood at the top of the step of the veranda yelling far into the night.

'Mamusiu, please come back. Please don't leave me with Poppa. I'll be good. I'll take care of you. Mamusiu, please come back, I'll be good. I'll listen to you'.

I sobbed the litany over and over again intersperced with prayers to the Virgin Mary that she would bring Momma back, as my despair deepened that I would ever see her again. Standing at the top step of the veranda I sobbed and wailed far into that dark night until it grew cold and I became wet from the dew that was forming around me. Shaking with despair, I backed into the silent house and tucked myself into my bed behind the large stove.

The anguish that I had betrayed her and that she would leave me grew in me and exploded into a miasma of sadness that dogged my whole life. The happy little girl became a tormented misplaced immigrant as we sailed toward America but the fear of desertion never left me. No matter where I went or what I did it was always there with me. As I grew up it intensified into a kind of inner gnawing that filled my life as I seemed to consume myself from within. As a teen ager I bit my nails to the nub until my fingers bled, twirled my hair wth such vehemence that a bald spot appeared on my skull, picked my face until it looked like chopped meat, wet the bed, cramped over for two weeks before my periods, feared human encounters using sarcasm that I thought was clever. I fought off bouts of depression, helplessness, my mind raced, talked to itself, and filled me with stories about what I should have done, how I could get even., how I could get attention, how I would show them. My days were filled with daydreams and my nights were filled with night MARES and there was Joya at the ranch riding by on her horse.

It took me a while for me to come to terms what Joya had done for me. The experience of trauma to the heart had to be faced head on as close to the original experience as it was possible. I had to relive the anguish of betraying my mother by betraying the only other MA in my life and that was Joya. That is how she worked. One way or another she forced people to face their fears and used what she called that tube or well of energy that flowed through her to carry away the burdens, like Hercules diverted the two rivers and flushed out the dung from the Augean stables,(the horse again). She had called it 'eating it'. Since I couldn't 'eat it' she forced me to face it head on. Her initial rejection of me was part of the process at my touchiness at being rejected and fear of desertion. It was her way of forcing me to face my upsets at being pushed away and to deal with it. I didn't understand any of that at the time. She forced me to face the horse in the direction that it was going to free me from the anguish of my original betrayal and the havoc that it played in my life.

CORKSCREW SWAMP
SANCTUARY IN FLORIDA

After I left the ashram I still didn't know what to do with myself, hoping that my last encounter with MA would show
me the way. I had asked to understand, along with healing my hip
and voice, was the source of the religious experience. The current human madness seemed to be mysteriously locked in The
Word of the Holy Bible. With the Kundalini experience coursing
through my body, I assumed that I had been given a glimpse of it.
It seemed so far away from going to church on Sunday, giggling
in the pews, aching with boredom during the sermons, watching
the priest as he moved his head back and forth, keeping his eyes
pretty much in one place. How were the two related, this feeling
that I had experienced on one side and the whole structure of
what had become practiced religion on the other. The two somehow as yet did not jell. What was there that united the two, "Who
was Jesus? Why the priests? What was the mass? Why were wom-
en left out? What was the stoned reality of Joya to do with any of
this? What was she? Who was she? What happened to me and the
others around her? Why did they all stay? What held them?

As I careened around Southern Florida with all these questions, some more clearly formed than others, rattling, surfacing,
subsiding in my brain, I sought out the bird sanctuaries and the
swamps. Although the woods fill me with awesome wonder, with
their cool cavernous silences and the ocean lifts my spirit and
clears my head, it is the swampy edges of the tidewater flats that
touch my heart and set my soul singing.

Something in me expands when I look out over an uninter-
rupted sea of grass swaying and changing color under the passing
clouds and the patches of dark shadow that spread over the water as the wind ripples and breaks its surface to chase the leaves

into swirls that eddy up and scatter about fragments of yesterdays loss. In the distance dark hammocks punctuated the swaying landscape. A containment of white birds, wary, patient, hovering with immeasurable hope of prey, rallied on the ragged edges of the swamp.

The birds had always been my most constant companions. I avoided people, picking up their chaos in my raw and opened state. Their tensions and fears vibrated in me and coupled with my own heightened receptivity made me edgy and uncomfortable. Sometimes only music sent me into that stoned ecstasy that left my rational mind behind.

I visited Everglades City and while there I found the Audubon Corkscrew Swamp Sanctuary and decided to see the cypress trees with their knees deep in water. Arriving there around 3:30 PM, it was a mellow time of day in Florida, still hot but with a coolness just edging in through a soft rustling of pines overhead. Turkey buzzards wheeled in the silent sky above and paths marked by cypress planks blended in the natural surroundings so as not to jar the tranquility of the place.

I parked my car, paid the fee, then walked through a partially cleared pine forest. An abrupt change occurred in the vegetation. As I left the pine forest behind me, a raised walkway snaked itself through the ubiquitous sea of grass ending in the far distance in a grove of trees which literally swept themselves up out of the water into tufted crowns draped with Spanish moss. Bits and pieces, something left over, something not quite whole but segmented, tattered gray laundry, holding its own tentatively, adamantly like an unresolved question, gently riding the wind in the far distance.

It wasn't like I entered the swamp, it was more like a pause that moved me forward in stillness, tiptoeing carefully cradling my Birkenstocks against the wooden planks, so as not to shatter the stillness.

As I left the shelter of the canopy of pines behind me, I felt myself moving through some invisible curtain into a different space. Nothing defined or qualified it. It seemed more like a move from the darkness of night into dawn and then into daylight. A gradual change but almost imperceptible as it occurred. Not a change in time or the quality of light but a move in space that had a feeling of time change in it.

A red winged blackbird swayed on a high stiff blade of grass, pools of water reflected the blue sky and disappeared into darkness under the planks which carried the path and me toward the waiting cypress trees. They grew larger, as my distance to them grew shorter. As I drew nearer to them over the open stillness of the grassy swamp, a wave of goose pimples swept over me, there was no apparent wind even though the grass and the Spanish moss lifted and fell as if on some unseen breath. I felt no chill in the air. The red winged blackbird crackled and spread the sound across the swamp, as another wave of puckered skin almost immobilized me. I could barely catch my breath and caught the railing on the curving walkway, rocking back and forth as wave, upon wave of heat and light swept over me. With great effort I kept walking as the ecstasy poured over me.

As I grew nearer to the giant trees which seemed to be growing upside down with their roots like branches thrust into the water, I could barely stand up. My knees lost their power and my legs buckled under me. I held onto the railing and hand over hand, led myself into the sanctuary of the trees to the first wooden bench that I could find. I became quite stoned, something in my head expanded, a sweetness filled the back of my throat, the bridge of my nose tingled, my body grew more and more straight, as I felt pulled back against the rough cypress logs of the bench as the ecstasy flooded me.

It was at that moment, with my body conducting some unseen unheard movement that a realization also filled me with its light. This movement that occurred in me and which seemed to be so magnified in a person like Joya, not only came through people but also through specific places and through trees, why not rocks and mountains and streams and caves.

In a flash, I understood the Druids, and the holy shrines and all those temples built on top of the ruins of former temples. It wasn't the view, or their accessibility, it was some sort of energy that the particular spot on the planet released which gave people a rush of ecstasy and rapture. How many people have died to protect those ancient shrines and the religions that grew around them in the name of God, never acknowledging the fact that it was the energy of the wild pleasure issuing up from the body of Mother Earth, that moved within them.

All those religious historians writing about the 'primitives' who worshipped the spirit of the trees, or the spirit of the mountains, patronizingly assuming how naive those early people must have been. They called it Animism and the worship of many Gods, little knowing that what the ancient people worshipped were people and places, and Mother Earth Herself, that filled them with ecstasy. From whence came that vengeful God of the Jews and that sour God of the Protestants. Little did they know that the ancients touched the secrets which we now are desperately trying to rediscover. How were they lost? What paths were taken that cut us off from this primordial ecstasy? As I sat meditating and hosting thoughts, it began to grow murky among my cypress trees and their shadows grew longer across the patches of open water.

An alligator moved in the shallows underneath the walk and floated like a silent log between a carpet of sea lettuce and a lily pad. A bittern stared at the sky with its eternally strained neck. Some roseate spoonbills flopped in and out of the trees of a distant hammock. I was the only human being there and I remained silent gathering the place to me, every cell of my body singing and jumping up and down with hosannas. As possible answers came to me, so did new questions. Is the road to 'spiritual' understanding paved with all this pleasure? If that is so, then why has it been kept such a secret?

Reluctantly I left the towering trees around me and knew for certain that the columns of the ancient Middle Eastern temples were not there to hold up the roof, the roof was there to keep the columns from toppling. What the ancients simulated in their temples and colonnades, was an ancient memory of a stand of trees.

They felt the movement of energy around trees and as the trees disappeared and the deserts took over, they chiseled synthetic trees of marble. I remembered that Egyptian columns were fashioned after trees and wondered why. The explanation by pundits was that they were phalluses, or that they were esthetically pleasing, or that they reached up to heaven, as all of us were admonished to do. What a travesty of the truth. They created marble trees because they remembered that actual trees were like some human beings in whom the energy was active before the Sahara became a desert. Many of the Greek columns still have the acanthus leaves as a laurel, a crown around their tops.

What other lies have we been told? So many that it was difficult to dig out from under them. But dig we must. The stakes must have been very high for all that information to have been so suppressed. There, after all, might have been a Garden of Eden, what killed it? What lies have we been fed to keep that Garden from being realized again? Eden and hedonism come from the same root and deal with pleasure. That should give us a clue.

Those ancient 'savages' which we so patronizingly paint in animal skins, also knew that certain places held the energy and made them stoned, so they placed their shrines and their pillared temples on sites they called holy and sacred. Then they peopled them with conductors, people who conducted this energy, who naturally became healers, prophets and often leaders, because they were like conductors of electricity. The current passed through them and turned other people around them on. It seems so simple.

I was being given answers to questions that I wasn't aware that I had been asking. It took many years for me to understand how the answers were flooding me. It took many years for me to catch up to them. What I didn't know at the time, was that I had been asking the wrong questions.

DREAM

Then I had one of mine lucid dreams.
—DREAM of Robert Oppenheimer, July 14, 1981.

"Now I am become death, the destroyer of worlds".

—Bhagavad-gita

F our years after my Kundalini experience, as my usually well crafted life was disintegrating into a chaos of loss and reorganizing frenzy, I woke up from the following dream.

In the dream I knew that I had gone through a very difficult time and sat facing the haggard face of Robert Oppenheimer, the American physicist who was instrumental for bringing into fruition the first successful explosion of the atomic bomb. He had been called 'the father' of that massive destructive force.

He was leaning forward toward me, across the small kitchen table. The anguish in his stricken eyes held me in place, for I knew that he was desperately trying to say something very important to me. It was something that he wanted for me to understand.

I leaned forward trying desperately to hear what his stricken eyes, riveting me to his anguished face were trying to say. There were many words that flew by me before I was able to transfer the meaning in his eyes, into audible sound. I asked him to repeat what he was saying to me, for it went by so quickly. He seemed impatient with my obtuseness, but made a concentrated effort to be more clearly understood.

He gazed levelly at me and shared with me that,

'I had moved my way in', and after a pause, that 'we have to become more aware of what comes to us, not only what we put out.' Which was the EST motto. He went on to say, that I had been given the opportunity to understand what he, and others like him were saying, because I had grasped the implications of the STAMPEDE OF THE NATIVES that night.' By understanding the implications of that flight, something had opened up in me and I would be able to get the information I was seeking from him, and from others like him.' What he said to me was difficult for me to grasp and I strained forward trying to remember as much as I could, for he said a great deal and I knew that what he was trying to make me understand was very important.

Then, as he continued to speak, and his lips continued to move on his face, I realized that I could no longer catch what he was trying to say to me, no matter how much I strained across the table to hear him. Both his anguished face and his voice filled with desperation receded into the middle distance and I began to wake up.

The dictionary defined STAMPEDE as that which was put to flight in a panic, that which broke away, fuelled by a common fear driven impulse. NATIVES defined a state, or characteristics that came with the package, were natural, emerged out of nature, were indigenous to the place and were not acquired. They were at home on the planet, be they plant, animal or human.

What emerged from my dream and what Robert Oppenheimer was trying to share with me, was that what he and his fellow physicists created, may very well bring on the end of the world as we know it. I also began to grasp that he was trying to give me some kind of information that would help me to understand what had created the possibility of the oncoming catastrophe. What he did actually say was how everything that was real, natural and NATIVE to planet Earth had become panicked into a stricken STAMPEDE toward oblivion. He did not give me any clues that led into a head long descent into the possible extinction of plants, animals, human beings and the planet itself. That, I had to figure out for myself. Tall order.

I realized that it was the question that I had been asking most of my life. How did women lose their cooperative clusters of peaceful centrality and how did men competitively take over the planet, tormenting all living creatures, enslaving women, abusing them and their children, making them into slaves, harems, subjugating them into unrelenting universal servitude, extending the same exploitative harassment to the body of Mother Earth.

Since the current human madness became petrified in THE WORD, it was to THE WORD that as language itself that I had to turn to find the answers to the questions that churned their way through my brain. I had also asked for the roots of religion that was sanctified in THE WORD. I realized that the Kundalini experience was given to me as an answer to that overwhelming question. As Robert Oppenheimer told me in the dream;

'We have to become more aware of what comes to us, not only what we put out'.

The content of my book STAMPEDE OF THE NATIVES came out of my life's experience, to which the Kundalini experience became like the crown, the icing on the cake, the door that opened into as yet unknown knowledge. I wondered how I was going to begin the great opus that the dream presented for me to pursue.

In time it became apparent to me that I had the answers to that problem at my fingertips, more specifically at the tip of my tongue. For it was language itself, that would give me the answers. It was only the sounds of language that survived from those ancient times of African dispersal, of female centrality (before male history), of a much more benign existence with other creatures and the planet Herself.

As the great cataclysms of famine, volcanic eruptions and ice ages occured, human beings took off on foot and in their dug-out canoes settling the far reaches of land, across the vast open oceans on the body of Mother Earth. They left everything behind, except what they could carry, their tattoos, the sounds that they used as communication, and the stories that those sounds imprinted on their minds.

It was those original sounds of human communication out of that ancient time of female centrality that I had to rediscover. To that end, I began to pour over as many foreign language dictionaries as I could find.

There emerged a dual track. The specific SHAPES and SOUNDS of the capital letters of the Western Alphabet came to my aid. All the other alphabets of the world are secret scribbles, are in code, available only to the cognoscenti.

Once you learn how to synchronize most of the capital letters of the Western Alphabet with the various organs on the mother's face, and the surFACE of Mother Earth, you will come to the realization that you don't need secret decoders to understand what is being written.

Existing in the right hemisphere of the human brain, and having access to the other side across the corpus collosum, our ancient mothers did not need to send secret scribbled messages in order to communicate. If you know how to find their original SOUND, SHAPE and meaning, each capital letter of the Western Alphabet begins to share with you its own story.

To find those original sounds of human communication using the capital letters of the Western Alphabet, I had to devise what became the twenty-five RULES of ORIGINAL SOUND DISCOVERY (ROSD) page 289, that would assist me in my search. The content of that research emerges in the, SHAPE OF SOUND. There are no potsherds out of that lost and neglected period of our heritage. Except for a few bone fragments, the only artifact that we do have to that ancient prehistoric time of female centrality is SOUND itself.

The results of that linguistic research, guided my way to finding many of the answers dealing with the Kundalini experience and how it became suppressed. STAMPEDE OF THE NATIVES emerges carrying the seeds of that discovery.

THE MYSTICAL KUNDALINI
CHACRAS AND LEY (LEA) LINES

"The curfew tolls the knell of parting day,

The lowing herd wind slowly o'er the LEA,

The plowman homeward plods his weary way,

And leaves the world to darkness and to me."

—Elegy Written in a Country Churchyard
by Thomas Gray

Along the way in my linguistic research, I began to realize that there existed a multi thousand years of female centrality, an age where mothers were at the center and defined reality from their point of view. It was a time before male HISTORY (his story) emerged as central and swamped humanity's HERITAGE (her-it age, the AGE that belonged to HER), the time that belonged to the ancient mothers.

There also was a time when the two hemispheres of the brain worked in concert. They were yoked together by the corpus collosum. The right hemisphere of the brain associated with the left hand of the mother worked in tandem with the left hemisphere of the brain associated with the right hand of the emerging father. The shift from left handedness to right handedness is illustrated in the direction that writing took in the Middle Eastern countries. Hebrew, Brahmin and Etruscan were written from right to left as if written by the left hand.

For ancient mothers, what happened on the individual female level also expanded to embrace the body of Mother Earth. They considered themselves as extensions, as daughters of Mother Earth in the creation of smaller replicas of themselves. They also believed that they not only shared the same organs but the same qualities, processes and functions as their overwhelming context, the great magnificent creative body of Mother Earth.

If they gave birth, then Mother Earth also gave birth. If they ate and digested food then so did She. If they developed a system of care and nourishment for their children, then so did their great Maternal context. She became joyful when they were joyful. She became sad when they succumbed to sadness. The surrogate mothers on Her plane, not only shared the same organs but also shared all of the same emotions, feelings, thoughts, wishes and disappointments with Her.

They knew that in the last stages of their labors with the high panting breath, their bodies exploded with the energy of heat and light to defuse the mother's pain during birthing. The experience pushed them to establish a class of rulers, awaken the forces of healing, delve into the realms of prophecy, play with the gifts of wish-fulfillment and activate the dormant streams of ecstasy. They shared that experience with long distance runners who with their high panting breath also sucummed to the ecatasy of trance.

The same or similar systems must have existed on the body of Mother Earth. With this perception we have to reach much further back into our linguistic heritage, than male history envisions.

FEAR
Male role in procreation unknown

Within the ancient human experience at the time of female centrality, the system of anguish defusion that Joya Ma used on me, evolved as an understanding of how the energy that existed within the body of Mother Earth could be shared with shamanic adepts, laboring mothers, and long distance runners.

Due to massive evolutionary changes and shifts in sensory perception, as the human creature became bi-pedal; in the male, the major shift occurred from the nose of smelling, to the eye of seeing, shifting his major activity to the left hemisphere of the brain dealing with the linear focus of image accumulation and genetically established unrelenting sexual imperatives.

In the female, the shift to bi-pedalism brought with it a narrow pelvis and monthly, rather than seasonal estral bloodletting.

There was another consideration. To get through that narrow pelvis of the mother, the large headed human baby had to be born with a skull that became smaller and smaller, less finished, even collapsing on itself in order to push itself through the narrow birth canal. As a result, the baby emerged less and less finished, needing more and more time to mature and more time to learn how to fend for itself. It needed a loving extended social structure around it, in order to survive. This was provided by an expansive matriarchy of female relatives.

The seeds of panic had been planted in the baby right after birth and bore a series of unanticipated fruits. The human infant was born not only helpless, but consciously aware of its helplessness and <u>panic stricken at its helpless condition</u>. There was nothing that it could do for itself. It couldn't turn over when a muscle needed stretching. It couldn't scratch an itch. A hungry stomach could not be filled. A full diaper could not be jettisoned. A mosquito sitting on a nose could not be swatted. All it could do was to search for the face that looked down at it and learn to get attention from that face.

The human baby became an attention getting machine. Realizing that it was helpless with the panic that accompanied that helplessness, the new born child began to lay the tracks of its subsequent habitual life through a filter of its total infantile helplessness.

The human being, no matter how accomplished, how successful, how carefully masked, carries within it the habits locked through a filter of fear during a helpless infancy, that as irreversible destructive tracks or canals, dog its whole life.

It is those locked in destructive infantile habits, understood by our ancient mothers that needed to be neutralized, needed to be burned out for the creature to survive with any freedom and joy. The seeds of that panic laid its irreversible tracks to gestate in the brain.

There was an early understanding that it wasn't the whole brain that caused the problem. They also understood that there were two sides to the brain. It was one side, the left hemisphere of the brain that gave them the problems dealing with fear retention.

As the human being became bi-pedal, the process of recognition on many levels shifted from the nose of smelling to the eye of seeing. No longer could the male humanoid smell the female in heat. He began to search for spots of blood on her flanks. This caused a great deal of confusion for blood on her flanks did not necessarily represent fecundity or receptivity. What followed was rape and the beginning of females being stalked through the tall grass of the savannahs. There was no concept of fatherhood to protect the offspring. Expressing the mating imperative at one end of the year didn't seem to have any connection with the blood stopping its flow on a mother's body and the delivery of a baby, ten lunar months later.

To survive, mothers began to create systems to protect themselves and their children. The most ancient one that is linguistically documented was to castrate their first born sons to act as protectors and uncles to the subsequent sisters children. Male role in procreation was unknown at the time that the most ancient tracks of codified SOUND were being laid down.

There were other factors that fed into the evolution of unrelenting panic, along with the laying of tracks through a prism of panic at birth and then the systemic rape of women.

Our ancient ancestors existed in the open savannahs once they came down from the trees. The grasslands of the savannahs were filled with lurking predators. Everyone, everywhere at all times was always hungry. Everyone, everywhere was always stalking for food. Some hunted alone like the cheetahs and leopards. Some hunted in prides like the lionesses and in packs like the wild dogs and hyenas. Nighttime was the horrific time when the prowling large cats assisted by their night time vision, turned to serious carnage.

Human beings, still part of the animal kingdom copied the animals in learning how to survive. They followed the chimps and baboons up rocky ledges and tall trees to get away from the slaughter that the descending night time always brought.

They couldn't outrun the carnivores. They had no fangs to protect them. Claws did not sprout from their paws. Even in packs, their skinny bodies were always at a disadvantage. There was no place to hide. Often they must have felt helpless as the images of present panic found a home that had been created during the time of their helpless infancy.

The images of panic moving in a single focused straight line through the left hemisphere of the brain began its march into the future. The panic of a helpless infancy, of kidnapping and rape, of death lurking in the tall grass became attached to the image forming, sex and violence activating, left hemisphere of the brain.

The panic laden image became more and more locked in the hemisphere of the brain that lacked compassion, lacked the ability to create relationships, lacked cooperation, dealing only with selfish extremes, beginnings and ends, black and white perception of reality, the idea as real, fantasy, competition, violence and war.

Fight and flight were not their only options. There was also fright, which rooted them to the spot, becoming the next snack on those open savage savannahs. When the moment of panic hit them, it also created a suspension of thought, they could fight, they could flee, or they could freeze in place. Outrunning the carnivores was not an option. Whacking them with sticks in those early days did little good. Freezing in place and thinking small, would lead to the end of the specie.

THE BIRTHING BREATH

In women it also took a corollary route. Due to bi-pedal loco-motion the birthing mother always had a more or less hard time getting the large headed baby out of her narrow hipped body. She panted hard and fast in the last stages of labor. The blasts of air acting like a bellows fanned the flames of the Kundalini energy lying at the base of her spine. It rose as a serpentine coil of heat and light within her body and as goosepimples across her skin. As the energy of ecstasy poured through her, she forgot her pain and on the crest of her ecstasy bonded with the fruit of her great labor.

It was with the birthing breath of the mother that the life of mysticism began to lay down its tracks. Birthing mothers could experience the internal spin of fire and light that erased their pain and brought them such joy.

On some level they understood that the energy that emerged as the shape of the spiral spin of tornadoes, dust devils, hurricanes, and whirlpools on the body of Mother Earth, was the same shape of the energy that spun its way through their bodies. They drew pictures of that ancient spiral spin on cave walls and overhangs. They also understood that there were places on the body of Mother Earth that seized them with the same ecstatic experience.

To exemplify the process, since there were two sides to the body, they developed a model, the double helexical snake-like spin up the spine burning out the trapped images locked in the left hemisphere of the brain that held the panic in place. The Tantrists called this system the Chacras, or spinning wheels, more like spirals of segmented energy trapped into specific physical form.

Since they believed that the same systems of panic defusion must have been shared by the body of Mother Earth, right under their feet, they charted the body of Mother Earth with the same attention to detail that they charted the chacras within the human body. They called their charting, a grid, as ley lines to the body of Mother Earth. They held the same transformative possibilities as the electrical movement of the Kundalini did to the human body.

The grid lines on the body of Mother Earth also held the same possibility for the experience of leadership, healing, prophecy, wish-fulfillment and ecstasy. There are clues in contemporary languages and in ancient ones through which the potsherds of linguistic evolution can be rediscovered. All else has been lost. Not quite.

What makes some places on the body of Mother Earth more desirable than others? What is it that some areas will drive men to kill each other to keep them, beyond their need to kill for territory? Location, location, location may be the answer.

THE NEANDERTHAL

The ancients understood the workings of nature and the cosmos, on a much more nuanced and intuitive level than even does the modern day scientific community. The definition of Stone Age cave men is an aberration of human history and singularly linear in its perception. The Stone Age fur clad, shuffling cave men and women survived some kind of a natural global catastrophic disaster that obliterated their ancient highly advanced civilizations. To the few that survived, it left them to huddle in caves, wear animal skins, to hunt the mammoth, and also to paint magnificent animal painting on those sequestered cave walls in France and Spain in which they found shelter.

At one ancient time on the planet there were two species of human. One was the Homo Sapiens and the other was the Neanderthal. They existed on the planet for over seven thousand years perhaps more, and their paths crossed on many areas of the globe. In the Carmel caves in Northern Israel bones of both the Homo Sapiens and the Neanderthal have been found on the same archeological level.

Even though the brain of the Neanderthal has been measured as being larger than the Homo Sapiens, especially in the back of the skull area, there is little doubt that they met and mated. That means that their mating produced hybrids. Who were those hybrids? What did they look like? How did they move into the future as their extended Neanderthal family disappeared around them? Or did it?

There was extensive human history before the great catastrophic disasters, such as glaciations, or even a universal flood. Mythologies the world over deal with those ancient often repeated stories.

Periodically Mother Earth went through massive changes.

Asteroids found their way to Her surface with astonishing precision. Volcanic eruptions and earthquakes toppled mountains, carved out great rifts, canyons and created tsunamis. Clouds of dust created year round winters. Melting ice caps helped to raise the water levels. Coastal land must have been inundated. A coastal flood is not that which happens because of heavy rain. A coastal flood is what happens due to a massive tsunami. In between the floods there were ice ages, many documented ice ages. Then the ice caps melted, the inundations began and ancient coastal civilizations disappeared.

The documented Homo Sapien brain has been the same size for at least two hundred-thousand years, maybe longer. We have less information about the Neanderthal. Many civilizations could have come and gone during those ancient epochs. Traces of their knowledge occur through newly discovered, if often buried ruins and singularly through the languages that they carried with them, as they fled from the repeatedly traumatized African continent and settled the far reaches of the world.

They also understood the workings of nature on levels that we can only surmise. It led them to the understanding of how the energy of ecstasy that brought with it leadership, healing, prophecy, wisdom and wish fulfillment, could be intensified, could be experienced everywhere on the planet.

Both species were human beings like us, with a need for some stability and control, so they made diagrams. Those diagrams lasted for thousands of years and served them well but they could not control natural cataclysms. Some of those diagrams we still have with us. Others peek through in myths, legends and poetry. Still others have been called fanciful, irrational and have been brushed aside to languish as superstitions and aspects of Paganism.

It may seem ironic that the nuch maligned Neanderthal not only had a larger brain than their contemporary Homo Sapiens, but it was in the back of the skull and their foreheads were flatter. Both of these characteristics surface in other native peoples who copied them as mothers flattend the foreheads of babies and elongated their skulls. You don't copy those who are inferior; you copy only those who are superior. In Egypt the pharaohs in sculptures on their temple walls have elongated skulls and a snood lke covering extending from the back of their heads.

THE SOLAR WIND

There were three areas that the ecstatic electrical essence that they wanted to understand needed to be chartered. One dealt with the human body and that charting the Tantrists called the chacras and the Chinese called meridians. Both dealt with a movement of the electrical Kundalini energy through the body.

The second charting, or grid, dealt with the body of Mother Earth and their awareness that certain areas on Her surFACE filled them with a state of transformative bliss.

The third category of charting dealt with the night sky and the wheel of stars that spun its way across the heavens. It became a map that evolved as Astrology, and an area of wish-fulfillment prophesy and a hope filled hook on certainty.

Studying the sky, they also realized that there were times during the year that the solar energy flowed with a concentrated intensity that could be charted and anticipated. During the year it was most intense at the equinoxes and solstices which they incorporated in the placement of their massive stone constructions. They also became aware that there were changes in the intensity of the lunar energy flow during the month based on the 'shape shifting' moon. The most immediate cycle that they encountered was the daily passage around them that was marked by the curve of the sun across the great expanse of the sky.

They seemed to understand that the body of Mother Earth like a massive magnet attracted the electrified wind of the sun. The solar wind barreled toward the body of Mother Earth and made its turbulent flashing appearance at the opposite poles as the Aurora Borealis, of the Northern lights in the Northern hemisphere and the Aurora Australis, as the Southern lights in the Southern hemisphere.

Uniting with the body of Mother Earth, the solar wind was

the 'helping hands' that carried the potential for the creation and maintenance of all of existence. So in the very beginning, during the time of female centrality and a balance between the two hemispheres of the brain, the solar wind and the body of Mother Earth were considered to be a single, constantly interacting unit. As the solar wind attracted to the body of Mother Earth pursued Her through space, it caught her and entered Her, not only at the poles but caressed Her, as it crossed Her surface. An aspect of cosmic sensuality enters here.

There was a dual activity that the solar wind expressed as it was drawn to and descended upon the body of Mother Earth. One was a magnetic penetration at the poles. The other was a direct falling down from the sky upon Her surFACE creating a crackling electrical passage across Her planetary skin.

The solar energy that entered at the poles, passed through the boiling cauldron within the body of Mother Earth, was cooked clean in Her oven, rose up through Her mantle along the ley lines and became available to living creatures, as the life giving solar Kundalini energy. The other swath of power came directly out of the sun, to fall precipitously upon Her surface, to spread across Her skin, the planetary plane of Mother Earth.

For the Tantrists, during the time of female centrality with their left handed path of the mother, the solar energy, after it passed through Her center, rose up from the body of Mother Earth, entering the soles of the feet while standing and the anus while sitting in the lotus position. It moved upward through the body to exit either at the forehead, the Egyptian Uraeus or cobra, or the Hindu thousand petalled lotus at the top of the head. For the Hopi Indians and Tibetans the solar energy flowed down directly from the sun, entering the top of the head.

The Tantrists evolved their chacra system out of the most ancient female centrality dealing with Mother Earth, and the solar energy rising up and out of Her, as the singular source of creation.

The Hopi Indians and Tibetans moved into male centrality, with the solar energy plunging down from the sky, at the same time separating the sun away from the body of Mother Earth.

Separation myths the world over document this celestial separation as the left hemisphere of the brain begins its separation from the right hemisphere and barrels into its dangerous right handed journey into the future.

What accompanied this perfect storm of separation and devaluation of the right hemisphere of the brain, is the beginning of understanding of male role in paternity and the shift of writing to the right hand, escalating into a universal movement into male centrality. As these concepts evolved, the energy rising out of the body of Mother Earth was considered to be female. The energy falling directly down from the sun was considered to be male.

THE CHARTERED GRID

There were those among them, usually birthing mothers, witches, shamans, the eunuch uncles and often homosexual males, who were not as yet burned at the stake, or split open on the rack. Those ancient shamans felt in their bodies the Kundalini ecstatic energy of healing and prophecy rising upward out of the body of Mother Earth and they charted or mapped the planet where they felt that the energy was the strongest. They called their mapping the ley or lea lines in England, for they LAy upon the LAnd of the LAdy, the beloved body of Mother Earth. It was upon those ley lines that they built their sacred temples to their Goddesses, for their Goddesses represented different specific aspects of Mother Earth. Their worship was not of individual personified Goddesses. Their worship was of the body of Mother Earth as the singular creative source that those Goddesses represented.

In England the trail of temples crisscrossing the landscape, is called the dragon's way, relating it to the ancient snake as guiding the sun through the dark nocturnal intestines within the body of Mother Earth to make its reappearance in the Eastern sky at dawn. Those same mappings occur all over the planet. The placement of temples and churches along those ancient ley lines cross the English Channel and continue across France past Italy into the Middle East.

Large concentrations of this ecstatic energy also exist under what have been called sacred cities, like Jerusalem, the 'city of peace', for the warring Jews, Christians and Muslims. The Muslims also have Mecca and Medina on the Saudi Arabian peninsula that they consider sacred. In Catholic Poland at Czestochowa there is Jasna Gora (the mountain of light). In France, Lourdes has the same reputation. The Vatican is built over a cave of an ancient

Goddess. Are they too planted on that sacred grid?

Ancient remains of great stone works harken back to a time when different systems of megalithic construction defy modern day understanding, like Stonehenge in England, Easter Island in the Pacific Ocean, Puma Punku in Bolivia, Chalala Pyramid in Mexico, Machu Pichu in Peru, Karnak in Brittany, Kara Hunge in Armenia, Zone of Silence in the Americas, Tihuanako in Peru, Mahanjo Daro in Pakistan, Ankor Wat in Cambodia, Gobekli Tepi in Turkey, Nasca lines in Peru, Baalbek in Lebanon. Were those ancient stone megaliths constructed by people whose brains were larger; or do they go further back?

The Australian Aborigines still in contact with the ancient mother based knowledge are directly connected to those ancient grid lines and as they 'walk about' they experience their 'dream time', and communicate with each other across great distances. As the Western civilized world has stopped using them for target practice, we may be able to learn from them how they accomplished those states of mind and to understand what makes Ayers Rock, or Uluru a sacred place.

Could it be that the insistent appearance of the crop circles are part of that ancient grid? The awesome possibility that Mother Earth dealing with Her greatest gift, Her talent for design, is trying to tell us something. All over the world, there are caves, wells, bodies of water, stones, trees, that ancient peoples have considered sacred, for when they experienced them, they felt the energy within them move and flush them with stoned ecstasy.

After I had the Kundalini experience and wandered through the Corkscrew Swamp Sanctuary in Florida, I was given the singularly awesome experience of having the ecstatic energy of Mother Earth manifest itself in me as I stepped onto that hallowed ground.

Years before, when my niece Michelle and I rummaged through some discarded plants behind the greenhouse in the City of Glass in Farmingdale, Long Island, we held onto each other's hands to climb over the top of the pile. At that moment we were both seized by an immensely pleasant rocking sensation that scared the both of us. We had no frame of reference to understand what caused that singular onset of pleasure. That sacred place still exists behind the City of Glass in Farmingdale and no one knows that it is there. As Christ said, '… when two or more are gathered in my name, I am there.'

It is of a piece, but we have lost the whole puzzle. The same thing may be happening at what they call the Bermuda Triangle. It may be that the planetary grid exists under water also, why not. The ancients were not only migrants on land but also, out of necessity, on water. Were they transported, not only physically but also for a lack of a better word 'spiritually', as they wandered all over the planetary plane?

RULES OF ORIGINAL SOUND DISCOVERY

(ROSD) from the SHAPE of SOUND

In Hebrew the word for 'transport', is hovana.

Human beings with extra sensory powers still exist among us but they have to keep a low profile, so as not to be called crazy, or part of the lunatic fringe, in spite of the fact that psychics often solve crimes and aid the reluctant, single focused, left hemispheric brained police, in their investigations.

Dealing with the solar energy moving up from the body of Mother Earth during the most ancient time of female centrality, we come to the realization that the human body is a system that really works dealing with the individual healing process, search for prophecy, wish-fulfillment and a rush into ecstasy. It is through the mapping of the human body that we begin to understand not only the charts on the body of Mother Earth but the chacras on the body of a living human being.

There are seven Tantric Chacras on either side of the spinal column that the solar and lunar energies spin around. They either rise up from the Earth or plunge down from the sky depending on where you stand in the time of female or male centrality. Therefore there must originally have been fourteen actual spiral wheels that did the spinning. As they spun across the two sides of the human body, at the different evolutionary levels, they segmented and then fused into seven spiral chacral spins around the spine.

The original fourteen chacral wheels evolved into the helping solar hands that defused panic and emerged as the hovering protective angels that rocked babies to sleep. The chacras may have evolved into the fused number seven, but the fourteen angels still exist in the memory of lullabying mothers.

'When at night I go to sleep, fourteen angels watch do-o keep'. Where did that protective lullaby come from, if not the Tantric ecstasy hovering around the seven spinning chacras, on either side of the spinal column? If you stay in female centrality, you get the Tantric movement up from the body of Mother Earth.

As male role in procreation was becoming realized and they created their 'source' away from the body of Mother Earth, for the Hopi Indians and Tibetans the movement was down directly from the sky, out of the sun, and subsequently out of the 'hidden' male mind of God, in the far reaches of space.

When I was still associated with EST, Werner Erhart asked me to assist the Karmapa, the Dalai Lama of Tibet, in rounding up his monks for the various festivities that they all had to attend when they were in Los Angeles. They were staying in one of the canyons, in James Coburns elegant house. Rounding up the monks and getting them into various vans, was not an easy task. They did not stay put and wandered around the compound, leaving and disappearing at a moment's notice. It was like corralling a bunch of cats, or a bag of beans. But for the few days that I was there, the experience left me with questions that the subsequent Kundalini experience began to answer.

Not realizing how blessed I had been, I reveled in the presence of the smiling, ever peaceful and gracious Dalai Lama for the few days that we shared together. Dozens of people prostrated themselves before him, as he blessed them. Initiating me with an orange string around my neck, I learned to hum and chant with him. It was as if I were being prepared for something. This was in the middle seventies, before I had the Kundalini experience in May 22, 1977.

One day he was explaining to some of his guests why he was visiting the United States, as a guest of Werner's and staying at James Coburns house. He was heading east to the Hopi Indian reservation because he wanted to explore how the energy systems of the

Hopi Indians were similar to the energy systems of the Tibetans. He claimed that they were related, that they were brothers. It was years later that I began to understand what he was saying. Both of these energy systems, moved directly down from the sky. They did not rise up from the body of Mother Earth, as they did for the mother centered Tantrists. It seems that living in a male centered world, he wanted to clarify the issue and to establish his 'source' out of the male centered heavens, away from the body of Mother Earth. Perhaps. I never got a chance to ask him how they were related.

SOL, SOLE, SOUL, HEEL
The guru's feet are holy

W hen you are standing with your feet planted on the ground, the magical energy of Mother Earth enters through the bottom of your soles. It is the energy of the sun, as the solar wind, after entering the poles and moving through the molten core of Mother Earth then exiting up onto the surface, that carries with it all the powers of leadership, healing, prophecy, wish-fulfillment and ecstasy.

In Latin the sole of the foot is called 'planta'. Not only plants rose up out of the body of Mother Earth but the same energy moving up and through the soles of the feet gave Mother Earth another name, as the planet. One dealt with stationary plants. The other dealt with a movement of the solar energy up the soles of the feet and during the time of female centrality, it was the common heritage of humanity. 'The gurus feet are holy' comes out of that ancient observation, for they are planted fitmly on the sacred body of Mother Earth at all times. It was the area that the solar energy entered the bottom of their feet when they were standing.

RULE TEN: Place the H (huh) sound before words beginning with a vowel. The word EL, becomes HEL and is one of the oldest names of an ancient Middle Eastern solar deity.

RULE NINE; Place the (AH) sound behind every consonant and HEL becomes HALA. HALA emerges as the Hebrew solar God, supreme deity of the Semites and in the Cannonite myth as the 'strong one', the helper. It also harkens back to one of the most ancient Mother Earth sourced names for the Hebrew sun. In Lithuanian the sun appears as saule (IS HALA).

RULE ELEVEN; The letter S is an EMPHATIC, remove it from the beginning of words. The Lithuanian sun as saule becomes (IS AULE).

RULE TEN; place the letter (H) before words beginning with a vowel. (IS AULE) becomes (IS HAULE).

RULE NINE; replace the existing vowels with the (AH) sound. (IS HAULE) becomes (IS HALA) establishing its links with the ancient sun. The phoneme (HA) deals with the belly of air above the body of Mother Earth through which the sun, having risen in the East passes. (LA) deals with the angular SHAPE of the suns emergence in the East out of the flat surFACE, of Mother Earth. Hillel (HALALA) is the Hebrew 'hymn of joy' to the rising sun at dawn. Halel (HALALA) also in Hebrew, means 'to praise'. The LA LA at the end of (HALALA) deals with the lallating tongue, filled with the joy of praising the rising sun and pushing it out, or regurgetating it at dawn. In Polish chalas (HALASA) stands for 'noise'. It seems that the 'noise' dealt with the cries of welcome for the rising sun at dawn, sol (IS HALA) in Spanish. For the British their ancient tribe of Celts (IS HALATA-) echoes with a similar linguistic construct as 'noise' does for the ancient Poles.

Greeting the sun at dawn was a universal rite. In Lithuanian the sun on its way to becoming (IS HALA) passes through (IS HOULE) which sounds very much like howling out of the hole on the face. In Greek the sun becomes eelyos (HALA-) and their sun God is Helios (HALA-), establishes him as the solar healer (HALA-).

When Christ was tormented on the cross His last words were 'Eli (HALA), Eli (HALA)' why hast thou forsaken me? Did He realize in His last moments of agony on the cross that transformation came through the physical body of the mother and not through the rational mind of the father? Were the ancient links with the solar energy as part of Mother Earth that had been considered sacred and then severed, revealed in that anguished cry? The subsequent words dealing with the sun follow the same pattern, with one addition. In Latin the sun is 'sol' (IS HALA), as it also is in Spanish and French.

RULE ELEVEN; The letter S is an EMPHATIC, standing for 'it is', remove it from the words beginning with the S sound. Remove the letter S at the beginning of sol, it becomes (IS OL).

RULE TEN; place the H sound at the beginning of (IS OL), you get (IS HOL).

RULE NINE; place a vowel behind every consonant and sol

(IS HOL) also emerges out of its ancient past as (IS HALA). It establishes its ancient links with the Hebrew solar deity as EL (HALA). It also expands to include the sole (IS HALA) of the foot and subsequently the soul (IS HALA) as the remaining segment after death. All of these words have their links in the sun AFTER it enters and travels through the body of Mother Earth and rises up to the surface. <u>Since the sun died to its light at night but rose predictably with light every morning, it was considered to be immortal.</u> It may have set in the West, died to its light but it always returned at dawn, fresh and new in the Eastern sky. Human longing for immortality, or even re-incarnation, attached the human soul (IS HALA) to the journey of the sun, Latin sol (IS HALA).

Gilgamesh in his epic myth debunked the belief that the soul travelled through the body of Mother Earth to be reborn into a new life, as the sun (SOL) completing the same journey was reborn to a new day. He threw the Middle East into turmoil, as for many, the belief in reincarnation was shattered.

In Finnish the sun made its descent and fell off the edge in the West. Ulos (HALASA) stands for 'exit'. Once it made its exit in the West it could go in a variety of directions. In Hebrew it became sheol (IS HALA) the sun in the netherworld transforming to be reborn in the East. For the Germans Hel (HALA) became 'fire', the gestating mountain of transformation where the sun waited to be reborn at dawn. Hellir (HALARA) for the Norse became the cave of rebirth of the sun. If it went in the other direction, then it moved further up in the sky through the celestial (IS HALAS-) realms and after death ending up in the Elysian (HALASA-) fields of great joy and happiness. Further up North for the Norse it became Valhalla (vala HALA) their ultimate journey into the sun drenched heaven.

RULE SEVEN; ANLAUT, the first consonant sound often establishes the meaning of a word. In Swahili mahali (maHALA) is 'place'. The place deals with (MA) the body of Mother Earth, through which the sun, the Latin sol (IS HALA) emerges at dawn and sets at twilight. In Finnish Maa is ground, soil, Earth.

Mahala is also a mountain range in the Rift Valley in Africa, the Swahili 'place'. The mountains were considered to be the gestating bellies for the sun to emerge out of them at dawn; one of the reasons mountains and their pyramids were worshipped.. It is the same concept on the other side of the world as the Australian Ayers Rock or Uluru (HALARA). In Sanskrit Mahalla (maHALA) is a eunuch. After he was castrated to act as a protective uncle to his sister's subsequent children, he originally assisted the mothers in the rites of the rising and the setting sun. In time as his power increased he singularly took over the duties of the setting sun. Also in Sanskrit mahila (maHALA) is 'female' who as the ancient matriarch was the original greeter of the sun with hallelujas (HALALA-) and hailing (HALA-) plus aves at dawn and the wailer at the setting sun at the Western wall of death at twilight. For the ancient Hebrews mahala as 'the curse' is based on the original (AH) sound construct and has very ancient linguistic roots. It could go in a variety of directions but primarily it deals with (MA) the body of Mother Earth and the sun (HALA) at night within Her body, cursed to dwell in darkness as Her creatures above dealt with predators and the panic of the long night.

Since male role in procreation was unknown at the time that these concepts were becoming codified, the ancient mothers believed that <u>the blood in a mother's body once it stopped flowing on the outside, coagulated to create a baby on the inside</u>. The solid bloody body of the liver was perceived to be the seat of that coagulation. To beget a baby was to deliver (DALAVARA) it. It became the 'gift of' (DA) the liver (LAVARA).

The word deliver (DALAVARA) takes us to the body of Mother Earth. What to the individual mothers body was the coagulated menstrual blood that made a baby, the same process extended to the body of Mother Earth. Her menstrual blood was the LAVA flow out of Her creative source, the volcanic crater, (KARATARA), the greatest creator (KARATARA) that erupted with Her baby, the land that solidified on Her surface. It was a baptism of fire that brought forth the plane of existence out of the body of Mother Earth, out of Her liver (LAVARA). It was the fires of the setting sun (RA) in the Western sky that caused the immolation that turned the menstrual LAVA into solid land. Ironically the word deliver (DALAVARA) sounds very much like Delaware (DALAWARA). (The (V) and (W) are interchangeable. For the Greeks, Prometheus may have been given the gift of fire to humans but that wasn't his major problem. It only means that he was in touch with the energy of Mother Earth and Her major expression as lavic fire. Chained to a rock he had his liver eaten by an eagle every day. Since he, like the sun, was immortal, the liver grew back and he went through the process over and over again. Pometheus represents the fecundity of Motherhood on a vatiety of levels. Menstruation in women returned monthly, as did the moon. The process of menstruation was also considered to be immortal. On the body of Mother Earth volcanic eruptions must have been seen as an disgorgement of the liver. The LAVA as the liver (LAVARA) flow, had its links with the sun (RA) and was also considered immortal. Since paternity was unknown and a baby was perceived to have been created out of the coagulated blood in the mothers body and the seat of that coagulation was the liver, then the role of Prometheus having his liver pecked out by a predatory bird takes on a different meaning.

The same process was shared with the body of Mother Earth which seemed to be how the sun that had set into the splattered bloody waters in the Western horizon shattered into a thousand pieces as Mother Earth swallowed it, ate it and went through a process of coagulation and transformation. It reconstituted it-self within Her body, transformed itself from a bloody liquid, back into a solar disc to be born round and pale at dawn. It went through an 'accursed' transformative state within the dark noc-turnal body of Mother Earth before it was reborn at dawn. The similar concept surfaces in the Hawaiian hala also based on the most ancient (AH) sound. It echoes the Hebrew concept of being 'accursed' for in Hawaiian hala means 'sin', 'error', and 'offense'. There is another aspect that has to be dealt with in Prometheus. It is an eagle, a predatory bird that pecks at and destroys his liver.

<u>Anytime a bird of prey attacks a Goddess, a snake or even a eunuch we are dealing with the patriarchy killing the matriarchy.</u>

THE SUN

Mother Earth was considered to be a surFACE and a body upon whom they had their being. She existed in a relatively flat circle around them as far as their eyes could see, ending at the horizon line. Where ever they went the circle followed them. They felt protected as if existing in a large airy womb. Out of Her surFACE she gave birth to everything that emerged out of Her ground of being and out of Her watery depths. Out of Her rim she also gave birth to the heavenly bodies and birds. They emerged at an angle out of Her flat side, passed above Her belly of air and sank, disappeared, was swallowed back into Her body on the other side. Her greatest off spring and 'helping hands' was the sun. The sun was dependable, rising every morning to do its job of lightening up the sky, awakening the sleeping creatures to do their work and was considered to be at one with the body of Mother Earth. It was as if She carried the sun pick a back, like some baboons did with their young. The sun was considered a child of Mother Earth, a small replica of Her, emerging daily out of Her flat side at dawn, being 'born again' over and over.

Everything that emerged, or was born out of the body of Mother Earth was smaller than she, was Her child. The individual mothers of the specie, also acted as Her surrogates in the creation of smaller replicas of themselves. The defining adjective for these words dealing with the sun as the solar wind moving up through the body of Mother Earth was holy (HALA). It was considered that the rising energy was not only holy (HALA) but it made you whole (HALA).

RULE FOUR; Go to the SOUND of the CONSONANT, not in the way in was written. The letter W in the word Whole (HALA) deals with water, the other expanse on the body of Mother Earth along with the soil (IS HALA). That creates the whole picture. In the word soil (IS HALA) an ancient clue surfaces. For soil was considered to be the result of volcanic eruptions. When the sun set in the bloody Western waters travelling through the underground entrails within the body of Mother Earth, one of its emanations was exploding up and out of the volcanic craters, as metaphoric menstrual period to the body of Mother Earth, Her bloody lava based in the solar wind creating the land on the surface or soil (IS HALA).

With the W at the beginning of 'whole' what you are dealing with is water, the other planetary surface that completes the expanse of creation on the body of Mother Earth. The sole (IS HALA) has close links with the heel (HALA). Achilles was vulnerable on his heel because that is where it was perceived by the Greeks that his solar (IS HALA-) Earth based energy carrying all the power, entered his body. If you punctured his heel (HALA), you either drained or dammed up the flow of this energy. The (R) at the end of the word solAR deals with the Egyptian sun, the doer (-ER), the hands that helped Mother Earth. The (-ER-AR-OR) at the ends of English words establishes the concept of the sun as 'the doer' or 'one who does'; (maker), (baker), (molar), (tailor).

SACRAL, SACRED

W hen a human being sat on the ground, not only the two buttocks but the anus (HANASA) was in direct contact with the soil. At the anus is the sacral bone. Sacral and sacred sound very much alike, for sacred is (DA) the 'gift of" the sacral. Why would the sacral bone at the anus be sacred? For two reasons. One is that the Kundalini creative solar energy of existence after moving through the oven within the body of Mother Earth when an adept is sitting in the lotus position, enters the anus at the level of the sacral bone.

The other is, that it lies coiled there like a snake ready to erupt when it is called into play through a variety of means. Like the evolution of talent gives the gifted person an extra energy for long sought for attention, so the Kundalini gives a human creature an extra boost of ecstatic survival to get through the evolving, unrelenting, chattering, panic driven left hemisphere of the brain.

What it does is, it puts to sleep the linear image driven, rational, forever judging left hemisphere of the brain and lets the holistic right hemisphere to flow through with the energies of leadership healing, prophecy, wish-fulfillment and ecstasy. To be DAMNED is to have the right hemispheric energies DAMMED up. To function with joy, the DAM has to be released. Otherwise you become DAMNED. Since the word dam (DAMA) establishes its links with the dam (DAMA) or lady of the land, it establishes the energy of the electrifying solar wind as sourced upward out of the body of Mother Earth. The phoneme (DA) is the'gift of' the MA, or mother. The anus (HANASA) has links with the journey of sun (IS HANA).

The most ancient names for the sun in English establish the consonant sounds of the Western Alphabet without the (ER) of the sun at the end as the doER. The RA sound phonetically speaking is of a relatively recent evolution. The most ancient

consonants dealt with the many qualities that the sun represented without the doer at the end.The phoneme (HA) deals with the
belly of air that the sun sailed through.

MOST ANCIENT NAMES FOR THE SUN

HABA is the sun in its aspect of 'two in one', as the process of
rising at dawn and setting at twilight. Its origin is of the two
lips on the mothers face creating the mouth in profile. Oba
(HABA) in Polish means 'two together'. It is the source of
the concept of repetition and habit (HABA-). and ultimate
obsession (HABA-).

HADA is (DA) 'the gift of' the setting sun. Had (HADA) becomes the past tense in English with a movement into Hades
(HADASA) after the sun had set. A womans organization
in Hebrew as Hadassah (HADASA), establishes the ancient
mothers as the wailers at the loss of the sun. In not so ancient Europe, Jewish and Gypsy women were hired to follow
a funeral procession and to wail and tear at their hair wearing sack clothes and ashes. Hid (HADA) deals with the sun
hidden (HADA-) in the body of Mother Earth after it set in
the west.

HAFA deals with the five fingers of fire that rend the fabric of
dawn in half (HAFA), out of the darkness of night into the
light of a new day.

HAGA is the break at the side on the circular flat body of Mother
Earth out of which the sun was reGURgetated out of Her neo-
mountainous surFACE, or beGOTten out of Her body.

HAKA represents the shape of the jaw as the hook (HAKA) on
the human face that hacks (HAKA) food into small (KA)
pieces. On the body of Mother Earth it is the water, aqua
(HAKA) that hacks (HAKA) reality in two; one above as life,
the reflection in the waters below as death.

HALA deals with the angular shape of the suns emergence upon the surface at dawn and the hailing (HALA-) of creatures. It also deals with the angle of the tongue (LA) pushing the sun out of the mountainous mouth on the rim of Mother Earth.

HAMA deals with the bloody aspect of the sun as it sets into the flaming blood splattered waters in the Western horizon after Mother Earth bit it, swallowed it and sent it on its way home (HAMA).

HANA is the sun (IS HANA) with the (NA) of 'emergence on the surfce' and 'a change from a former state', as it continues to shine (IS HANA). In Finnish han (HANA) is the name for 'she', a female. It is the most ancient name when the sun (IS HANA) was considered to be at one with the celestial female clan. In Basque hun (HANA) stands for 'good'.

HARA the belly of air (HARA) above the surFACE contains the possibility of the rebirth of the sun, as do the gestating mountains on the edge. HARA is a form of 'belly' in both Hebrew and Japanese. For the Maori maHARA stands for 'intestines'.

HASA as has (HASA) deals with containment and holding in the present. The sun as life (isness), blood (sange, sanguis), light (swiatlo Polish) and survival.

HAVA as 'to have' (HAVA) the blood out of the vulva, in the eve (HAVA) of evening, the lunar ritual of menstruation. It has links with the hidden bee hive (HAVA) the metaphor for Mother Earth.

THE SEVEN CHACRAS

The root chacra to the human body, at the base of the spine, is like the first step in the evolution of life is to the body of Mother Earth.

THE FIRST CHACRA
THE MULADHARA ROOT CHACRA

Earth, Kundalini, sense of smell, physical sensation, red, LAM EAT AND BE EATEN. Life on planet Earth deals with the primal activity of finding enough food to survive. The same process of eating was believed to have been shared with the body of Mother Earth.

RULE SIXTEEN; OVERLAPPING TRYADS Muladhara (MALADAHARA) (MALA-LADA-DAHA-HARA) chacra. MALA deals with the milling (MALA-) of food, making the pieces smaller (IS MALA-) so that they could be swallowed. In Polish MALA means the 'small she'. LADA deals with the lady (LADA) either of the land as Mother Earth, or the individual mother. DAHA is the 'gift of" (DA)of air (HA). In Polish DACH (DAHA) is the word for roof. HARA is the name for the 'pregnant belly' or ' mountain' in Hebrew and 'belly' in Japanese. What they are dealing with is the belly of air (HA) through which the sun (RA) passes during the day.

The root chacra covers many bases dealing with survival. First it deals with the carnivore mouth that not only does the killing of prey but the masticating of food into smaller pieces. Then it establishes the gender of the food partaker as the lady, the mother who smothers it. As the food travels down into the belly, the belly expands to take in the food, transform it and expel it as feces which came close to the expulsion of a baby out of that same general area.

On the body of Mother Earth an eternal battle that has been life itself, had been playing itself out for millions of years. Every creature was always hungry. It was always stalking its prey to assuage that hunger. Bigger creatures ate smaller creatures. The Russian Easter eggs, a smaller one hidden in a larger one, and the larger one hidden in a still larger one, establish an understanding of how the system of eating operates. The largest one ate all of the subsequent smaller ones.

The mothers of the specie, especially the carnivorous with their never satiated young did most of the hunting. It was perceived that the same process must have existed for the body of Mother Earth. Since they reflected each other's activities concerning motherhood, then Mother Earth must also have gotten hungry. What could She eat to satisfy that shared hunger? They came up with a very creative idea. Since the sun disappeared into the Western WALL of water at twilight, then She must have sWALLowed it. The SHAPE of that disappearance with the round disc of the sun reflecting itself in the waters below, became a pun bridging two perceptions.

RULE SEVENTEEN; HONONYMS puns within the same language.On one level the SHAPE of that solar descent reflected on the water became the number <u>eight</u>. On another level it became an activity. 'She ATE it'. (8)

Another number emerged out of that same observation. For when the sun sank in the West, the angular SHAPE of that sinking, the fall off the side of the flat surFACE of Mother Earth came to define the number seven of 'separation', and in time death establishing it as the ubiquitous sacred number.

As male awareness began to develop concerning their input in procreation and the shift to the left hemisphere of the brain, they began to create their own Gods away from the body of Mother Earth. Their major solar hero became the sun which they appropriated from the wailing eunuchs at the Western wall of death of the setting sun.

The activity of life associated with the mother's during the daylight hours was above the planetary surFACE. The activity of darkness and death was below the reflected surFACE associated with the sun that had set and with the emerging power base of the castrated eunuchs and the heterosexual 'band of brothers'.

The same configuration that emerged as letters existing on the face of the mother was shared with the surFACE of Mother Earth. The M of the top lip reflected the W of the bottom lip. On the body of Mother Earth the M of the top lip were the mountains, the gestating bellies that reGURgitated the sun at dawn. On the other side in the West was the great W of the reflected watery maw that swallowed the sun at twilight.

As males began to realize their role in procreation, they began to fight for control, for their own power base and their own creative source. That power base became the sun. The eunuch uncles were already esconsed there. On many levels they joined forces.

What had been occurring on the planet, the bloody gender based fight between the mothers and the emerging fathers was echoed in the emerging language. It was also happening to the body of Mother Earth and the emerging male creative source, the sun.

The phoneme (WA) on the human mothers face was the shape of the bottom lip. It was considered to be a reflection of the top lip. Together with (MA) they formed the mouth. At the time these concepts began to emerge the (WA) expanded to include the bottom lip, the WAtery aspect on the body of Mother Earth. It was the WAtery aspect on the body of Mother Earth that sWAllowed the sun in the West. The sun as RA, the Egyptian sun God had to fight back. So the WA of the Mother got the RA of the father.

WA plus RA became war (WARA) and linguistically WAR emerged on the scene. It reflected the reality of that what was happening between mothers and the emerging fathers on the planetary plane.

What came with the concept of war was the shift from the right hemisphere of the brain and left handedness of the mother's, to the left hemisphere of the brain and the right handedness of the emerging fathers.

Early writing in the Middle East had been written from right to left, as if written by the left hand. With writing itself and the linear shift in the hemispheres of the brain, what had been the oral heritage of the mother's became the written secretive history of the father's.

RULE SEVENTEEN; HONONYMS puns within a language. Writing came to define what was right because it was written by the right hand of the emerging feathers. The left hand of the mothers was left behind.

Originally, during the time of female centrality it was the right hand that was the dextral (DA) 'gift of' the extra hand. With the movement into male centrality and a shift into the left hemisphere of the brain that activated the right side of the body, the right hand gained in supremacy. The left hand as sinestral became the sinister hand. To this day in India food must be eaten with the right hand. The left hand emerged to clean away the remains of digested feces.

In Poland before the Second World War, the left hand was considered by some to be the hand of Satan.

I was born left handed and was considered to be cursed by the devil. My left hand was enclosed in a sock and tied tightly around my wrist. I had to learn to write and to use the scissors with my right hand. Everything else, the things that I do naturally, I still do and have done, with my left hand. The tension that the activity of changing my left handedness to my right handedness plagued me all my life with pain, arthritis and subsequently shoulder replacement.

Another unfortunate habit dogged my foot steps. Because I was naturally left handed writing with the right hand always caused me to make the initial mistake as I tried to create the elusive symbols. I cringed, twisted the tongue in my mouth to help me, gouged the paper trying to write with my right hand. It left me with an unfortunate habit of making a mistake at the first try no matter what I embarked to do. After I made the initial mistake, I could go on and correct the blunder but it left me hesitant, especially when I had to audition for the Broadway shows that paid my way through college. I could always blame it on nerves, as I corrected the problem. I knew better, but didn't know that it was a long standing habit that came with the forced use of my right hand.

The left hand of the mother's at the time of male centrality evolved as the evil hand of Satan and the writing right hand of the father's emerged triumphant. There is a clue that the right hand associated with the left hemisphere of the brain carried with it the seeds of panic. It resides in the word FRIGHT (FARATA). For FRIGHT is associated with the fingers (FA) of the RIGHT hand and the left hemisphere of the brain in which are stored the images to which fear (FARA) has become wedded.

It was Christ who was supposed to have said 'I am all right in me there is no left'. I find it difficult to believe that he said that. His message was the message of compassion and love of the ancient left handed mothers. It was Jehovah astride in male centrality who said 'sit on the right hand of God the Father almighty'.

Human speech and writing with the right hand shifted the power from the cooperative ancient left handed mothers living in relative peace, to the emerging competitive right handed fathers and a descent into unrelenting competitive war.

The begats of male descent in the Bible document the shift from female to male centrality.

RULE NINE; Replace the existing vowel with the (AH) sound. The WAR that had plagued mankind became petrified into dogma with the word (WARADA). The word (WARADA) with emerging male dominance became the 'gift of' (DA) war (WARA). If the word didn't work then the extension of the hand as the weapon was used and the sword (IS WARADA) came into play.

The story of King Arthur in England was an effort to bring back the relative peace and a movement into transcendence that existed at the time of female centrality. To have peace you couldn't have the Alpha male as one leader. So Arthur created an enormous round table. There would be no one to sit at the head of that enormous round table. All of the knights would be considered equal. No Alpha male here. His kingdom called Avalon (HAVA(LA)NA) had links to the River Avon (HAVANA) at Stonehenge with the (L) of the lady halving its linguistic center (HAVA(LA)NA). There was another aspect to King Arthur. He was the only one who could pull the SWORD out of the stone. When the meaning of the 'stone' becomes apparent, it will fully reveal to what lengths the legend goes to bring back the magical 'stoned' centrality of the ancient mothers.

To work (WARAKA) establishes its own origins. On one level to work (WARAKA), has its roots in war (WARA) and the subsequent curse of bondage and slavery. On another level, reka (RAKA) in Polish means 'hand' and hand deals with laboring and making smaller pieces (KA) of replicated matter. Work (WARAKA) also means small (KA) war (WARA). The nobility of labor has no place here. Another name for Mother Earth is WORLD (WARALADA), the planetary battlefield that was the 'gift of' (WA) the all encompassing lady (LADA) of the land. Eat and be eaten furfaces here.

The word 'weapon' (WAPANA) in Polish tells its own story. For in Polish lapa (WAPA) is the 'paw' of an animal. It may be the mouth of the carnivore mother that does the smothering but it is her paws as weapons (WAPA-) that do the clutching of the prey in place. jThe carnivore paw(PAWA) estabishes its power (PAWA-) base and its relationship to killing and war (WARA).

The concept of killing having its roots in the mouth expands to include other animals, especially among the carnivores. For in Polish WARga (VARAGA) is a word defining the lips. It is the lips of a carnivore that asphyxiate the prey when a kill is made. In German 'to eat' is essen (HASASANA). In order to eat you have you becme an assassin (HASASANA). It echoes the same concept using different sounds. From whence Essene (HASASANA)? Did they understand the 'eating' of trauma as Joya Ma advocated?.

RULE NINETEEN; METAPLASM, or transposition, adding or deleting letters in a word. The battle between the ancient mothers and the emerging fathers grew to such massive proportions that the planet itself was redefined. Trying to anchor it back to the mothers, the ancient women took the word (WARADA) and placed the letter (L) in the center, almost begging for some peace and balance. The WORD as the gift of WAR, came to define the world (WARA(LA)DA), still the home of the LAdy of the LAnd, or Mother Earth. The same construct surfaces in the name of King Arthurs city Avalon (HAVA(LA)NA). It didn't last long for that was the last gasp, as women lost to 'THE WORD' written by the right hand, petrified in stone, on papyrus, paper and bark along with male violence and war, overran the body of Mother Earth and all of Her creatures, the STAMPEDE OF THE NATIVES is upon us. No one is being spared.

Since human beings considered themselves part of the scene of life, they did not consider animals inferior to themselves. They knew that animals felt and thought as they did. They were limited by their bodies not their hearts and minds. As they began to lose their instinctual certainty due to the over evolution of fear, they turned to other creatures to give them a clue how to survive on the open savannahs.

The queen bee became the metaphor for Being, as the sole creative source, same as Mother Earth. The ant may have been the example for the endless succession of sisters as aunts. They held animals in awe and wonder for their specific qualities. It was the lioness that caught and held their imaginations, in time surfacing as the monumental Sphynx in Egypt. The Sphynx is Mother Earth with the body of a lioness and is much more ancient than male history proclaims.

With a movement into male centrality the lion, not the lioness became the king of the jungle, actually the savannah. With a shift into male centrality it surfaces as the symbol of kingship and majesty in England for reasons that will become apparent.

It was the lioness and the other mother carnivores that created life and death on the open savannahs. They had to feed their cubs. So the lionesses stalked and in organized feline groups brought down their prey. The activity dealing with killing their prey became a word that defined the action. For it was the mothers of the lioness pride, or alone as the leopard and cheetah, that SMOTHERED the hapless antelope or wild pig.

The activity of smothering (IS MATARA-) dealt with the mouth (MATA) or jaws of the feline mother grasping the throat and cutting off the breath, thus killing its prey. MATA doesn't only mean mouth (MATA). It also means mot (MATA) or 'death' in Amharic. Also in Amharic mata defines 'evening', the time of day when the sun was killed to its light and the darkness of death covered the perilous land. In Bugotu the concept of killing is delegated to the whole face, not only the mouth of the mother. The word for 'face' in Bugotu is also mata. It becomes even clearer when to 'bite' or 'chew off', also in Bugotu is (gamMATA).

In Basque the name for 'boy' is mutila (MATALA). Was his young boyhood mutilated (MATALA-) or killed in the service of the Mother, the LAdy of the Land? In Polish motyl (MATALA) is a butterfly, a transformed pupae. A butterfly in Spanish is mariposa and mariposa is a derogatory Spanish name for a homosexual male having links with the unreproductive eunuch.

In Finnish sur MATA also means 'to kill.' There seems to be little doubt that the job of killing prey was delegated originally to the most fantastic creature of the savannahs the lioness and to the mouth (MATA) of the carnivore mother (MATA-). An English word smite (IS MATA) joins the Biblical construct.

If the name of a 'boy' in Basque is mutila (MATALA) then we are dealing with a variety of clues. He was castrated, his body was mutilated (MATALA-) to become a eunuch. The eunuchs and the homosexual males joined forces facing the same derogatory remarks. It also means that the Basque language on the peninsula of Iberia emerges out of the most ancient linguistic roots, not unlike Finnish, Lithuanian and Hungarian.

RULE EIGHTEEN; HOMOPHONES, puns across languages.

It was the mouth (MATA) of the carnivore mother (MATARA) that did the Smothering. What the feline mother accomplished was asphyxiation and murder (MARADARA) of the struggling prey. In Polish a crude word for the mouth surfaces as morda (MARADA) covering both linguistic bases. For it was the mouth, morda (MARADA) in Polish, that did the murder (MARADA-) in English.

The concept of destruction expands to include Mother Earth as Her marine environment. The war that existed between Mother Earth and the sun whom she swallowed in the West, echoing the battle of the sexes on Her Earthly plane, comes down to us as MA, Mother Earth as water and RA the male solar deity who died every night, was swallowed by Her. The linguistic construct became MA plus RA-MARA. With the addition of SA at the end to establish 'isness', you get Mars (MARASA), or the God of War. As the solar deity, he began to fight for his life, resisting being swallowed every night by the watery maw on the body of Mother Earth. Since he could not win on the planetary plane, he was pushed up into the heavens to reign supreme in space as the male God of War.

The gender battles that were happening across the globe became reflected in the creation of words. As male power began to establish its own foothold, paternity became a real issue. Males wanted to know which children they had fathered. The first inkling of marriage surfaces when the male had to leave his 'band of brothers' and live with the clan of his intended. That system still exists in China around Lake Mugu where the boss is the old matriarch and there are no marriage vows. Men live with their mothers and have a 'walker' marriage. They do not have primacy in the home. A similar system still exists in the Wadabe tribe where the brothers and uncles take care of the children. The girls choose their mates and live with their mothers.

When during the time of female centralty a girl still lived with her mother then she had the protection of the female clan. When she became housed in the family of her husband, after the shift into male centrality deepened, she became the slave of her husband's relatives. She had little to say about her fate.

There must have been a massive battle as women resisted their constrained circumstances. Two words surface that give meaning to the battle. One is marital (MARATALA) dealing with marriage (MARA-). The other is martial (MARATALA) dealing with war. They contain within their linguistic folds the (MARA) dyad establishing the battle between the body of Mother Earth (MA) and the sun (RA) that reflected the reality on the planetary plane.

Along with the sexual power battle there surfaces a word that gives meaning to the new perceptions as the knowledge of emerging paternity. The father is the one who made HER FAT/ FAT HER. We are in the land of the anastrophe (reflection).

The root chacra on the level of life on the planet is the first organizational spin of life dealing with violent survival, based on the killing of prey, ingestion of food through the mouth, its digestion through the digestive organs, and its elimination through the anal aperture. Without the ingestion of food on some level and its transformation into energy, there would be no life on the planet.

The edibility of food is based first on the sense of smell then on the sense of taste. A snake does both. It smells the air with its tongue.

The sense of smell also deals with recognition; the male smells the female in heat and commences to mate, assuring survival of the specie. The mother smells and hears her baby, especially among birds and hurries to empty her gizzard into its waiting open maw, thus assuring its survival.

THE NOSE KNOWS

Animals mark their territory and recognize the marking scent with their noses. The protection of the territory assures a steady food supply. 'The nose knows' is an old adage. It also establishes the fact that knowledge is in the NOW moment of physical experience. 'To know' is not an idea in the mind. 'To know' is an experience in the body. The mind was considered to be like a troop of screeching, scattering monkeys high up in the jungle vanopy. It was the body that could be counted on. It always knew what to do.

All the senses crisscross between the eyebrows at the forehead. The right hemisphere of the brain controls the left side of the body. The left hemisphere of the brain controls the right side of the body. The only sense that goes directly to the brain is the nose that goes on a parallel track through the two nostrils straight into the olfactory bulb in the brain without crisscrossing. Therefore the sense of smell is the oldest organ based on the chemistry of the universe. The sense of smell may very well be the basic characteristic of the atom.

Human beings have lost their capacity to smell like other creatures, when they became bi-pedal and shifted away from the multidimensional nose into the single focused, linear image making capacity of the eye.

The base chacra establishes the expanding plan for the survival of life on planet Earth. All of the subsequent chacras are contained in the base chacra of survival, like in the Russian Easter egg.

Human beings possibility of endurance is based on their ability to ingest and digest food. Problems with the appetite to ingest food dealing with survival, means that the Kundalini energy is trapped on that first root level and has to be burned out for the creature to survive and prosper. If problems with eating continue then the creature will have trouble surviving. Eating problems dealing with famine, starvation, addiction to food, obesity, boulemia, deal with energy entrapment or damming up on the most basic level.

There are three sins. One is jealousy, the second is greed, the third is revenge.

The panic of losing the food supply surfaces when a nursing baby at the breast is replaced by a new arrival, the rival for the milk supply. It is when the seeds of helplessness that have already been planted right after birth, are joined by the seeds of fear at being deserted and resentment at being pushed away. Part of that fear accompanies the child for the rest of its life and may cause eating problems in adulthood.

In the African language and the country of Bemba they understood the problem and even defined it with the word lunse (LANASA). It deals with the mother becoming pregnant before the child is weaned. It is the source of much human misery based on the loss of the breast. The jealousey born of such rejection may follow the victim for the rest of its life.

RULE SIXTEEN; OVERLAPPING DYADS. The Bemba word of lunse (LANASA) is rich in meaning. The first dyad (LANA), deals with the mother giving birth in concert with the cycles of the moon, Luna (LANA) in Latin. The moon was considered to be responsible for menstruation and the coagulated blood within the mother's body that created the baby. (NASA) the second dyad deals with the Latin nasence (NASANASA) meaning 'to be born'. The birth of a new baby assured the replacement of the nursing infant at the breast and the beginning of its jealous sourced agony.

The root chacra on its primary level deals with eating, digesting and defacating. With the LAM (LAMA) syllable associated with it, there comes a realization that LA deals with the LAnd, and MA deals with the Earth Mother as the LAdy of the LAnd. For the Maya LA as Mother Earth was the 'eternal sound of creation.' As far as the Middle Easterners were concerned, it was RA, the sun. The LA of pleasure (PALASARA) dealing with the sensuality of the ancient mothers was replaced by the RA of pressure (PARASARA) release dealing with the sexuality of the emerging fathers.

It was the land that came first as the volcanic eruption splayed LAva out across the surface to create the foundation upon which the drama of life could be played out.

The letter L in its most primal shape deals with the tongue, the angle that lies in the cavity of the mouth and does a variety of things. It lallates lullaby's to a baby and licks it into a peaceful sleep. It also creates meaning to the sounds that leave the oral cavity.

    As the angle that lies in the cavity of the mouth, the tongue also tells lies. Language cannot be trusted. Body language can be relied on but not the convolutions of speech.

The most important activity of the tongue (lengua in Latin) is its milling ability, to create small enough pieces for the masticator to swallow. It was first associated with the eating and the swallowing of food, the chore of the first chacra. It does the same thing with SOUND, segmenting it into small understandable pieces that in time have evolved into words.

The letter L has confusing antecedents for in its most ancient evolution also deals with the SHAPE of the emergence of the sun out of the Eastern, either mouth or vulvic hole, out of the flat circular body of Mother Earth. As Mother Earth regurgetated her most recent solar meal, it was perceived that it was the tongue that pushed the sun out of Her mouth onto Her surFACE at dawn. The five, fingers of fire come later. The organs out of the mothers face, like the tongue, have first linguistic priority.

Ironically the word Karma (KARAMA) in Hindu deals with accumulated negativity from a former life and the possibility of creating more negativity in this life. In Polish a similar linguistic structure surfaces in karmic (KARAMA-) which means to feed, or 'to eat'. Joya said that she would 'eat' an indiscretion committed in this life but if it happened again the adept would have to 'eat it'. It seems that she could either lift it from you, or you had to face it and chew through it yourself; echoes of essen and the Essenes.

In Sanskrit Karma (KARAMA) deals with mixed caste, shoemaker, worker, one who is paying for his past life's sins by being born to do the lowest work with leather and the cobbling of shoes. It deals with the stratification along caste lines first noticed among bees and ants. Also in Sanskrit karmara (KARAMA-) is a smith and a smith (IS MATA) was the mutilated (MATA-) subsequent son who took over the workings at the forge. He was maimed to keep him from running away. The same thing happened to the shepherd.

In Finnish the word kaarme (KARAMA) takes another tack, for it drags the 'serpent' in. It was the evil serpent that did in the two inhabitants of the Garden of Eden. He created their everlasting karma (KARAMA). There seemed to be no one to 'eat it' for them as they were banished from their joy, until Christ came along.

In Homers tale of the hero's transformative journey in the Odyssey, Hercules has to clean out the Augean stables. He takes a look at the accumulated piles of manure and diverts two rivers to plunge through the stable and carry out all of the accumulated garbage. The horse stables surface in Homers Odyssey as the metaphoric stable within the psyche that has to be cleaned out. Every time that some aspect of the horse surfaces in dream time or myth, we are dealing with the journey of the Kundalini energy as a cleaning out agent. The two streams of water are kin to the Ida and Pingali of the Tsntrists that do the same job, both dealing with the Kundalini energy rising up the spine as a double ribbon of coiling snakes.

What Homer was dealing with was the ritual journey of the hero through the chacras and the cleaning out of the accumulated debris of infantile entrapped destructive habit. The Tantrists used the metaphor of the fire or serpent energy doing the job. The Greeks surrounded by plenty of ocean, opted for water. Ironically they kept the double winding snake, the Caduceus as part of the healing aspect of the sun. They left he moon behind with female centrality.

Caduceus (KADASASA) strains to be revealed. There are two dyads that bear closer scrutiny. One is (KADA) and it comes from the 'gift of '(DA), the maker of smaller (KA) objects. The Kundalini mystical energy, is the energy that accompanies the birthing process. The birthing process creates smaller objects, as in kid (KADA). The 'gift of' (DA), of (KA) the smaller object that is made.

The other is the (SASA) on the end establishing the healing rod (i.e. spine) as containing the bloody life force of the indivisual mother (SA) and the all embracing life force out of the body of Mother Earth (SA).

The (SASA) construct had originally been associated with mothers who gave birth, as in princess (paranaSASA), carrying both energies. A further clue surfaces. (PARANA) of princess (PARANAsasa) shares its linguistic root with prana (PARANA) establishing its links with the Hindu Shakti, or the electrical current that is awakened during birthing and blasts its ecstatic way up the spine. In Polish the name of that electrical energy is prand (PARANADA), or the 'gift of' (DA) prana (PARANA). In English the electrical current as Shakti (IS HAKA-) also establishes its electrifying quality as a shock (IS HAKA). A shock is that which blasts or hacks (HAKA) you free from the pain drenched extended labors of birthing, on one level and the stultifying burden of habit on another.

THE SECOND CHACRA
THE SEXUAL CHACRA
THE SVADHISTHANA OR SACRAL CHACRA
Water, emotions, genitals, reproduction, moon, orange, VAM

RULE SIXTEEN; OVERLAPPING TRYADS and more.

The sexual chacra, the SVADHISTHANA (IS VADA-DASA-SATA-TANA) hides in its linguistic folds a variety of clues. VADA is the 'gift of' (DA) the vulva (VA) and (VA) vagina on the mother's body. DASA deals with the 'gift of' (DA) of 'is-ness' (SA) or the beginning of life as the breath, (aspiration), or blood (sangre), and the spin of the spiral energy. The last tryad gives us the most salient clue, for SATANA (SATANA) with the last two dyads combined, sits at the end of the name of the sexual chacra. Based on the (AH) sound, it is one of the most ancient concepts to be codified. At this point in Tantric understanding sexuality was considered to be the basis of the negative energy of Satanism.

The Hopi Indians and Tibetans disagree with the Tantrists on the division of the chacras. They claim that there are five chacras. The two top chacras and the two bottom chacras are the same. That could only happen if you believe that sexuality is on the same level as eating and digestion. It could only happen in male centrality. You can live without sex but you can't live without food.

Males have to fight the Alpha male to get to the female and to mate. Territoriality establishes the food supply. So territoriality and mating became intermingled. In the male brain, sex and violence come out of the same area.

There are a variety of problems that sexuality presents to the contemporary human creature. One deals with the definition of gender. Another problem deals with the sexual molestation of women and children, of rape, pornography and of slavery. Then there is the problem of fertility. The most universal problem in males deals with sexual performance.

The definition of gender is tricky and full of many pitfalls for Mother Nature is not that specific in Her creation of what had become defined as female and male. The varieties are endless. Many males are so heterosexual that the thought of a male lover sends them into paroxysms of denial. Then there are some who are more flexible and a male lover is not that far out of the picture. Then there are male homosexuals who cross over and are able to love women along with men. And there are others who find women totally distasteful.

Then there are the some, including both females and males who feel that they are in the wrong bodies. They go through sex changes to feel more comfortable. There are some men who can only get an erection watching pornography, snuff films and there are others who like to be beaten. The combinations are endless.

Conversation

'I think that homosexuality is a sin, and homosexuals should be ostracized.'

'Do you believe in God?'

'Yes, but what has God to do with it ?'

'Do you believe that God created everything?'

'Yes. '

'Then if God created everything, then God created homosexuals'

Huh?

And so it goes.

Women go through similar problems but they in most cases seem to be more forgiving. Mothers fall in love with their children no matter what they look like, or who they may become. Some may reject their homosexual off spring primarily for the fact that there may not be any grandchildren. For mothers sexuality in their children may not be as defining a factor as it is for the fathers, since it is the father that can only create male children. The ignorance and madness out of Afghanistan, that a husband killed his wife for giving birth to a baby girl, reaches cosmic proportions, since it is only the father who can generate male offspring.

Then there is the other factor that gives human beings a monstrous amount of angst.

For the male it is his erection,

It deals with its size, durability and dependability. The size deals with bigger is better which translates into more is better, then most and ultimately into greed and ostentacious display of wealth. The durability deals with lasting longer and not having a premature ejaculation leaving the partner sexually unsatisfied. The dependability deals with becoming erect when the time seems to be right and not becoming erect when an erection is not appropriate. The problems dealing with impotence are universal and never ending.

For the female, it deals with the orgasm.

It hides in its folds the roots of mysticism

The female orgasm did not evolve out of intercourse. The female orgasm evolved out of the birthing experience. The reason that the female orgasm has been dealt with so much misinformation and secrecy, is that it was not only the woman's power base, but it also at a very ancient time of female centrality established the roots of the mysterious mysticism. It also deals with a primal male fear that the penis does not do its job. It shouldn't. It didn't evolve to give most women orgasms. It evolved to deposit the sperm as far up the vagina as it could reach.

Then what is the function of a mother's orgasm? It is to get the large headed baby out of her narrow birth canal. Due to bipedal locomotion the mothers hips did not spread out enough to make room for the large head of the baby. When the labor contractions begin, it only means that the birth canal is beginning to spasm. As it spasms, it begins to contract around the head of the baby pushing it down and out of the mother's body. The head of the baby, on its way out rubs against the stretched clitoris that is impeding its progress. This is accompanied by unrelenting spasms, or orgasms. As the baby's head keeps rubbing against the beak of the clitoris that is stretched around its head, it spasms the clitoris into a cascading rush of orgasmic pleasure which helps to accelerate the uterine and vaginal peristalsis. That is why mothers have multiple orgasms. It's to get the large headed baby out of their bodies. Male sexuality and female sexuality are very different. Just because a male has one orgasm doesn't mean that the same activity must be part of the female experience. Male orgasm deals with ejaculation. The female orgasm is much more ancient and deals with spasming the baby out of her body.

It did evolve that some women (twenty-five per cent) have orgasms with a penis during intercourse. The clue exists in the perception that the <u>head</u> of the penis rubbing the clitoris from the outside does the same job as the <u>head</u> of a baby rubbing the clitoris from the inside. That is why the tip of the penis is called a <u>head</u>. Some have misinterpreted it as the penis having a mind of its own, but I think that it goes back to something much more ancient.

There was a time when women were either masturbated or masturbated themselves to help squeeze their large headed babies out of their bodies.

RULE NINETEEN; METAPLASM the transposition , addition or deletion of letters in a word.

An ORGASM creates a new ORGA(NI) SM. The (NI) in the center of ORGASM is the new arrival on the planet. Ni (NA) deals with either 'emergence of the surface', or 'a change from a former state'. The linguistic example may be very explicit, or for some it may be too close for comfort.

There must have been an ancient perception that masturbation brought forth a baby. At the time of male centrality, the Egyptian God Amun in his sanctum sanctorum masturbated all of existence into being every night. Where could his priests have gotten that idea if not by watching women give birth? This must have been before the time that semen took its proper place as the co-genitor of a baby.

In the last stages of labor, the birthing mother automatically begins to pant like a dog, with the Bastrika breath of the Tantrists to accelerate the spasming activity of the uterus and vagina. The high fast panting breath like a bellows fans the flames of the Kundalini energy that is lying dormant at the bottom of the spine. As it uncoils and rises, it not only activates great pleasure in the mother's body but burns out the traces of pain that she has suffered during her labors. She is then able to look at the product of her great labors and through a haze of ecstasy, bond with her off spring. It is that high panting breath that also opens up the doors of mysticism, of obliteration of the left hemisphere of the brain, as the mother suspended in her trance, is borne on the wings of her ecstatic creation.

It is ironic that the Hebrew God Jehovah, onto the women he said Gen 4:16 'I will greatly multiply the sorrow and thy conception, in sorrow shalt thou bring forth children and thy desire shalt be to thy husband for he shall rule over thee'.

Does that mean that there was a time that women bore their children without pain? Did the practice of clitorectomies enter the picture around this ancient male centered Biblical time? <u>If you remove the clitoris then you take away not only joyful birthing, but the possibility of mysticism associated with the birthing experience that males could not share.</u> With mysticism came the powers of ruling, of healing, prophecy, wish-fulfillment, wisdom and ecstasy.

The power that had been attributed to women because of their seductive sexuality was the power of the birthing breath that had to be destroyed. The only way to negate the power inherent in the mystical Kundalini experience was to excise the whole clitoral structure. As male centrality became established this is what the fathers demanded and the crushed subservient mothers provided. In Northern Arica and the Middle East a young girl cannot be married if she did not have her clitoris removed. It is a point of honor for Arab men who also masturbate to pictures of women who have been so mutilated.

Some contemporary pundits deal with this 'problem' in women as nymphomania that has to be controlled. It has nothing to do with nymphomania. It has to do with the fact that the birthing breath was the source of female power, the roots of mysticism and all the gifts that the Kundalini experience blessed upon birthing mothers. Since males could not share in that process it therefore had to be destroyed. Women are not sexually disfunctional because they donn't 'come' during intercourse; they were never meant to. It was an evolutionary plus with males for the ones that did.

Subsequent male rulers claimed a link with that process but it came out of a totally different direction. The pharaohs of Egypt claimed to be partially Gods. So did most ancient kings and Roman caesars.

If the birthing energy came alive in them, then they were either castrated males, or homosexuals in whom the female energy had been internalized before birth.

In castrated males as eunuchs the male energy was neutralized due to the removal of their testes. The Kundalini energy as the energy rising up from the body of Mother Earth is female energy and is mostly alien to male bodies. That may be the reason as males gained the supremacy of the planet all the powers that had been associated with Mother Earth and joyful motherhood had to be obliterated.

There are clues in the names of what became male leaders and heroes. At the end of some of the most important names of male leaders there is a construct of (SASA). The first (SA) deals with the blood of the personal mothers; sanguis, sangre. The second(SA) deals with the shape of 'ISNESS' of the spiral on the body of Mother Earth.The list spreads out in many directions. Ramses (RAMA SASA), Moses (MA SASA), Zeus (SASA), Theseus (TA SASA), Perseus (PARA SASA), Odysseus (HADA SASA), Jesus (JA SASA). Ancient people like the Anasazi (HANASASA), even places like the oasis (HASASA) come into play.

The SHAPE and SOUND of the letter S is one of the few consonants that emerged singularly out of the sissing vents on the body of Mother Earth. It deals with the shape of spiral spins, hurricanes, tornadoes, dust devils and establishes the concept of, 'isness' or 'being'. Becoming associated with human beings, halved laterally through its center, the top half of the letter S deals with the ocular cavity and the eye of C-ing and with life above the surface. The bottom half facing in the opposite direction deals with caves and corpses and life below the surface. Thus above the plane and below the plane the letter S embraces both possibilities dealing with life and death. The letter S may also be a simplified form of the two orbs of the setting sun one above the surface and the other one reflected below which surface in the ancient Chinese Yin Yang.

Originally at the time of female centrality, the double SS as (SASA) was at the end of female names such as Goddess (GADASASA), princess (PARANASASA), Mount Parnssus (PARANASASA) may have been the original home of the princess (PARANASASA), mistress (MASATARASASA), hostess (HASATASASA). To have the double SASA at the end of your name, you had to have had both alive in you; the individual personal mother energy of 'isness' , (SA) and the energy of Mother Earth as 'isness', the other (SA). With the birthing breath it came naturally to women but it had to be ritually created in men who became leaders, as male centrality overran the planet. That is why many of the subsequent men who became kings, leaders, pharaohs, caesars emerged with the (SASA) at the end of their names attaching themselves to the ruling powers inherent in the ancient mothers.

We have to become aware that we are deep in male territory when actresses drop the SASA at the end of their names and become affiliated with the more important moniker, the male actor.

COSMIC ORGASM

I often tried to explain to friends what had happened to me at the Topanga Canyon retreat when I experienced the Kundalini energy exploding in me. Most faces grew slack with pity and their glassy eyes took on a look of vague disbelief, but not all the time. As I was telling my neighbor about what had happened to me, her eyes grew wide and she looked around furtively to make sure that no one was listening. Not knowing what to call it, she claimed that she too had what she called a cosmic orgasm. But it wasn't during sex. She almost apologized. She didn't know that it even existed but when she gave birth to what became her fifth child she had an experience of the Kundalini rising, except she didn't know what it was. She was going through natural childbirth and in the last stages of labor, as she was panting, her breath came faster and faster and her accelerating contractions became orgasmic. Great waves of pleasure swept over her body as she gave birth to her son. Wondering what had happened to her and trying to explain it to the male doctor, who brushed it off as her imagination.

She had been a librarian and began to do some research. Coming across the experience that she had, she found out that it wasn't that uncommon except that male doctors didn't know anything about it and didn't want to deal with it, funneling it into Aristotle's female 'hysteria' bandwagon.

Except for a minor few, the penis didn't evolve to give their partners sexual satisfaction, pleasure yes, but not full sexual satisfaction. It is the fingers, when the creature became bi-pedal that began to rest at the area of the genitals providing comfort by playing with that forbidden area.

Blaming women for being frigid because the penis didn't do its job and the partner didn't know how to use his fingers or tongue to bring his partner to orgasm, only deals with the universal ignorance that males have with female bodies. When males learned their role in procreation, one of the things that issued forth from that awareness was that the penis and the seed that emanated from it were both holy. It is a universal tragedy that we don't have the ancient houris or temple prostitutes, the holy women who taught young men how to pleasure their partners. It would have taken both sexes off the tormented sexual hook.

Some women fought back demanding sexual satisfaction. It was sometimes easier to achieve an orgasm during intercourse with the woman on top, so that her clitoris was in direct contact with the penis stretched around it as it was during birthing around the head of the emerging struggling fetus.

As we see in the Lilith (LALATA) story, the happy, singing, lallating (LALATA-) first bride of Adam. She and Adam were equal and both came out of the soil of Mother Earth. He wanted to be the boss and remain on top in order to maintain the soon to be deified missionary position. She said no and left. Since she still stood for ancient female power, as male centrality took hold, she was delegated to becoming a demon, killer of children, generator of nightmares and nocturnal emissions to men. So the male God Jehovah came along and created another bride for Adam but this time out of Adams rib. He called her Eve of evening as secondary in importance to the sun of daylight. The sun, after male centrality took hold, became associated with men and the moon with women.

The birth out of Adams side or rib, goes back to the flat circular surFACE, or body of Mother Earth who gave birth to the heavenly bodies out of Her planetary side.

As males took center stage then they too had to give birth. Not only did Adam give birth to Eve out of his rib, or side, but as male centrality made its appearance and established its locus in the left hemisphere of the brain, a similar story is echoed in the Greek myth of Zeus giving birth to Athena out of his mind.

All these permutations deal with the power that women had with the sharing of their birthing pleasure with men. The pleasure couldn't remain out of female bodies. It had to shift to the primacy of the penis. As men pump away trying to satisfy their partners, they never realize that the pumping will not do it. The contact cannot be made by endurance. Other means have to be employed. Since the penis has been defined as holy, the blame for a lack of sexual satisfaction has been laid at the feet, or vaginas, of women. Women to please their partners and get over all that straining activity have become universal actresses, (cum actors), in faking orgasms.

Since all male based religious texts demand female acceptance of whatever their husbands bring to their beds, what we now have is a universal miasma of religiously sanctioned ignorance. It is not only universal ignorance but a psychological mess. Men blame themselves for not being able to satisfy their partners and women scream for a release of their frustrations due to unsatisfying sex.

During the sex act as the uterus and vagina contract, they are accompanied by the contractions of the anus and lower colon. The singular act of sex through the anal opening is called sodomy and is practiced by homosexual men, for good reason, as it spasms it is their seat of pleasure. Because they share that orgasmic pleasure with birthing mothers, it may be why so many of the 'spiritual' males are not only gay but considered as second class citizens, a moniker they share with women.

In days gone by, if males did not begin their lives as being gay, then to become leaders they were either castrated or went on great TESTs, great transformative mythological journeys to reach that status. It may be partly that the test of TESTosterone that creates the separation and the imbalance between the two hemispheres of the brain. Originally at the time of female centrality when male role was undefined, the male gnitalia had been perceived as the emergence on the surface of the inTESTines. They really didn't understand male role in the production of babies and wondered what the role of the extra body parts was about. Unfortunately many ugly activities were tried to make a boy more like a girl so that he too could have children. Freud with his 'penis envy' really missed the point. These concepts have very ancient roots.

In the system of Astrology Libra holds up the scales that are balanced. Libra also means liberty and liberty deals with freedom. Lib means to be castrated. To be free from the unrelenting pressures of violence and sexuality it was believed at the time of female centrality that the young boy had to be castrated, to go through the process of liberation.

To be free, you must have the two hemispheres balanced. One cannot be stronger than the other, as the left hemisphere carrying the male essence has become, carrying with it violence, war, secrecy, domination and competition.

The name gay (GAYA) does not necessarily mean that homosexuals are cheerful people. The linguistic source gives us a clue. Gay (GAYA) people are in contact with the body of Mother Earth as Gaya, the begetter (GA) of light (AYA). Aya is 'light' in Persian and 'dawn' in Assyrian. Mother Earth at the time these concepts came into being, either regurgitated the heavenly bodies out of Her mountainous mouth at the edge, or gave birth or begotted them out of Her vulvic side at the Eastern horizon. Then She swallowed them in the west on the other side at the end of their journeys. A double process occurred above and below. Gay people were the creation of the great Mother GAYA. They were Her creations, were like Her, existing as 'two in one', both female and male. She was their androgynous Mother.

The concept expands in Hebrew into the word goyem (GAYAMA). A goy (GAYA) was not a Jew. A goy (GAYA) was the child of the ancient mother who as a 'pagan' worshipped the body of Mother Earth (GAYA), not a creation of the Hebrew father (YHVH), the hidden vowelless mind of God in the sky.

The sound in the second chacra is VAM and VAM deals with the V on the female body as the vulva and vagina and on the body of Mother Earth as the volcanic vent. The vulva (VALAVA) is the valve (VALAVA) that creates the passage back and forth into the possibility of life. It also deals with the moon of the menstrual flow and water, for it is the moon that not only brings on the menstrual flow in individual females but pulls the tides back and forth on the body of Mother Earth.

In two Slavic languages there is a fusion of meaning that can bring clarity. It deals with the word 'hinge', and it may be far from Stonehenge but it went in its own direction. A door hinge is like a valve. It is a turnaround, back and forth, in this case between life and death. In Polish 'zawias (IS HAVASA) is a 'hinge'. In Russian zaviaz (IS HAVASA) is an 'ovary'.

The problems with sexuality based in the second chacra are endless, dealing with gender identity, reproduction, expression of love and the sharing of pleasure on the one hand and the expression of sexuality through violence, abuse, pornography and serial murder on the other. The male monotheistic patriarchial religions give homosexuals the short shrift and delegate them to similar realms as they have delegated women. Having the female sexual energy internalized before birth, because it is female sexual energy, sets them apart as not being acceptable. What has not been understood is that because the gay man has gathered the female energy to him before birth, he may be able to experience similar aspects of mysticism through the practice of sodomy that the birthing mother does through the activation of the Kundalini orgasm during birthing. That may be why sodomy has come to be so vilified and outlawed. The word sodomy (IS HADAMA) may give us a clue. It is the 'gift of' (DA) the mother (MA), dealing with past tense of had (HADA). The anus may have been considered to exist behind the vulva on the female body and as a passage of the sun into night on the Western rim was behind the body of Mother Earth.

Beautiful Asinet out of the Hebrew Bible establishes prehistoric links with the Kundalimi experience. She falls in love with Joseph of the multicolored cloak (already ritually transformaed). She is not a Jew and can't marry him. Despair, sack cloak and ashes cover her as do seven days of chest beating. She devours a honey comb. Bees surround her. She becomes transformed.

Bees at the time of mothers centrally were metaphors for the singular creative capacity of Mother Earth, in Her 'hidden' hive (HAVA) of creation. The hive (HAVA) in Polish is chova (HAVA) or 'hidden'. As male centrally overwhelmed the worship at Mother Earth the 'hidden' God of the ethers became JEHOVA (-HAVA) Asinets experience of the Kundalimi emergers not out of the bithing breath and the cosmic orgasm of birthing but out of her despair. Her anguish awakens the Mother Kundalini engery in her and she becomes a Jew. What does that tell us about the ancient Hebraic source?

The bee Goddess of the Greeks as Deborah (DABARA) or the 'gift' of (DA), the (BARA) or brother (BARA-) establishes links with the encient brothers as eunochs in the service to the Mother.

Another majestic woman surfaces in the Sahara, as the Tuareq Queen, who was a leader, mother, warrior, mystic led her 'free people' against the Arabs. She was ALKAHINA (HALAKAHANA). She has links with the sun (IS HANA) (enlightenment) coming and going. The sun as the solar wind moved through her as the Kundalini when she was still privy to her birthing breaths of ecstasy. (KAHANA) with the small (KA) sun (IS HANA) or enlightenment.

One ancient tribe of Jews, the Lemba, migrated out of the dessicating Sahara, claim to be the descendents of a priestly class called the KOHANIN (KAHANANA).

As they peopled the world due to catastrophic disasters the ALKAHINA cum KOHANIN became;
COHEN (KAHANA) in Europe,
COHAN (KANANA) in Ireland,
KHAN (KAHANA) in the Middle East and Asia,
KUHN (KAHAHA) in Germany,
but their source goes further back in pre-history for ...
COCHINA is a sacred object of the Hopi
COCHINA is kitchen in Italian; Kitchen is a place of cooking in English.
KOCHANA (KAHANA) is 'beloved' in Polish. It is Mother Earth as the beloved cook that gave birth to all the KAHANAS.
The "Big Kahuna (KAHANA) is Mother Earth.

THE THIRD CHACRA

THE MANIPURA CHACRA
THE SOLAR PLEXUS POWER CHACRA
Sun, fire, power, will, self identity, yellow, RAM

THE MALE LINE-UP

All creatures who exist within a hierarchy based on birth, caste, class, size, importance, wealth, organization, detachment, pugnacity, job distribution, exist in a line-up. A line-up goes up in a straight line and goes down in a straight line.

Whenever you have a cluster of creatures you have some aspect of a hierarchy. It begins with insects such as ants, who are not only birthed by one mother ant, are not only aunts to each other but have specific hierarchial functions that they have to perform. The same construct happens with bees, they too have a rigid structure with the queen bee laying all the eggs and the workers performing all the jobs. Because of the queen bee doing all of the work of creation, she became a metaphor for Mother Earth, who also did all the work of creation. Linguistically the queen bee came to represent the B of 'being'. Then there are the termite mounds who follow the same mother based system. Those may be the most universal. Most other insects like the spider, praying mantis, butterflies, moths, beetles, centipedes, cocaroaches are loners. Butterflies may group together for their migratory flights but most of the time they are on their own.

Whether birds have a hierarchy is a moot point. They do exist in colonies and many are loners except at the time of chick creation. Some like to pair up and often stay together for life. Penguins huddle in specific inland colonies but territorial hierarchy doesn't seem to be part of their experience. Some fish do have territories that they patrol under the sea but the large sea mammals travel over the far reaches of the oceans.

Then there are the creatures of the African savannah. Some are loners like the cheetah and leopard, while others like the lions live in very structured prides usually with one male Alpha lion to mate with. The wildebeest and zebra when not endlessly migrating seem to have territorial aspirations. The elephants, hyenas, wild dogs, chimpanzees and baboons, all live in more or less flexible hierarchical configurations. Horses also live in family groups.

There is one universal constant.

In order to mate the males have to fight and depose the Alpha male.

So for the males, whether carnivore or herbivore when the pressures of sexuality unfold their nets, the male smells the air to find a female to mate with. He has to get past the Alpha male. Violent confrontations ensue. So to get to the female and have sex the male has to fight his way in. Very early in evolutionary history, sex and violence became intermingled. It exists in the same area of the human male brain to this day.

Females do not have to fight to mate. Nature takes care of them by moving the female into estrus, by spotting her flanks with red blood that can be read by the male to tell him that she is ready. So in human sexuality male violence and female readiness have very ancient and very different roots.

The line-up of importance can be very rigid. Among human males, it was originally based on the strength in the arms of the upper torso, to keep the female in place, then also among men it was on the size of the penis. In time it became the size of the money belt. As society expanded there were always those who were bigger, stronger, smarter, richer, more detached, less vulnerable, who took advantage of the smaller, weaker, dumber, poorer, more compassionate and more vulnerable creatures.

The ultimate thrust in males is to WIN, to topple the Alpha male and get both his territory and the females esconsed there. Homage may be verbally paid to 'how the game is played' but the truth is it doesn't matter how the game is played, the end result, no matter at what price, is to WIN. This leads to the use of any and all means to attain the power and control that winning provides.

The most ambitious, ruthless, competitive, vicious Alpha males will scheme and fight their way to the top and destroy anyone who might undermine their power base. In the name of selfish 'individuality' the Alpha male has become the 'self made man' and his power is unassailable. His dictum is 'you owe me'. A balance of power is established using that phrase.

Women can't perform on this 'you owe me' level. There is no way that a mother can say to a new born baby, 'you owe me'. There is no thing that a baby can give back to its mother at that helpless time.

The process lays its tracks in different ways across gender lines. Between males the 'you owe me', deals with favors, bribes, secret agreements, loyalty, corruption, lying, and jockeying for position on the line up. With women 'you owe me' deals with sexual payback. Most women resent the set up but can do little about it. There are others who have learned to play the male game and they have come under the curse of being called 'bitches'. At this time of male centrality, humanity has come under the multilevelled curse of the universal Alpha male. They have surfaced in politics, business, sports, entertainment, religion and all areas where more than one man seeks to be the 'top dog'. There is a misunderstanding that men fight for an 'ideal', be it love of country, love of religion, love of language, love of tradition, love of a woman, you name it. That is not why men fight. Men fight because they are primed to fight. Fighting is the most exciting thing that they can do. Whether or not there is a violence gene in the male molecular makeup is a moot point. All male animals butt heads in order to establish territory and corral the females. What would make the human male different? Except in the present moment with the nuclear Democles sword hanging over our heads, the thrust to fight will reap a nasty harvest.

The line up exists for both sexes but not to the same degree. When women enter a party, they look so see who is younger, prettier, has a slimmer body, and what clothes and jewelry she may be wearing. When men enter a room they look to see who is their competition, who is more important and who is less important.

The more important competitor will get a full dose of charm. The less important competitor will be summarily dismissed.

In a male line up, your job is to try and tear down the one above you and watch out that the one below you doesn't tear you down. The jockeying for position is never ending. It is a battle of endless competition. <u>As males fight to WIN, women slave to GET THE JOB DONE.</u>

The battles between male opponents at the time of the rut or must gives us a clue of how the power play evolved as animal male adversaries pound their heads together, lock their antlers, gore each other with tusks, stalk their competition through the bushes. The same activities occur among human males in the hierarchy of military campaigns, competitive business, religious systems and sports. The means become the end as males battle it out for power and control and the prize, the female and the subsequent baby gets lost in the shuffle.

As the power chacra, the solar plexus deals with status and standing in a society. It is the chacra of self identity, and self worth. It is the chacra of gameplaying.

Since it is associated with the power of the sun, then the primary expression of this chacra deals with males. This perception is expanded with the sound of RAM (RAMA) and RAM is the male sheep. RA deals with the sun and MA deals with the body of Mother Earth. But RA of the male sun comes first and MA of the body of Mother Earth follows it. It wasn't always that way. Originally the dyad was MARA. In Hebrew MARA means master and it dealt with the watery aspect of Mother Earth.

RULE EIGHT; ANASTROPHE, PALENDROME. reflection or inversion.

During the time of female centrality when the body of Mother Earth was worshipped as the sole creator, she was considered as a dual expression. One aspect of Her was the land. The other aspect of Her was water. The existence of life was the part that flourished above Her surface on land. But there existed another reality. The existence of life on land was reflected below on the surface of the water. Both survival systems above and below were considered to be real. The reality above dealt with life and the reflected reality in the waters below dealt with the mysterious passage into death.

Originally MARA was one of the great rivers in Africa. It came out of the time of female centrality and the MA of Mother Earth came first. She was followed by Her greatest creation and helper, RA the sun. For the sun was perceived to be born out of Her side in the Eastern sky at dawn. She was the life above the surface and the sun was the reflected reality below the surface out of which it emerged in the East. She dealt with life and he dealt with death. The evolution of names followed the same progression.

When males shifted the burden of primacy to the sun as lord and master then MARA above the plane in life became RAMA, the reflected reality in death (MARA/RAMA). The same progression followed all of the other Mother Goddesses as they were redefined as male Gods.

Maya as the holder (MA) of the light (AYA), ' light' in Persian, 'dawn' in Assyrian, became the reflected male god Yama, (MAYA/YAMA) the Japanese 'lord of death'. In the African language of Bemba YAMA is the 'maternal uncle'. In the most ancient prehistoric times he was the castrated first born son who not only protected his sister's children as their maternal uncle but officiated at his mother's side over the rites of the setting sun as it died to its light. Also in Bemba MUN YAMA was a 'ritual murderer', who wept and wailed as Mother Earth ate the sun in the Western sky, as it slid out of sight into the blood splattered waters below. As the 'ritual murderer' he became associated with the death of the sun, the loss of its light and the approach of total darkness.

When human beings feel powerless, it means that they haven't found a place in the line-up, or the place in the line-up doesn't satisfy them. They have not assumed their place in the hierarchy of status. It leads to most of the social dislocations as they scratch their way up and always find someone to look down on. To establish their power base, males will create other male adversaries that they can topple. <u>Males always need someone to surmount.</u>

The contemporary dislocation that men are facing is that there are fewer and fewer people that they can look down on. The blacks have been more or less liberated. They, as emerging bosses can tell the former owners what to do. Definitions of intellectual superiority no longer hold water.

Then there are the women who could always be counted on to be made inferior. Fewer are marrying, more are becoming financially independent. Many are having babies out of wedlock. Who will the human male look down on and feel superior to. It is an enigma and a massive social problem. The Western world has added to the problem with the liberation of women. That is not true for the rest of humanity as women are veiled, stoned, clitorectomized, abused, raped and killed. War, that used to be singularly a man's game has become a detached massacre, as missiles strike the male, female and child alike.

Hoping for still possible future adversaries the mostly male UFO enthusiasts yearn for some male enemies that may appear from out of space and create another 'other' that can be stalked and killed.

The lower three chacras deal with the violent physicality of mostly male behavior. No one has escaped the fear that has been planted after birth and its accompanying helplessness.

The hunting and killing to eat of the first chacra can be shared by all. The sexuality of the second chacra emerges as violence from the male side and the unrelenting reproductive capacity on the female side. The third chacra dealing with power establishes the violence that on a universal scale countries flexing their military muscles exhibit in their competition for global supremacy.

Human beings who have problems with status and finding their place in society will have the Kundalini energy trapped at the power chacra. Once a baby is born, the power play begins. It lasts for most of human lifetime. In the Western world status has been defined by class. Like it or not you were born into a class. There was usually no escape. Aristocracy and nobility ruled the domain and the rest of feudal humanity serviced them. Usually the name of God was invoked to make the aristocracy valid. In the ancient male centered left-hemispheric past, rulers were in one way or another related to God. Like Ramses in Egypt and

Caligula in Rome they actually defined themselves as God. In time hereditary ruling classes supported by God as 'divine right of kings' sanctioned by the church, were enough to keep the peasants in line.

In India the ancient Manu women hating priests, ironically set up the caste system structured on the mother based bee hive. Each person and all their future descendents was born to do a specific function forever. There was no escape. You were cursed with karma and to pay for your sins you had to do what was demanded from the state. To this day birth into a caste determines your destiny.

A country emerged on the shores of a newly discovered continent that denied the right of kings to rule and birth was not the ultimate trap. It was called the United States of America and the battle has been to keep it from becoming a class warfare state of the few powerful rich and the many unlucky poor, with a caste system based on an economic oligarchy. Time will tell.

THE FOURTH CHACRA
THE HEART CHACRA—THE ANAHATA CHACRA
Air, compassion, love, self-acceptance, relationships, green, YAM

RULE EIGHT; ANASTROPHE or PALENDROME, reflection or inversion, read forward and backwards in a word of cluster.

The heart chacra as ANAHATA (HANAHATA) contains in it the reflection of HANA as the sun (IS HANA) above the plane and the NAHA as the sun under the plane. (HANA/NAHA). The heart chacra establishes the balance between the two hemispheres of the brain using the complete journey of the sun moving above and below the body of Mother Earth resulting in the love that the journey established between the sun and the body of Mother Earth.

It is the love of the mother that creates the balance. When we move into the heart chacra we are dealing with all mothers and some fathers who bond at birth with their off spring and who love and nourish their children. When we move into the heart chacra, we are moving into the territory of motherhood. It's not only a human condition, for birds also share in the love of their offspring, as do carnivores and herbivores. Even crocodile mothers love and protect their babies. The open heart of the mother assures the survival of the child. She will die to protect it.

The heart establishes the possibility for relationships that transcend the need for lactating nourishment. The mother becomes the master of teaching the baby how to survive. The hum (HAMA) of the mother while masticating food in her mouth tells the infant what is edible and what should be spat out. The only sound that you can make when your mouth is closed and chewing is going on inside, is the sound of humming. A variety of concepts emerged out of that initial chewing activity. What also emerged is the true shape of the top lip that did the humming, emerging as the M of the Mouth of the Mother.

Someone defined the hummer as a human (HAMANA) being. In ancient times it was the mother's who defined HUManity as in time the emerging father's defined MANkind. It seems that being called a hummer was done as an observation made by someone who was not a hummer. There was another human creature that existed at the time that these concepts were being codified.

It also brought up the concepts that the human hummer was somehow different, that it came out of the humus (HAMA-) or the body of Mother Earth as did Adam of the Bible. The human mother as the joyful birther of children, with her high panting breath and a movement into ecstasy, possessed not only joy but a great deal of humor (HAMA-). In Finnish, that may have its roots in Phoenician, the 'smile' is hymy (HAMA) and to gossip was to spread 'rumors', humu (HAMA). Most of all, she was humble (HAMA-) and filled with gratitude to the great Mother Earth who provided for all. Hubris was not part of her makeup.

Ironically that the Egyptian God Amun who masturbated existence into being every night has hidden in his name Amun (HAMANA), links to the ancient human (HAMANA) mother who also masturbated existence into being every time she gave birth.

The humming sound created another ancilliary gift. Originally when the mother hummed, she vibrated her palate. The palate sat under the pituitary gland. When the pituitary gland was activated it sent forth endorphins filling the mother's body with pleasure. It gave her an added incentive to keep chewing and to keep humming.

The humming sound not only defined the humming human mother but the HUM (HAMA), or AUM (HAMA), or OM (HAMA), in time became the sacred syllable that was associated with a ritualized movement into the ecstatic trance, or the suspended dream state. In time a hymn (HAMANA) grew out of human humming. A male aspect enters here with the male him (HAMA). Was the ancient eunuch (HANAKA), uncle (HANAKALA) part of that ancient humming group, or was he a singer (IS HANAGA-)? The letters (K) and (G) are interchangeable.

Most religions deal with the open heart. In Roman Catholicism it is Mother Mary who holds the baby in her arms and her heart flushes with the mothers spilled blood. The dyad HAMA is associated with blood. In Greek, hemophilia (HAMA-) deals with a blood disease where the blood doesn't clot.

The mother and child configuration surfaces in most of the ancient religions of the world. In Egypt it is Isis with Horus as Mother Earth and her son (SUN). Also in Catholicism, Christ as the son emerges with the open heart, bleeding for humanity. In Hinduism it is Hanuman (HANAMANA) the monkey God whose open heart also bleeds for humanity. He has links with the sun (IS HANA) and the moon (MANA) echoing the balance that is expressed through the two currents carrying the solar and lunar serpentine spirals that rise up the spine as the Ida and Pingali of the Kundalini energy. That echoes the open bleeding heart and a balance in the two hemispheres of the mother and her love.

Hanuman (HANAMANA) the monkey God of humility contains in his name not only the sun (IS HANA) but the last two syllables fused, create (NAMANA) which is an anastrophe (NAMA/MANA), a reflection within his name and the realization that he also was balanced in his two brain hemispheres and capable of unconditional love. In Hinduism the dance of the open heart is also performed by the two lovers, Shakti and Siva.

As males gained their supremacy during the time of their ascendance most of what came before and was associated with the power inherent in mothers and their birthing breath had not only to be destroyed but vilified. The open bleeding heart of the mother brought with it not only the curse (KA(RA)SA) out of the coos (KASA) but shame (IS HAMA) for the spilled blood out of the wound on the mothers body.

There seems to be a heartfelt progression and it deals with a warning.

First we have the AB of the Egyptian 'heart soul'. The (AH)

sound stands for the first breath of a baby. On the body of Mother Earth it is the shape of the volcanic cone out of which not only Her breath but also land is born out of Her lavic blood, as Her most formidable creation. The (B) is what came after the mother and that was either the baby, or the BA as the Middle Eastern father. I opt for the baby, for it goes back to before paternity was known.

The AB of the Egyptian 'heart soul' establishes the bonding and love between the mother (AH) and the baby (BA) that emerged from her ABdomen.

Then you move to Hinduism and emerge with the male and female, the Shakti and Siva dancing in the heart. Mother love branches out to include love between woman and man. Except I thought that Siva was gay, that Mother Kali took care of his violence and liberated him from his heterosexual destiny. LIB means to be castrated. Libra deals with a balance of the scales of destiny, the two hemispheres of the brain balanced, liberated, working in concert, the Kundalini energy doing its job and burning out the dammed up vestiges of left hemispheric violence. To liberate a male child was to set them free. To castrate, is to create the concept of 'two in one' as the letter B in lib (LABA) illustrates. The 'two in one' of castration deals with both the male body and the female essence having become balanced and opened to the possibilities of transformative trance.

The lib (LABA) construct has very questionable and dark overtones for labios (LABA-) in Latin means lips. In Hebrew during a circumcision ceremony a special rabbi (moyil) bites off the fore skin of the poor unsuspecting male child. The links with a much more ancient ceremony of castration cannot really be questioned. Once the foreskin was bitten off, it was often buried under a mountain altar close to the solar deity. The name of the ceremony of circumcision was called a 'bris' and the discarded foreskin became the 'gift of' (DA) the bris, or DEBRIS.

With the ceremony of circumcision the ancient Hebrews gained great power. The circumcised male not only became the rabbi (RABA), dealing with the rising and the setting (BA) of the sun (RA), but he also gained the powers inherent in mysticism. He became a prophet, a healer, a ruler and he could ride on the wings of ecstasy.

It is not an accident that Hebrew (HABARA) comes out of the same linguistic construct as hubris (HABARASA). The ancient Jews set themselves apart from the others around them, as 'the chosen' because they followed a very ancient custom of modified castration.

The end dyad in hubris (HABARASA) is BRIS (BARASA) dealing with the often arrogant power inherent in the ceremonial removal of part of the penis having links with ancient castration and the powers inherent in the birthing breath of the mothers.

The most ancient belief at the time of female centrality was that Mother Earth was the single overwhelming creative context. She made everything, all the creatures on Her surFACE, all the plants and trees. She even gave birth, or regurgetated the sun, moon, stars and even birds out of Her flat surFACE. They were all considered Her children and were smaller than she was. She was their overwhelming context. Female mothers of the specie were Her surrogates in creating smaller replicas of themselves.

Then came the next step. The need to give thanks for their endless bounty drove human mothers to create specific aspects of their expansive maternal context to give thanks to. They created Goddesses and endowed them with specific powers. One could insure fertility. Another was blessed with the gift of rain. Still another could find a handsome lover and the gift of wealth. The worship of Goddesses expanded to cover as many bases as there were human needs. Animals were always part of the picture and assisted the Goddesses in fulfilling human wishes. This construct existed for many, many thousands of years. Then as male centrality began to take over, some of the animals remained but male Gods began to replace the female Goddesses. The male Gods took over the celestial realms of the air. They moved into the secrecy of the mind and became the hidden movers, the wind through the trees, the thought through the head. As they made solid their opinions they gave us another clue. The letter O deals with the disc of the sun and as zeros the permanently empty male womb. Pinion means wing on a bird. The word pinion as a wing on a bird uses the air as a vehicle for its flight, as does opinion.

Then a mjor shift occurred. As the Gods became sourced by the male mind, the males who sourced the Gods became at one with them. They became made in the God's image.

A conversation with a devotee wrapped in a winding sheet at the ashram.

'You know, I think that I'm God'. He shared with me as we circled the lake.

'What makes you say that? Ever ready to get some answers.

'Because when I talk to God, I talk to myself'. Out of sheet clad air heads words of wisdom.

Something like this must have happened at the time of ancient male centrality as they struggled to find their bases of not only power, but faith. We are made in the image of God must have been a very new idea since Gods and Goddesses were perceived to have been outside of human bodies. To be made in the image of God took a lot of nerve. The Greeks must have been part of the ancient scene for when they took one look at their neighbors, the Hebrews (HABARASA) they came up with a name defining them with 'hubris.' (HABARASA)

Then we come to someone more contemporary with an open heart. It is Christ who says for us 'to love thy neighbor,' 'turn the other cheek,' 'help the poor.' He is bringing us the message of the ancient mothers. Born of a virgin, as were so many of the ancient messiahs and heroes, he may have been an un-reproductive male, who not only replaced SIVA but extended his plea and said, you had better shape up and treat each other better, or you are in for a lot of trouble.

It's not enough to love your baby. It's not enough to love the beloved. You also have to love thy neighbor, the stranger. His message was thwarted, as had been most of the messages of the ancient mothers. The message became thwarted as religion took over spirituality with the faith of the fathers. Christ didn't bring us reason and rationality to deal with. That had been going on for thousands of years and it didn't work. He was trying to deal with the experience of mysticism which Mary Magdalene, his closest disciple shared with him. He knew that it was the only way to save warring left hemispheric mankind. But the petrified word out of Peter shut down the open heart. Politics took over the word of the messiah. Brutal politics replaced the love in the open heart of the mothers and their emerging peaceful Son.

The heart is attached to the skin. The nose smells, the tongue tastes, the eyes see, the ears hear, BUT the heart feels and the skin feels. So the heart and the skin are in some way connected. It is the touching of the skin that assists in the process of bonding.

Primates groom each other. All that means is that while looking for insects such as fleas, lice and ticks, they touch each other. They comb through their pelts with delicate fingers. As they comb through their pelts, they share the pleasure of activating the sense of touch which is connected to the heart. That brings with it sensuality and social bonding. It creates extended family groups that our ancestors copied. We may never know how much hair they had on their bodies but running the hands over their skins has very ancient antecedents. The human creature is addicted to pleasure. Sharing the touch of their bodies added to the emergence of sensuality.

The sharing of the touch began between the mother and the child. It expanded to the touch of the beloved. In time as the 'idea' became real, the love expanded to include all aspects of God.

In caressing the skin you make the skin feel wonderful. That wonder moving across the arms and into the chest also fills the heart with love. Adepts on the path of spirituality strive for the open heart, for unconditional love, for lack of judgment, for detachment.

There is a pitfall that has to be avoided, for detachment can often lead to indifference. Indifference can destroy the mutuality that love can awaken. It can lead the adept into selfish pursuits of power and control.

During the Second World War in England because of the bombing of the cities and the mothers working in defense factories, babies were relocated to nurseries in the country. There was no one available to pick them up, to touch them and to make that initial contact with the mother. Many of those babies died. Love as emotional nourishment is just as important as mother's milk for the infant to survive.

When Israel was putting itself together, the egalitarian Kibbutz was an important place to raise children. There was no parental input especially from the mothers. Everybody had to work hard to create a new land. There was little individual touching and tender care. What they found that those children raised in the egalitarian Kibbutz were incapable of intimacy later on in life. The possibility of intimacy with the beloved is established at the breast with the touch from the mother.

Related to Venus (VANASA) as the passage of the mother's blood through the veins (VANASA), the heart chacra embraces motherhood. Associated with the YAM sound it establishes its links with the Y shape of the female pubis. As YAM (YAMA) it can go in a variety of directions. Originally it dealt with the gorge on both the female body and the body of Mother Earth. In Polish a jama (YAMA) is an abyss, an open pit like crevasse. It was that crevasse between the mountains that the sun either rose out of, or sank into at the beginning and end of each day.

In Japanese it emerged as Yama 'the lord of death' and it dealt with the setting of the sun into the crevasse, or body of Mother Earth and dying to its light. The Bemba yama as the 'maternal uncle' sets up the eunuch uncle as protector of his sisters children assisting his mother in the rites of the setting sun. As the mun yama he establishes himself as the 'ritual murderer' of the sun, as it died to its light at twilight.

YIN YANG

The process of the sun moving in and out of the body of Mother Earth is also exemplified in the Chinese Yin and Yang. In contemporary male centrality it is explained as the male and female forever spinning through space. The S circle containing the Yin Yang is Mother Earth containing within Her, the dual S of 'isness', as the ultimate androgyny.

During the ancient time of female centrality the Yin and Yang were considered as one unit and dealt with the dual aspects of the sun. The Yin was the sun above the plane in daylight and the Yang was the sun under the plane in darkness.

When male centrality co-opted the scene, the Yin (YANA or HAYANA) above the plane stayed female but the Yang (YANAGA or HAYANAGA) below the plane became male. They became redefined as female and male and lost their links to the sun.

The shape of the letter Y not only deals with the female pubis but also with the Y shape of the break between two mountain peaks, the crevasse on the body of Mother Earth, out of which and into which, the sun rose and sank each day.

The Yin (YANA or HAYANA) dealt with the light that rose out of the tomb of darkness, to light up not only the sky above but the body of Mother Earth below. In Persian AYA (HAYA) means 'light'. In Assyrian AYA (HAYA) means 'dawn'. When Mother Earth and the heavenly bodies were considered to be one indivisible unit, that solar aspect of Yin above the plane in time became redefined as female dealing with Mother Earth as <u>life</u> above the surface. Yin as the female aspect in Chinese is echoed in Hindu as the yoni (HAYA, HAYANA) and ione (HAYA, HAYANA) in the Semitic countries.

The Yang (HAYANAGA) also dealt with the sun, as the (HAYA) in its name suggests but it is the (NAGA) that moves in to define the male aspect. The (NAGA) deals with the snake (IS

NAKA, NAGA), the guide of the sun through the subterranean dark caverns within the body of Mother Earth, it wouldn't get lost on its way back up to the light. The ritual process dealing with the rising and the setting of the sun came to be represented by the eunuch (HANAKA, NAGA) uncle (HANAKALA).

The snake began its journey as a guide to the sun. In time it was replaced by male ferrymen and psychopomps who guided the sun through the underground maze to its rebirth.

The snake not only became the guide of the sun but was also considered to be very smart, for it always found its way out of the dark convoluted intestines within the body of Mother Earth and like the tongue pushed the sun up and out of her maw to emerge at dawn. With that quality of smartness because it had been associated with female centrality as males took center stage, it became the evil serpent in the Garden of Eden who tempted the two human creations to defy the laws of the male God.

So Yin and Yang have their own history which delineates the passage from female centrality to the centrality of the males. In Chinese a subtle plus for women came to light with kouYIN and it defines 'oral sex'. With the YIN in its name it is telling us that Chinese men from that ancient prehistoric time didn't singularly rely on their penis but knew how to satisfy their sex partners orally.

The Kundalini energy is neutral.

If it is dammed up in the three lower chacras, then it can lead to the expression of evil. When it reaches the heart chacra then it can usually be considered on the side of the good. When the Kundalini energy moves through the three lower chacras it can activate the negative karma based on survival, rape and power associated with dictators, killers, authoritarians; Alexanders, Ramses11, Hitlers, Stalins, Napoleons, Genghis Khans, Maos. When it moves through the heart chacra it can activate the positive charisma of mothers, care takers and some performers.

Rev. Rosalyn Bruyere, the minister who saw auras around people, shared with us that great performers who had the Kundalini energy alive in them could expand it out into the audience until it embraced the whole assemblage.

One day I was standing on the corner of Seventy Second Street and Broadway in New York City when all of a sudden I began to rock and the feeling of being stoned burst through me. Looking around for the cause, I at first thought that I was standing on a ley line. But that thought was quickly dismissed as Liza Minelli passed by me. As she passed I could feel the rush of charismatic energy that she as a performer carried.

When people live with a closed heart they could be in pain. Joy has left their lives. They could also be dangerous, for compassion has also left them. They are privy to the singular focus of the left hemisphere of the brain which doesn't deal with relationships and is totally focused on obsessive repetitive control. There may be evolutionary roots of autism in that singular focused orientation.

THE FIFTH CHACRA
VISHUDDHA CHACRA THE THROAT CHACRA
Creative identity, sound, blue, HAM

T he throat chacra is the chacra of communication, sound and creativity. There is a dual aspect to this chacra; one deals with the SOUND that issues forth from the throat, the other is the experience of resonance that SOUND can create within the human body.

It is the singing voice that can send goose pimples coursing across the skin. The female voice at its most sublime is associated with a diva and diva is not only the 'gift' (DA) of (VA), the 'voice' but it is also divine. It has links with divinity or as SOUND, a movement into transcendence. It is the amplified SOUND of a chorus chanting that can add to the enchanting trance of transformation.

The other aspect of SOUND deals with our almost forgotten ancestors who built those enormous citadels of stone. Who were they if not our ancient mothers in whom the two hemispheres were conjoined and yoked together? The power of that yoking has yet to be realized. There is also a factor of a larger brain case. Before the last wobble of the Earths axis, or a glacial winter, there existed people who had powers that we have yet to understand. They seem to have known how to move enormous stones from place to place. Some speculate that those great stones must have been levitated into place. But fit together like clay in some areas? We do not have the answer. Could our ancient mothers have gifts that blessed them with the nullification of gravity?

The word levitate (LAVA-) should give us a clue. It hides in its linguistic folds two possibilities. One deals with a Polish word for left which is leva (LAVA) and has links with our ancient left handed mothers and the creative body of Mother Earth recreating Herself as lava. The other deals with a tribe of Hebrew priests called the Levites (LAVA-). Could they also have been mother centered and left handed? Did they understand the process of levitation? They did worship the Leviathon or Mother Earth as the ubiquitous watwey snake before they hilled her.

It's ironic that the word Hebrew (HABARA) has links with hybrid (HABARADA), hubris (HABARASA), Iberia (HABARA), and zebra (IS HABARA). HABA is one of the most ancient names for the sun. It deals with the dual activity of the sun rising in the East at dawn and setting in the West at twilight establishing B of the 'two in one' concept. It echoes the 'two in one' shape of the two lips in profile on the individual mothers face.

STONE, ROCK

As SOUND in the fifth chacra, there are two curious words that have to be dealt with. One is STONE. The other is ROCK. Both of these two words have double meanings. How come to be moved to ecstasy is to be stoned? What does the stone have to do with being stoned? The word ROCK deals with a stone and the verb to rock. You have to take it apart to its most basic ancient SOUNDS.

RULE ONE; MONOGENESIS, there are no border lines between languages.

Stone can be (is tone) or sound. What is a tone? A tone is a sound that holds a certain vibration. A tone (TANA) also deals with holding. In Latin tenere (TANA-) means 'to hold'. It goes even further back into the ten (TANA) fingers that do the holding. As the ten (TANA) fingers that touch and awaken the pleasure on the skin, so the tone (TANA) as SOUND, activates the same response to the whole body.

The SOUND as tone (TANA the first syllable TA) deals with things that occur on the edge, on the tip, like the teeth are on the edge of the gums, toes are on the edge of the feet, teats are on the edge of the chest, things are on the edge or surFACE on the body of Mother Earth. (NA) having its origins in the nose as seen in profile deals with either 'emergence on the surface' or 'change from another state'. It originally dealt with breathing in and out, smelling offensive food and shoving it out with the tongue.

It is the thumb that does the thumping on a drum that causes a tonal and vibrational response in the body. When the rhythm is constant and the thumping goes on for a long period of time and dancing accompanies it, then trance creates an entrance into the center creating the yoking of the two hemispheres of the brain working in concert. It is a power that has yet to be understood and realized. It's what happened to me at the TV store on Madison Avenue in New York City with the Indians thumping on their drums.

The drum (DARAMA) creates the 'dream (DARAMA) time' that the Australian Aborigines talk about. The drum and the dream also create the drama (DARAMA) that unfolds as the trance state takes over. It is in that 'dream state' that the opening occurs into alternate levels of reality that brings with it healing, prophecy, wish fulfillment and ecstasy.

There is ongoing research that Stonehenge as a large stone circle created a powerful area of transformation. Drummers sat inside of the stones and drummed together sending an echo that vibrated not only the stones but the human brain into Alpha wave states that created a movement into trance. King Arthur removing the sword from the stone had wider implications. He may have been removing the violence of war that the sword represented and moved into the transcendence of being stoned that the mythological stone embodied.

That may have been the reason that massive stones around the planet were used not only as buildings but as places of ecstatic ritual.

<u>Human beings have always been addicted to pleasure.</u>

Why else would they have sent themselves into states of stoned ecstasy? They didn't align their structures with the solar solstices and full moons in order to know when to plant their seeds. The American Indians planted their corn when the leaves on the oak trees were the size of a mouses ear. They aligned those ancient megaliths because they knew that at certain times of the year, at certain times of the month and even certain times of the day, the solar Kundalimi energy moving up from the body of Mother Earth was the strongest. They knew that if they got together at those times that they could get stoned. Like the Chassidim at the stone wall in Israel and the Muslims in the madrases they could rock back and forth in ecstasy as they recounted their secret words.

Another curious word comes out of the same mine. It is rock (RAKA). A rock is also a stone. When the Kundalini energy awakens in you, one of the things that you do is rock back and forth, as I have gleefully done a variety of times. It is ironic that caged primates in mankind's zoos rock back and forth. The same activity has been observed in autistic children. There must be a memory of comfort reminiscent of the rocking in the womb as the mother walked. It was a time when both the rocking primates and the autistic human child must have felt total safety and peace. That safety and peace plus much more has become ritualized in the activity of rocking back and forth.

A Finnish word for 'stone' is kivi (KAVA). In Polish the word for rocking is kiva (KAVA). The word kiva (KAVA) takes us into ancient prehistory. It has its origins out of the cave (KAVA), the body of Mother Earth where they must have felt the original grid energy the strongest. It was the womb of creation in Her magnificent abdomen. They built their altars inside of those caves and buried their dead for a quick return to rebirth through Her voluminous womb. A cove (KAVA) is also a safe harbor.

The (VA) in cave (KAVA) deals with the volcanic vulva that created land on the surFACE, and all the smaller aspects (KA) out of Her great creative body.

Mother Earth had been considered the matriarch that created and sustained everything. Like other matriarchs, specifically the oldest and wisest elephant, she was the oldest member of both the human and celestial family. In Bugotu of the South Pacific kave (KAVA) is the name for the 'grandmother'. Any 'old woman' is KAE KAVE or (KAKAVA). A curious dyad surfaces in Finnish and it is kives (KAVASA) standing for testicles. Were ceremonies of castration committed in those ancient caves? As young males were indoctrinated into the service of the family.

When the ice age descended on those original ancient migratory trekkers and subsequent builders of megalithic cities, they hid in those caves and survived the great glacial onslaught. In time with their memories intact they built other caves into the ground and covered them with wooden planks. In the Hopi Indian tradition those ancient caves are called kivas (KAVA-) or the caves (KAVA) dug into the body of Mother Earth. It was in those kivas that they activated their ceremonies dealing with dancing, rocking back and forth in trance which brought them all the blessings of the Kundalini energy. The coven (KAVA- of the covenant (KAVA-) surfaces here.)

The roofs of those Hopi kivas were called clouds. The clouds along with the blessed rain brought with them dramatically changing shapes across the celestial landscape, especially faces of humans, of animals and even monsters. A whole drama could be played out with the changing cloud faces up in the sky. In Polish a cloud is called a chmura (HAMARA). A very similar word in Greek is chimera (KAMARA or HAMARA) and it defines a monster. Looking up at the cloudy sky with the drama of change being played out, is it too far to imagine that the ancients believed that Mother Earth was trying to tell them something, not unlike the crop circles?

Modern UFO enthusiasts define the cloud roof on a Hopi kiva as the work of extraterrestrials, <u>anything to give credit away from the body of Mother Earth as 'source.'</u>

When you deal with transformation you have to face the worst in yourself. You have to face the fears that have trapped the panic stricken images in place and to burn them out. In Finnish kuva (KAVA) stands for 'image' that which is trapped by fear.

In Polish, 'kava' surfaces intact, as the name for coffee. It must have been at some ancient time a hallucinogen. It does jack people up but something else much more substantial must have given it at that ancient name based on the (AH) sound, that relates it to an ancient ritual.

RULE SIXTEEN; OVERLAPPING tryads; The word trance

(TARANASA) as the overlapping tryad TARA-RANA-NASA
sheds some light on the understanding of the special condition
dealing with transformation. Reading from right to left; (NASA)
deals with birth. In Latin nascence (NASANASA) means birth. It
is the 'emergence on the surface '(NA) of the 'life force' (SA).

Then rana in Polish gives us a clue that establishes its relationship with the body of Mother Earth. Rana in Polish means both
'wound' and 'dawn'. It was out of the 'wound of dawn' in the Eastern
sky on the body of Mother Earth that the sun was born at dawn.
(RA) deals with the sun and (NA) also deals with 'a change from a
former state' or 'emergence on the surface'.

Then comes (TARA) and TARA is the terrain (TARANA), the
tar (TARA), the tor (TARA), the terrace (TARA-) on the body of
Mother Earth out of which the sun (RA) emerged up onto Her
surFACE or top (TA). Tara was the primal Mother Earth Goddess
who was worshipped throughout Ireland, Southern Russia, the
Middle East, India and Europe.

A trance (TARANASA) is the new birth that emerges (NASA),
out of the wound of a new dawn (RANA), out of the body of
Mother Earth (TARA).

It is a poetic description of the Kundalini energy as the heat
and light of the solar wind emerging up and out of the ley lines
on the body of Mother Earth, bringing with it the burning out of
the entrenched habits of a panic stricken infancy and an opening
into leadership healing, prophecy and ecstasy.

On the 'spiritual' level it is the movement into self-realization.
For self-realization is the self realized without the burden of fear.
Being 'born again' takes on new meaning. Along with drugs, the
rituals of meditaion, singing and dancing, there was a more ancient process to defuse the habitual panic that had been stored in
humanitys panic stricken infancy.

The habit (HABATA) having links with the repetitive habitual passage of the sun, could be dealt with by spending time in
the abaton (HABATANA) a cave under the temple of a Goddess.
During the time of female centrality the male adept longing for
the transformative state would spend time in that abaton until he

faced his most intense habit entrenched fears and emerged fearless and self-realized. A Hittite Goddess represented the struggling soul, her name was Hebat (HABATA). In Anatolia she was Eve Habat (HABATA) having links with the moon and night.

The struggling for universal transformation during the time of female centrality became redefined as a day of rest as male centrality gained momentum. It happened on a specific day of the week, the Hebrew Sabbath (IS HABATA) or Saturday. In Amharic sabatt (IS HABATA) means 'seven'. It also means that the sabbath (IS HABATA) declares that 'the hair turns white'. There have been stories that when someone went through a horrific fear his hair turned white. It was usually associated with having fallen ubder a speeding train. The survival victim emerged alive but with a mop of white hair. In Basque the same weekly day of Saturday surfaces as zapatu (IS HAPATA).

Abad (HABADA) means 'to perish' in Hebrew. For the Egyptians abtu (HABATA) was the abyss, the fish of Isis who swallowed the penis of Osiris. It dealt with Mother Earth swallowing the rays of the sun, (the hair on Samsons head), the virility of the sun in the Western sky.

Two English words further our understanding of how the establishment of habit (HABATA) moved through and disrupted the psyche. It has links with the sun (IS HANA) for the sun was privy to the ultimate habit. It rose and fell everyday of its life. Like a human habit the sun could not get off the hamster wheel of repetition. To inhabit (HANA HABATA) was to live in the habit. When the habit became destructive, it moved into the role of inhibit (HANA HABATA) or damming up the free flow of the Kundalini energy. The obsession (HABA-) of habit was not a welcome guest that could be jettisoned without help.

When I was in India and trudged to the glorious establishment in Arunachala, I was eager to see the cave under one of the massive temples in which Ramana Mahashi spent an extended period of time until he re-emerged transformed. He did not see the light of day for many years. Food was slipped under his door until he was ready to emerge as a new soul, to be 'born again' minus his old fear driven self.

Standing in the bowels of the temple and looking down into the tiny grotto in which Ramana Mahashi had spent all that time, I found it difficult to believe that the desire for transformation could exact such penance. After he emerged transformed, he became a guru and became a universlly known wise man and teacher. There was no indication that his hair turned white.

RULE SIX; PHONOLOGICAL CORRESTONDENCE, SOUNDS that replace each other .

The (T) in abaton is replaced by the (D) in abaddon.

As male knowledge in paternity was bcoming established and the left hemisphere of the brain was separating itself and plunging into the abyss of selfish individuality, the ancient Hebrews redefined the abaton (HABATANA) as 'the bottomless pit', the dreaded abaddon (HABADANA). It came out of abad (HABADA) the word representing 'to perish' in Hebrew, with links to the abyss.

The transformative energy of Mother Earth had to be vilified as the systems dealing with fear defusion (or of 'eating it', 'facing it') disappeared into the mists of prehistory. The stay in the abaton dealt not only with isolation but complete silence. It was in that silence that the self could be faced completely. It was in that silence that the self without fear could be born.

The SOUND that exists in the throat chacra contains in its folds a double edged sword. On one level the SOUND made by the human voice as extended singing and chanting can lead to an altered state of consciousness. An extension of that activity, the SOUND made by vibrating stones responding to the SOUNDS made by repetitive drumming, leads to becoming stoned and to rocking back and forth in ecstasy.

On another level, the SOUNDS that human beings have codified as linear speech and then linear writing have fed the linear oriented left hemisphere of the human brain in which the image-fear laden combine exists. One side creates the mess and negatively repeats over and over that the glass is half empty. The other side trying for some balance and positivity says that the glass is half full. The human creature is caught in the middle.

Through the experience of trance our ancient mothers and contemporary shamans, witch doctors and psychics have tried to keep the ancient knowledge alive and to share it with the rest of suffering humanity.

There are many roads into the trance state. Drugs create one of the pathways. People take drugs for many reasons. One is for entertainment and as an enhancement to sex. Another more pragmatic reason is to still the voice over of the fear driven left hemisphere of the brain, to keep it from prattling on without stop with all the stuff that is driven by helpless inadequacy and the fear of exposure. The third reason which includes the former two, deals with reaching a state of consciousness that transcends ordinary reality. All three could be dangerous and research needs to be done to ease human pain without further expanding the penitentiary industry.

God (GADA) is the 'gift of' (DA) of beGETting. In Polish the ancient (ah) based word 'gada' mans 'to prattle on'. It was understood that the place where the male God resided was the place where He talked forever to the tormented fear driven creature. He resided in the left hemisphere of the brain and gave humanity no rest. To set the left hemisphere voice over to rest, meditation, drugs, singing, dancing, chanting and all the other rituals were used to still the voice over mind.

THE THYROID GLAND

The throat also deals with the thyroid gland and the role that it plays in the creation of speech. I tried everything that I could think of trying to get my voice to work. I even sat in a box at a Columbia University Research Center in New York City with electrodes plastered to my throat and body, as Japanese doctors tried to determine why my voice periodically failed me.

Cortizone injections did not help. Nutrition did not help. Therapy didn't help. New voice teachers did not help. Hoarseness plagued my singing career. Then when my mother died and I almost lost my will to live, the doctors couldn't find my pulse and finally decided to do some tests on my thyroid gland.

Lo and behold I was hypothyroid. It all began to fall into place.

The thyroid gland sits at the side of the vocal cords and out of its side there also sits a gland that squirts a fluid every time that you phonate, or make a SOUND. It lubricates the vocal cords so that they don't whack together and cause callouses or temporary swelling which leads to raspiness and the loss of the voice. If you are hypothyroid you do not produce enough fluid to lubricate the cords. It took me half of a lifetime to finally discover what the problem was. By the time that the answers came to me the boat had sailed. The theatre went West with the emergence of television. I had to stay in New York so that my son could continue going to the same school and not have his life disrupted by my chasing acting parts around the country.

I found that many women my age had thyroid problems and after Chernobyl the universal nuclear science expanded its destructive net. Many Russian, Polish and Ukranian women downwind of the nuclear plant came down with an enlarged goiter. I realized that the atomic tests of the fifties of the United States and Russia in the Western deserts and in outer space had done a similar number on so many of our thyroid glands. It's no wonder that Robert Oppenheimer was burdened by so many reasons to be so guilt ridden.

Not always sure where the journey that he so vehemently admonished me to make was taking me, I resolved to somehow keep going.

HILDA CHARLTON

During one of my more extended stays in New York tending to my home in Rockland County and patrolling the erstwhile tenants that I harbored on my property, I met another guru named Hilda Charlton. Every Thursday night she held services in the Manse of the church of Saint John the Devine up town on the West Side in New York City. In the late sixties and early seventies she had been part of the triad of Joya Ma and Ram Dass. Rumors floated around and reasons were given why the trio broke up and scattered to the four winds. Joya Ma settled in Florida and Hilda stayed in New York City.

Not wanting to waste what I had experienced with Joya MA,

HILDA CHARLTON

who was in Florida, I joined the trekkers from Rockland County to the Manse every Thursday night. There were quite a few of us and I became very popular for I always had a car. It was with Hilda, along with Synthroid, a thyroid supplement that the healing of my voice started to take place.

The Manse contained a long relatively narrow room at the end of which was a stage. It was on that stage that Hilda shared her gifts of the Kundalini energy with all who came to be with her. She had been a dancer and while on a concert tour in India she was overwhelmed by her experiences there and emerged years later as a guru. In front of her, mostly on the hard floor below, sat many of her disciples. They were smart enough to bring a lot of pillows. Some even brought chairs.

Because the church was in New York City, many of the people that I had known in the theatre found their way to Hilda. We fell into each other's arms with rediscovered glee. It was from them that Hilda found out that I could sing. Correcting my thyroid problem with Synthroid did not free me from the panic that had locked itself in me concerning that I would not be able to carry off the performance and that my voice would fail me. Rather than face the possibility of endless failure, I had stopped singing.

Hilda must have read something in me, for she too had been a performer. One of the first things that she advised me to do was to prepare an appropriate number for the next Thursday night service. I was going to 'eat it.'

At her suggestion to sing I began to shake with a growing panic. I prepared the first of many songs and faced my coming doom. Standing on the stage with no lights to hide the upturned faces waiting in anticipation below me, Hilda must have known what I had been experiencing. She stood very close to me and gave me her arm to hold on to. As I wove my way through the vocal selection, I must have left black and blue marks on her arm, I held on to it so tightly. My voice did not fail me. I came in on the right key and didn't forget the words. As I took my bows Hilda informed me that I had to have a song ready for every subsequent service.

It began a journey that I had wanted to experience all of my life. Never did I want to sing and girate my hips and be cute, and make men 'come in their jeans' as one singing teacher advised me to do. I had wanted to sing and move my listeners to the passion that I felt which was other than blatantly sexual. But I didn't know how to explain it. Hilda nodding her head with encouragement, gave me the opportunity while singing to send people into a stoned silence.

There were those who as they sat on the cold floor below me as I sang went into states of stiff and apparently rigid Samadhi. As we filed out past them, Hilda would admonish us to go around them and try not to 'tip them over.' Then she would stay with all of them them until they 'came down' and I redistributed the stoned disciples in my car all over the City and the far reaches of Rockland County.

All the seers, gurus, psychics that came through the City found their way to our meetings at the Manse. There was a man who claimed that he could transform our lead fillings into gold. The hugging guru MA from India was also made available to us. Swamis from all over the world shared their wisdom with us. They all knew Hilda and respected who she was and what she was able to share with us.

It was Hilda who said that we didn't need a guru as we worked our way up through the chacras cleaning them out with systematic meditation. The only place she warned us that we needed a guru is when the Kundalini energy moved past the third eye chacra and then into the lotus chacra of exit, on top of the head. Those were the places of the temporary Samadhi from which you returned and the permanent Maha Samadhi from which you didn't, for it meant death.

Most of my life I had been stuck in the throat chacra, so the warning didn't seem pertinent to me. After I had the Kundalini experience I began to experience the movement into the third eye chacra as the lights began to flash on the inner vision of my eyes.

The HUM (HAMA) SOUND dealing with the throat chacra may have its roots in the heart chacra with the loving relationship that the mother had with her baby. She not only hummed but as a human being communicated through the use of words. The use of actual specific sounds that began their life as a hum, then spread out into song, eventually emerged into words to communicate with her off spring. It set her apart from the rest of the creatures on the savannahs who used body language, vocal vowel sounds and raspy coughs to signal their concerns.

Other mothers may have loved their young as the heart chacra establishes, but only the human mother could use actual words with which to communicate. <u>Most of the SHAPES and SOUNDS of the capital letters of the Western Alphabet came out of the organs on her face that made them.</u> It all may have begun with the hum (HAMA) but it expanded into singing and then into speech.

The word HAM has other interesting ramifications and now I'm heading to the edge of the branch. In Stonehenge, archeologists have found many pig bones. The feasting that went on as part of their plunge into stoned ecstasy while rocking back and forth may have been accompanied by the ingestion of the suckling pig.

The most desirable part of the pig is the HAM. It may have been that while they drummed they also hummed (HAMA-).

The pig may have been part of that ritual.

In Polish the word for 'holy' is swienty (IS WANATA). It has a similar linguistic construct as swine (IS WANA) without the (TA) of 'place' at the edge or tip. Whenever you encounter the WA sound you are usually dealing with some aspect of water. NA deals with either 'emergence on the surface' or 'the change to another state'.

Stonehenge is on the River Avon (HAVANA) and it is a river of passage across water, and the water is the Atlantic Ocean. Most mythological rivers of passage are relatively narrow, like the Styx, Charon or even Jordan. But at Stonehenge they thought big. Their actual river of passage led to the Atlantic Ocean and it was the crossing of the Atlantic Ocean that led them to the stop over shoals of paradise in HAVANA. They were heading for the seven (IS HAVANA) sisters of the Pleiades but that's another story.

After the last glaciation, as people scattered all over the globe there was a desire to create specific traditions. To create specialness, customs had to be framed anew. Could it be that the Hebrews wanting to separate themselves from the goy group that wandered off to Britain rejected all, including the eating of pig meat. Just a thought.

It's ironic that the tragedy of my riding the horse backward and marrying into the closed class driven circle of theatrical royalty gave me a temporary name of HAMmerstein. Stein (IS HATANA) not only means stone, but stone is also (SATANA) or satan (SATANA). Are there really no accidents?

The inability to experience SOUND as communication or resonating ecstasy means that the Kundalini energy is trapped at the throat chacra of creativity and needs to be released.

THE SIXTH CHACRA
ANJA—THE THIRD EYE CHACRA

Light, intuition, separate reality from illusion, white, KSHAM

T he third eye chacra is the chacra of enlightenment for in its
name there exists the sun (IS HANA). The name Anja
(HANAJA) contains within it the sun (IS HANA) and the snake
(IS NAKA, NAGA, NAJA) the guide of the sun. Here we are dealing with the prehistoric, mother centered priesthood as eunochs
(HANAKA) and uncles (HANAKALA), who not only were the
castrated first born sons but at the sides of their mothers officiated originally over the rites of the rising and the setting sun.

Because there was no knowledge of paternity and fathers were
not there to protect their children, mothers had their first born
sons castrated to do the job of protecting the family. This ancient
practice spanned the ancient prehistoric globe as a result of the
glaciations and volcanic eruptions that scattered the terrified inhabitants of Africa far and wide.

The overlapping phonemes of avuncular (HAVANAKALARA)
as uncle (HANAKALA) spans so many bases needing to be
examined.

(HAVA-VANA-NAKA-KALA-LARA.) Reading right to left,
(LARA) is the left hand orientation of the ancient mothers and
their first born sons. (KALA) is the killer (KALA-) as time, Mother
Kali (KALA) in her aspect as the eater of the sun, with her tongue
extended and blood dripping from it. She is also standing on the
body of Siva whom in some way she has compromised. (NAKA)
deals with the snake (IS NAKA) who guides the sun through the
dark intestines within the body of Mother Earth. The next two
dyads HAVA and VANA should be conjoined for they represent
HAVANA. For an ancient people who had to disperse after a massive cataclysm their journey toward immortality or reincarnation

took them across the great divide of the Atlantic Ocean to the island of Cuba and to the city that bears the name of HAVANA.

The avuncular (HAVANAKALARA) uncle (HANAKALA) was not only a protector to his sister's children but he was kind and caring. Officiating over the rites of the rising and setting sun at the side of his mother he emerged as the priest who became the ritual master over the weeping and wailing as the sun died to its light. He became the 'ritual murderer' of the sun.

It is through the third eye of the sixth chacra that the CONSCIOUS journey using a variety of disciplines into mysticism could begin. It could begin by using a variety of means; fasting, dancing, drugs, sex, spinning, chanting, and meditation.

Meditation deals with the conscious focus of the mind and a concentration on both the third eye and the breath. Done diligently over a period of time it can lead to the activation of the Kundalini energy explosion in the body.

The letter K of Kundalini deals with the shape of the open beak of a bird making the COOing sound associated with birds. Since birds lay many eggs that become hatchlings, they became associated with fecundity and the universal makers of smaller (KA) replicas of themselves.

As an avian, (HAVANA)specie they make more anomatopoeic SOUNDS beginning with the sound of (K) than any other creature.The sound KA, at the end of many nouns the world over deals with the 'smaller she'.

Like the BEE emerged to define BE ing, so the letter K emerged out of bird sound and the fecundity of birds making smaller versions of themselves. The concept expanded to include women and the body of Mother Earth also creating small replicas of themselves.

KU is the energy of Mother Earth in Sanskrit.

KUN (KANA) is the energy of the female as mother.

KUNDA (KANADA) is the 'gift of' (DA) the energy of Mother Earth KUN, as the Hindu Goddess Kunda.

KUNDALI (KANADALA) with (LI) deals with movement like the angle of the tongue in the mouth moves, or the angle of the leg moves. It also includes the LAdy of the LAnd or Mother Earth as the ultimate mover into life and death.

KUNDALINI (KANADALANA) with (NI) deals with 'emergence on the surface' or 'a change from another state'.

RULE ONE; MONOGENESIS, there are no borders between languages. The surface or skin (IS KANA) on the body of Mother Earth, as Her surFACE is shared by Her creatures. As an extension of Her skin (IS KANA), the triangular volcanic cone (KANA) is Her most formidable aspect of creation. She creates the land from Her volcanic cone (KANA) that spreads a skin (IS KANA) across Her surFACE. It is that skin that she shares with all of Her subsequent creations. Skin (IS KANA) establishes the kin (KANA) that creates the possibility for the young to survive. If the survival is with an avuncular uncle, the survival is kind (KANADA), or the gift of the kin (KANA). It is usually to the kinder (KANADA-) or child, in German, to whom the kindness is expressed.

RULE TWENTY; BUZZ or DEROGATORY words for female body parts; The whole construct can extend from the coos (KASA) of birds into another direction. Coos (KASA) is also a container (KANATA-) such as casa (KASA) the Spanish house, and the hand in Finnish, as kasi (KASA) also when holding things, is a container. Birds are the ultimate makers of smaller things which the sound of (KA) represents. The smaller (KA) things are also made out of the mothers blood (SA). The same construct of (KA+SA) as the coos (KASA) is shared by the human mother.

The two derogatory words for the female genitalia as coos (KASA) and cunt (KANATA) have an extensive if more benign history. The coos (KASA) or kashi (KASA) cover a multitude of possibilities. In English the coos (KASA) emerge as the first cause (KASA). To 'begin' or 'to start' in Chinese is kaishi (KASA). In the language of Bemba, mwanakashi (mawana KASA) is a 'woman'. Kuso (KASA) deals with the 'left side' also in Bemba. In Sanskrit kushoto (KASA-) means 'left'; not 'right'.

It is out of the mother's blood (SA) that the 'beginning' into individual or small (KA) life can take place. In Sanskrit kashaya (KASA-) means reddish brown, the color of coagulated blood. In Bemba kashika (KASA-) is 'red', the color of blood. It is only through the coos (KASA) that there can be completion and fulfillment. In Bugotu kasa is to be 'complete' and kasa gna (GANA) means total 'fulfillment'. Completion and fulfillment deal with the activity of the female gyne (GANA) of gyneco-logy and gene. Both words are based on the (AH) sound and must be very ancient. In Bemba the sister who as the nanny helps to care for the children is nkashi (-KASA). It is she who when she grows up becomes the 'queen' in Bemba as yana kashi (KASA)). <u>The yana (HAYANA) as the 'queen' in Bemba establishes its links with the Hindu yoni (HAYANA), the Chinese yin (HAYANA) and the Semitic ione (HAYANA) all dealing with the female vulva.</u> They are all an aspect of the mother as the carrier of the light aya (HAYA) in Persian and dawn in Assyrian. The light that she carries is the light of the risen solar wind that shimmers across the internal landscape of her mind during her birthing experience of the Kundalini energy explosion of ecstasy leading to transformation.

RULE SIX; PHONOLOGICAL CORRESPONDENCE when made in the same area of the mouth, SOUNDS replace each other. (The letters (T) and (D) are interchangeable. A container (KANATA-) with the cunt (KANATA) in its linguistic folds is also the counter (KANATA-) of the passage of time. It is the moon that counts (KANATA-) the time in sink with the menstrual cycles of women's cunts (KANATA).

In Polish a kont (KANATA) is a corner, an angle, the V shape of the vulvic patch. Out of the body of Mother Earth it is the cone (KANA), the triangle of creation out of the volcanic vent that spews forth lava onto the surface. The lavic 'fires' that spew forth creating land on the surface in Sanskrit are kanda (KANADA). Also in Polish a corner is a rug (RAGA). It deals with the body of Mother Earth at Her edge where the sun (RA) is begotten (GA) at an angle, out of the corner of Her body.

RULE EIGHTEEN; HOMOPHONES, puns across languages.

The Polish corner 'rug' and the English carpet 'rug'. The flying rug or carpet of Alladin (HALADANA) having links with the sun, the Spanish sol (IS HALA) and Greek eelyos (HALA-), has interesting antecedents. When you have the Kundalini energy awaken in you, you often experience flying through the air, along with becoming stoned and rocking back and forth. A drug (DARAGA) is the 'gift of' (DA) the rug (RAGA) and one of the means of experiencing the flying carpet of Alladin. The other is the vulvic corner, the Polish rug out of which the the baby pushed out by the ecstatic birthing breath, emerges.

In Swedish the 'ten' lunar months of gestation, also counted by the cycles of the moon is kuni (KANA). The deeply worshipped Hindu Goddess Kunda (KANADA) when the shift into male centrality occurred became the vilified female cunt (KANATA).

Other names bridging similar concepts emerge linguistically. In Basque the word for 'language' is hizkuntza (hasaKANATA-). It establishes its links with the ancient mother and her ever present cunt (KANATA) as the counter of time along with the passage of the moon, the other counter (KANATA) of time. It also establishes her as the creatress of language. In Sanskrit kandala (KANADA-) deals with 'of a woman', Also in Sanskrit the 'beloved' or 'desirable' is kanta (KANATA), Polish kont (KANATA) or corner.

Paten Kunti (KANATA) in Lithuanin means to be 'content' (KANATA-), 'satisfied'. The Lithuanian mothers must still have had the birthing breath available to them. The paten (PATANA) contains within it the ten (TANA) either of the ten masturbating fingers or the ten months of lunar gestsation and the birthing breath experience at the end of that term. To make a baby in Bemba, to 'squat down' is makunda (MAKANADA), the mother (MA) in the process of squatting down and pushing the baby out of her body. It expands in Finnish into –kunta (KANATA) defining 'the people' and 'nation'.

Again we move into Finnish as the Great Creatress Goddess, Luoma Kunta (KANATA). Cunti (KANATA) establishes the

Oriental Great Goddess. In Sanskrit a 'well' is kunti (KANATA), Mother Earth as the source of water. Guari Kund (KANADA) is a holy lake in the Himalayas. Mem Kund (MAMA KANADA) is a mountain lake in the Himalayas, source of the Ganges.

Another aspect enters the picture dealing with the ever present nocturnal horse. In Polish a horse is kon (KANA) relating it to the body of Mother Earth and Her skin (IS KANA). For the horse gives birth to koniec (KANA-) and in Polish koniec (KANASA) means 'the end'. It was the return back under the skin (IS KANA) of Mother Earth after death that the horse played a major role. It was a creature that established itself as the guide of death. To return under the skin (IS KANA) of Mother Earth was to die, to reach the end of your life. All creatures who died, in one way or another were either dispatched through ingestion, or they decayed (DK). The horse was one of the symbols as a guide of that ultimate return. It is the four horsemen of the Apocalypse that hourney into the underworld.

Animals played a major role for our ancient ancestors. We have lost the keys to that understanding. Myths deal with human beings understanding the language of birds. Ancient Egyptians mummified the remains of the ibis, baboons, cats and other animals. Were the larger brained Neanderthal and their two hemispheres working in concert privy to processes that we have yet to discover?

When my sister was terminal, spending her last days in the hospital, we sat with her waiting for the inevitable end. As she was slipping in and out of our reality, one relatively lucid day she remarked. "I didn't know that they allowed cats in this hospital, how nice."

I looked at her and tried to understand.

"I don't think they do.What do you mean, Jane ?

'There's a nice grey cat sitting in that corner'. She pointed to the empty corner of the hospital room. A few days later shortly before her death, she again remarked that the nice gray cat was now sitting on the corner of her bed. She seemed to welcome it, as it came closer to her. What roles did animal play in that ultimate passage?

How we treat animals is unforgivable. Our ancient mothers

were in contact with the passage between life and death and the role that animals played in that passage. They were ancient guides to the other side. Civilizations have come and gone where they worshipped animals not because they were superstitious but because they knew that some animals were guides in that ultimate journey.

In Gobekli Tepi in Turkey there are prehistoric sculptures of a myriad of animals adorning the massive stone walls. We have lost that connection with our fellow creatures. They exist not only to be abused and butchered. They existed as an extension of out mortality. In touch with the Kundalini energy they are privy to a knowledge that exists only in the SOUNDS that have been left behind. Animals are limited by their bodies not by their minds or hearts.

Moving it further afield in Finnish kanta (KANATA) is base or heel. Here we are dealing not only with the angle of the ankle on the bottom of the leg but with the movement of the Kundalini energy within the female body. It exposes the same perception as the Greek hero Achilles searching for transformation being vulnerable on his heel or shin (IS HANA) where the energy of the sun (IS HANA) moving up from the body of Mother Earth when dammed up or damaged, led to his demise.

With the evolution of male centrality and male religious systems, that ancient connection has been lost as we wander around in our bifurcated brains wondering what is going to happen to us after we die. Our ancient mothers knew and worshipped the animals who carried the keys to that passage. The horse as the Polish kon (KANA) having links with koniec (KANA-) as 'the end', was one of those sacred creatures of passage. That may be why so many women love their horses so much. It also may be why the horse is the symbol of the psyche, of riding the creature of fate in the direction that it is going. It is ironic that Hercules as one of his twelve trials killed the Amazon queen Hippolyta named after a horse.

In Polish the name of the female horse, the mare, is kobyla (KABALA). Further back in time, the Mongols thundering across the steppes of Asia on their beloved horses were led by Kubla (KABALA) Khan (KAHANA). Both names have linguistic links with the centrality of the mothers. In Spanish the name of the horse is caballo (KABALA) also establishing its links with the Hebrew Caballah (KABALA). What has not been lost, redefined, suppressed, or rewritten? The clues to that loss exist in the words themselves.

The Hindu Goddess Kunda (KANADA) and the vilified cunt (KANATA) splay out in their own directions without leaving the North European Goddess Frigg behind. On the other side of the Atlantic Ocean, there is not only Havana but Canada (KANADA). Whence? Who created those ancient names that still pop up in contemporary languages on the Western side of the Atlantic?

Back to the onomatopoeia of birds and their awesome multi-sonar SOUNDS starting with their gurgling coos (KASA) relating them to the clitoric beak or coos (KASA) on the female body. In Polish the clitoris is affectionately called a dziobek (JABAKA), the small (KA) beak. In English, across a great linguistic divide what does a beak do? It jabs (JABA-).

Joya Ma named the ranch, the Kashi (KASA) Ashram. It dealt with human beings who in one way or another had deep emotional scars dealing with their mothers. She became the universal Ma who gave them the love that they yearned for. As she was sharing her love and shakti with them, she also filled them with the transformative Kundalini energy. Many became both male and female Mas who fed the hungry, housed the homeless and comforted the despairing. She knew that it was the mother energy that needed resuscitating on the planet. As she became a painter, many of her paintings dealt with both the male and female genitalia. Those may have been the roots of the cosmic orgasm and the name that the Kashi (KASA) Ashram represented.

SEVEN (IS EVEN), (IS HAVANA)

S ince most of the SHAPES and SOUNDS of the capital letters of the Western Alphabet had their singular origin out of the organs and features on the mothers face and the surFACE on the body of Mother Earth and since most of those letters evolved into specific concepts, then it is primarily to the SOUNDS out of the human mothers face that we have to turn to, for the answers of the origins, not only of speech but the concepts that emerged from those SOUNDS. Origins (HARA-) and organs (HARA-) give us another clue for the origins of SOUND, mostly emerged out of the organs on the Mother's face.

There was a very early perception that the human face reflected itself laterally. One side evenly reflected the other. There were two identical sides to the face and the two sides worked in tandem. They were joined at the center, at the septum of the nose. This perception expanded to the rest of the body. Facial symmetry was considered to be a sign of great beauty.

The letter (B) of the two lips in profile working together vertically to create the one unit of the mothers mouth became the symbol for the concept of 'two in one'. It surfaces in the buzia (BASA) as the face in Polish and body (BADA), the 'gift of' (DA) 'the two in one' (BA) in English. The 'two in one' concept encoded in the letter (B), expanded to the breasts, 'two in one', the brain 'two in one', buttocks 'two in one', brazos, arms in Spanish as 'two in one', book 'two pages in one.'

One side, closest to the heart, was called the left (LAFATA) side and became associated with the left handed mothers. The other side was the dextral hand, or the 'gift of' (DA) the extra hand, since the left had was the primal hand of the Mother. In time, as male centrality gained momentum it became the right hand of the fathers.

Whatever was experienced by the individual mothers, expanded to include the body of Mother Earth. If they had two sides to their faces and bodies then Mother Earth must also have had the same two sides. As they began to define their reality, the two sides on the body of Mother Earth spanned a host of expanding processes. A perception emerged as the bio (BAYA) of life, the 'two in one' (BA), concept was aided by the light (AYA) of the sun. It was out of that most ancient time Mother Earth and the sun were perceived to be working as a single unit.

One of the most enduring pictures that existed as their constant companion was the 'two in one' reflected reality that they could see daily across a still and quiescent body of water. They surmised that there must have been two sides to Mother Earth, like there were two sides to their faces and bodies.

Here they were dealing with their mortality. One side was above the surFACE where they lived. In the waters below that same reality was mysteriously, evenly reflected. It was as if Mother Earth was lying on Her side as the ground under their feet. The top part of Her body, defined as the left (LAFATA) side of life (LAFA) created an identical reflection in the waters below. The reflected side in the waters below was the mysterious realm that became associated with the right side of Her body and with death (DATA) or the 'gift of' (DA), the passage of the moon at the tip (TA), establishing the immutable journey of death that the passage of time brings. The moon was the original counter of time. It was the moon (MANA) that established the name for the original month (MANATA), the passage of time at the top (TA). It was the lunar hand, 'mana' in Spanish, at night that helped Mother Earth, as the solar hand (HANADA) did during the day.

What our ancient ancestors saw in the distance reflected in the still waters of the Okobongo Delta, the lakes in the Rift Valley or the verdant Sahara were the two sides on the face and body of Mother Earth. It looked to them like the reflection created an even distribution above Her body and below Her terrain. In Cambodia there is an enormous stone statue of the Buddha lying on his side as a male metaphor for that same ancient concept.

The concept of even (HAVANA) began to grow in their minds. The life on top and the death reflected below, created not only evenness but balance. Life was evenly balanced above the surFACE by death and death was evenly balanced under the reflected surFACE by life. As the individual creature body was balanced by having both sides, so was the body of Mother Earth balanced by having the same construct. The concept of evenness (IS EVEN-, HAVANA) began to take root and expanded to include a myriad of other processes.

It was at the time of the ancient migrations that the next set of phonemes began to surface. Due to massive changes in the evolutionary sexual history of our struggling mothers, they began to give birth year round. Every ten lunar months a new baby was born. The infant nursing at the breast was not yet weaned when the new arrival, the rival for the mother's milk supply, made its entrance out of the AR- (HARA) or belly of arrival. The ancient mothers solved the problem by following the semi annual migration of the herbivore herds to the greener pastures in the far distant savannahs (IS HAVANA).

The ancient year began at the time of the spring equinox in either March or early April. That was the time of the estral frenzy when all the creatures around them succumbed to their mating imperatives. As the wildebeest and zebra began galloping to the falling rains in the distant savannahs (IS HAVANA), they were carrying a small replica of the mother in their wombs. Human mothers knew that when they reached those verdant grasslands in the distant savannah that the mares would drop their foals and come into a milk supply. It was that milk supply that urged them on and showed them the way to the showers beyond the far horizon.

This migratory herbivore trek broke the year into two even halves. Time was reckoned by the thirteen cycles of the waxing and waning moon across the night sky. They began their march in March. In September the seventh month, if you begin to count the year in March, they began their journey back to their beloved mountains. In Latin the sept of September means not only 'seven' (IS HAVANA) but 'separation'.

So you had the two even sides of the face and body of the individual mother, the reflective surface on the body of Mother Earth, and the migratory YEAR broken up into two even halves. It didn't stop there.

The MONTH also had to be evenly broken up. Since the lunar month had twenty eight days, then the break had to be at the number fourteen. It was based on the waxing and the waning of the moon. There were two weeks of waxing in one direction toward the full moon and two weeks of waning in the other direction toward the new moon. The even (HAVANA) balance through the passage of lunar time was achieved. The number seven (IS EVEN or HAVANA) dealing with the days of the week gets buried under the number fourteen.

As they gazed up at the night sky, the light of the waxing moon must have filled them with great hope that the light of the moon would push away the dreaded predators who stalked the hunting grounds of the savannahs. As they looked up at the moonlit night sky they also saw the shimmering wings of white birds returning from their summer homes further North, winging their way to their winter nesting sites.

The birds were like a clock (KALAKA), (the reflection in the word of coming and going (KALA /LAKA) clacking (KALAKA) their way across the night sky and the beginning of the semi annual, back and forth, (like the word), herbivore migrations.

The birds (B) 'two in one', halving the migratory year in half were like messengers that the time for the journey and an added milk supply was at hand. As the moon grew heavy and waxed full in the night sky, the herbivore mothers grew heavy with their foals. The birth of new babies, the fullness of the moon, the shimmering of the birds flying high overhead must have looked to them like an awesome blessing that Mother Earth was handing them.

They called those avian messengers that brought with them a milk supply and a separation into the journey back to their beloved mountains, angels (HANAGALA-). The angles that as bird wings shimmering by the light of the moon were a blessing, not unlike their avuncular (HAVANAKALA) and kind uncles (HANAKALA).

In time the fourteen days of the lunar balance become the fourteen protective angels that mothers lullabied their babies to sleep.

'When at night I go to sleep, fourteen angels watch do-o keep'.

It explains the number fourteen as the two sets of protective angels that sit on each shoulder. They brought light out of the darkness and milk out of the bodies of herbivore mothers.

The waxing moon became associated with the mothers and goodness. The waning moon became associated with the emerging fathers and loss. It didn't stop there, for evenness and balance became an obcession. It extended to the DAILY passage of the sun rising in the East and setting in the West. When the sun set in the Western sky, it was either swallowed by the great mouth of Mother Earth, just fell off the edge into nothingness, or began its journey of transformation through Her intestines. It was also perceived that within the body of Mother Earth there were underground tunnels, or tubes that when the sun set in the West it had to travel through to be reborn in the East.They called those underground tunnels the intestines within Her great body. In Amharic angat (HANAGATA) deals with 'entrails', the intestinal solar track within the body of Mother Earth. The (HANA) in the Amharic 'entrails' deals with the sun (IS HANA). The snake (IS NAKA,NAGA) surfaces here as the guide of the sun. The (GATA) on the end looks suspiciousluy like the English gut (GATA). For the Maori the 'intestines' are called mahara, and deal with the belly (HARA) in Hebrew and Japanese in which the intestines are housed.

The passage of the sun overhead created an even 'separation' between DAY and NIGHT. It also created a 'separation' from light into darkness. Darkness was associated not only with the reflected mystery of under water and the passage underground, but with death. The SHAPE of that fall off the edge, off the flat body of Mother Earth at Her horizontal rim was at an angle. The angle of that fall became codified as the SHAPE of the number seven (IS HAVANA) of 'separaton' and death. It is out of that angle (HANAGALA) at the edge from which the birds emerged at a right angle that also fed into the concept of angels (HANAGALA). They, like the uncles (HANAKALA) were the protectors that not only brought shimmering light to the night sky but a promise of life sustaining milk. The HANA deals with the sun (IS HANA). The NAGA deals wit the snake (IS NAKA, NAGA) as the guide of the sun. The GALA establishes its links with the moon and milk.

Since all of this activity dealing with the oncoming of night happened at evening time, the even (HAVANA) of evening, broke the day and night cycle into two even halves which could only occur at the equator, more to the point at the Sahel and at the ancient Sahara desert at that ancient time when the sands flowed with bountiful water.

RULE SIX; PHONOLGICAL CORRESPONDENCE. Look for SOUNDS that replace each other.

The Sounds (KA) and (Q) in agua are interchangeable.

RULE TEN; place (HA) before words beginning with a vowel.

Aqua becomes (HAQUA)

Place the (AH) vowel behind every consonant.

HAQUA becomes (HAKA).

Aqua (HAKA) as the Latin reflective surface of water, emerges out of its most ancient past as the hacker (HAKA-) of reality in two. It establishes its links to the jaw, the hook (HAKA) on the bottom of the skull of the carnivore mother who hacked her prey into smaller (KA) pieces. On the body of Mother Earth. the hacker of reality into two parts on the bottom of Her surFACE, was the water, the Latin aqua (HAKA).The Latin aqua doesn't necessarily deal with evenness. It deals with 'separation'. That separation begins to usher in male centrality as the waters become the separating agent for the sun away from the body of Mother Earth, in time becoming a male deity.

Before the process of reflection and separation gained momentum on the body of Mother Earth, it had its origins out of the individual mothers face. In Polish the word for eye is oko (HAKA). It is the eye that along with the jaw, the hook (HAKA) on the mothers face that hacked, divided reality into two equal parts, one in front of the eye and the other behind the eye. Divison is the (D) 'gift of' vision. Division also creates the individual the specific aspect separate from the ground of being.

When you hack (HAKA) morsels with the hook (HAKA) on the bottom of the skull, you create smaller (KA) pieces that can be ingested. That is what they perceived that the eye, the oko (HAKA) in Polish, also did. It hacked reality into small enough images to be absorbed by the brain. It is not only the word hook (HAKA) that establishes the separation from life into death. It is also the word equal (HAKA-) that establishes the same ancient meaning.

The oko (HAKA) in Polish as the English eye makes a geographic as well as a linguistic journey. As a reflective surface associated with the human eye extending to the body of Mother Earth, it surfaces not only in Africa as the Okobongo (HAKA-) River Delta but high tails it across the Atlantic Ocean to the continent of North America to become the Okeefenokee (HAKA-) Swamp in Georgia and the Lake Okeechobie (HAKA-) in Florida. There are many other watery realms that have the (HAKA) dyad of aqueus (HAKA-) reflection representing them.

It joins the Savannah (IS HAVANA) River, the Suwanee (IS HAWANA) River and the city of Havana itself. Along with Canada (KANADA) as the Kunda (KANADA) of the Tantrists we are linguistically dealing with an ancient prehistoric time that has yet to be explored.

Since it is the eye on the face of the mother that linguistically came first, then how did it surface all the way up in Poland? There are echoes of the same shape in Spanish as ocho. Ocho also stands for the letter eight. Lay the letter eight on its side and you not only get 'infinity' but the way that the eye sees. It is an even distribution of two closed circles, one inside and one outside.

When the AHA moment hit our ancient ancestors, they must have cried out. 'Look ! The reflection of Mother Earth across the great expanse of standing water IS EVEN'.

The perception of what they saw as being IS EVEN came first, be it the eye of seeing or the reflective surface of water. The number seven (IS EVEN) as an even number, followed course as it also dealt with the ancient migrations to the savannahs (IS HAVANA) in the seventh (IS HAVANA) lunar month of September. It was also the time of the semi anuual avian (HAVANA) migrations that broke the year into two equal halves.

It established the concept of balance and evenness on the creature body, the body of Mother Earth, the migratory yearly trek to the savannahs (IS HAVANA), the even (HAVANA) fourteen day distribution of the month, the even (HAVANA) passage from day into night, in the evening (HAVANA-).

The -ing (HANAGA) at the end of English words deals with the continuous habitual movement of the sun (IS HANA) above, as the sun (IS HANA) and below as the guide of the sun, the snake (IS NAKA, NAGA) becoming (HANAGA).

Then where does the dyad HAVANA come from and how is it related to the number seven (IS EVEN)? When the concept of 'separation' became attached to the number seven (IS HAVANA), it tried to explain the concept of reincarnation. The sun, Spanish sol (IS HALA) set the pattern for the human soul (IS HALA). Since the sun as a child of Mother Earth was 'born again' every day at dawn, it was considered to be immortal. The same process must have been shared by the human soul. It too was a child of Mother Earth and like the sun it too must have gone on a journey of rebirth.

The sun not only fell off at a right angle off the body of Mother Earth in the Western sky, giving us the SHAPE of the number seven (IS HAVANA) but like the birds, it flew up to its newly found haven (HAVANA) in heaven (HAVANA). The separation myths pepper the ancient landscape as males begin to find their own 'source' at first in the sun, then the sky, then in the mind of a Father God.

It doesn't stop there, for as the ancient Africans dispersed due to climactic cataclysms, a few linguistic areas give us further clues. The ancient Hebrews possessed the rituals of fear defusion as they rocked back and forth. To rock back and forth in Hebrew is to d'aven (DAVANA), the 'gift of' (D) aven (HAVANA). Also in Hebrew aven (HAVANA) deals with 'nothingness'. It is either to ritualistically empty the mind in the individual, the goal of the Buddhists, or it deals with the setting sun as it fell off into the abyss of 'nothingness' and death.

Another group dispersed to the British Isles and settled on the banks of the Avon (HAVANA) River, next to Stonehenge. The pathway from the circular drumming circle of Stonehenge to the River Avon (HAVANA) could be reached by a wide avenue (HAVANA). The River Avon was the river of passage for the human soul. To make that journey you had to leave the British Isles and head West where the sun set across the great devide of the Atlantic Ocean, to HAVANA, Cuba. Something exists there that has not yet been discovered.

The thirteen regular phases of the moon were so deeply engrained with women's menstrual cycles, that when males made the shift into the twelve month irregular solar year, they had to villify and demonize the number thirteen. With male centrality came the irregular solar twelve month year, associated with the SUN away from the body of Mother Earth.

There must have been some reason for the Egyptians to create the seven step mastabas, seven steps above and seven steps below. It dealt with a much older concept dealing with the reflective surface of water. As such the ancient passage across water after death takes on new meaning, as other emerging civilizations come up with the reflective surfaces of rivers of passage, like the Charon, Styx and Jordan.

Egyptian mythology fuses many of these concepts together. For them the unending war that existed in the world was not between Mother Earth and the sun. It was a war between two brothers; the risen sun Osiris and the SETting sun Set.

We are dealing here with two actual male power bases. One was the eunuch priesthood who presided at the side of the mothers dealing with the rites of the solar passage. The other was the peripheral 'band of brothers' that have been shoved out of the female clan at the time of puberty.

The evil brother Set, of the SETting sun, kills his brother Osiris and cuts him up into fourteen parts. There must have been an important ritual that has been lost to us based on the division of the twenty eight day lunar month into two equal fourteen day halves. Set not only kills his brother, cuts him up into fourteen parts but won't tell his sister Isis (Auset) where he has hidden him. She has to know the secret word. THE WORD as a sacred secret rears its head. She gets it out of him and finds her brother and puts his FOURTEEN parts together without the phallus. Shades of Siva and Mother Kali. (The ice man found recently in the Alps had also been castrated). Isis (Auset) is Earth Mother and marries her castrated brother Osiris. Mother Earth prefers the risen sun to the setting sun. They beget Horus, the hero sun (son) of a new age. Since Osiris has been castrated, then Horus is the result of a virgin birth. Echoes of echoes, like the drumming sounds in Stonehenge.

The paintings and statues on temple walls and columns in Egypt depict human figures and all creatures in profile. They are represented as half figures. What they may have been trying to represent was that only half of their reality existed upon this plane. The other half which was just as real, existed under the skin of Mother Earth in the reflective quality of water. Only the pharaoh, as their representative could make the journey home, in an expensive gold laden barque that guaranteed all of them immortality.

They also believed in being joyful. The Goddess Maat weighed a feather (birds again) against a human heart soul. If the heart soul was heavier than the feather it couldn't pass and had to do it over again. Grief and sadness made the soul heavy. Joy made it light. The pursuit of joy was part and parcel of the political structure. It may be ironic that the Masons with their pyramids, obeliscs and the third eye in the forehead, would have included the 'pursuit of happiness' as part of the credo of their new nation.

At the time of ancient female centrality, the beginning of night at twilight was ritually the most important time. It is not an accident that the eve of evening broke the day evenly in half and was the time for ancient nocturnal lunar services. The eve of evening not only created the even distribution between day and night but also surfaced in the Bible as Eve, the second, not as important as Lilith, the first wife of Adam.

The ancient grid charts tell us the story that our ancient ancestors not only charted the body of Mother Earth but also the human body. They came up with two movements. One was solar and the other was lunar, the Ida and Pingali of the Tantrists. Both of these streams of energy lay coiled in three and a half coils at the base of the spine and rose seven times around the spinal column carrying with them all the potential of joyful living. It didn't work out that way. As the Kundalini rose upwards through the body through the Tantric chacras, it not only created them but put different evolutionary characteristics into each one. If any of the ascending characteristics got trapped by fear, they had to be released. This is where all the Kundalini systems of fear defusion come in. Layer by layer the seven chacras have to be cleansed.

A metaphor of the onion emerged to describe the process. The onion has to be peeled layer by layer. One skin has to be removed and you have another skin. When you remove that skin then there is another one underneath that has to be dealt with.

The dance of Salome (IS HALAMA) with her seven veils deals with that same metaphoric peeling away of the painful illusions that we have saddled ourselves with, to survive.

At the base chacra we deal with survival and will say and do anything to get fed. In the second sexual chacra the veils are endless dealing with identity, attractiveness, pleasure, denial, fantasy and shame. At the power chacra we deal with how important we are and how much attention we can get. At the heart chacra we set up how compassionate and caring we are. At the throat chacra we deal with creativity and communication. <u>When we get to the third eye we have to begin telling the truth.</u> We have to strip away all the veils, all the masks that we have created to survive, to be loved, to be accepted, to be attractive, to be important. We have to begin to stand naked, free of illusion and to tell the truth about who we are and how we have put ourselves together.

In male centrality Salome's dance of the seven veils became a dance of seduction. Originally it was the dance of fear defusion in the seven chacras, like Hercules rerouting the two rivers of the Kundalini energy carried by water as a conductor, to flush out the manure (fear) in the Augean stables.

The onion in Polish is cebula (IS HABALA), HABA is one of the ancient names of the sun the 'two in one' (BA) journey above and below the body of Mother Earth. There is a Goddess Cybele (IS HABALA) in Greek mythology who dealt with orgiastic violence and who may originally have been the symbol for the peeling of the onion of entrapped fear. Also in Greek Hebe (HABA) is the virgin form of the triple Goddess Hera. Hebe is a derogatory name for Hebrew (HABARA), the helper (-ER) of the sun.

The seven chacras moving up the spine echo the concept of 'separation', for when fear gripped a person and the fear driven image became the vehicle for action, the person became separated from their peace and joy.

More contemporary surfacing of the number seven deals with the Book of Revelation and the SEVEN seals that have to be broken for the ultimate separation, the end of the world to come to pass. Linear beginnings and ends exist in the left hemisphere of the human brain. St John, a lone hermit on the island of Padmos, not yet ready for the Kundalini energy to blast through him, unleashes the negative forces that his three lower chacras have trapped in him. He had a series of visions crackling through his third eye that spelled the end of the world through war, violence, pestilence, fire, famine, disease, you name it, all four, males riding on the backs of horses.

There is little doubt that Mother Nature has not been fair to the male gender. No babies pop out of them every ten lunar months. No birthing breath flushes them with ecstasy and makes them privy to all of the accompanying powers. It is not Freudian 'penis envy' that is the reality. What historically males have pondered over is their peripheral state. For thousands of early years their bodies have been mutilated in order for them to have a baby. Nothing worked. At first there was great jealousey and mimicking. Then the evil hiss of revenge raised its hooded head as they took after the individual mothers, condemming them to rape, harems, exploitation, slavery, and clitorectomies.

The fear and resentment toward the individual mother expanded to include the body of Mother Earth. Exploitation, destruction, pollution, forest depletion, ocean desecration, specie extinction, all followed the unrelenting pressure of more human babies, more money, more greed, until the body of Mother Earth, our planerary nest has been brought to Her knees. St John is only one of many men who would like to see all of the creations out of the body of Mother Earth and Mother Earth Herself to be destroyed. Consciously or unconsciously that is what is happening. As males try hard to find a home away from the body of Mother Earth and their 'source' in space, with satellites, and UFOs, the seven seals of 'separation' are upon us.

The (B) of 'two in one' also expanded to include the (B) of the brain. It has two exact halves that are encased in the skull. Our ancient mothers understood that it was only one side of the brain that gave them problems. They surmised that if one side on the body of Mother Earth dealt with life, then the reflected side dealt with death. The same process must have been occuring in the human brain. They understood the crisscrossing at the third eye. The right hemisphere of the brain dealt with motherhood, relationships, compassion, cooperation and was attached to the skin and the heart. It became associated with the left handed mothers. They also understood that the left hemisphere of the brain with its detachment, secrecy, violence, image accumulation and fear retention was the side that gave them trouble. If we have come to these conclusions after our five thousand year history, what could they have known since their brain has been the same size for at least 200,000 years? And then there were the Neandethal whose brains were bigger.

Since a balance and evenness existed with the body of Mother Earth and Her reflective surface, then that same balance must have to be pursued in the human brain. Like it or not they came up with the process of castration. When the testes were removed the male child became docile, no longer violent. That history existed for multithousands of years. It is not a pretty story but the words bear witness to its linguistic reality. Almost all languages have the word castration in their dictionaries. It was believed that to castrate a boy was to free him from his violence, to give him freedom. The word lib surfaces here as castration, and Libra holds the scales of balance. Libra deals with liberty and liberty deals with freedom.

To be free of male violence is to have had the balance in the brain between the two hemispheres restored through castration.

RULE EIGHT; ANASTROPHE or PALENDROME, reflection or inversion of words.

The reflective balance restoring peace that had been pursued to exist in the human brain, expanded to include other factors dealing with the reflective balance in words representing transformative places, cities, countries, processess and people;

Magma (MAGAMA) (MAGA/GAMA), (Ganga (GANA/NAGA), Tibet, (TABA/BATA), Cusco (KASA/SAKA), level (LAVA/VALA), clock, clack (KALA/LAKA), kayak (KAYA/YAKA), David (DAVA/VADA). Divide (DAVA/VADA), Miriam (MARA/RAMA), Druid (DARA/RADA).

The world of water also dealt with the MARA dyad. It surfaces in the MARine environment and as mar and mare. It not only gave the names of the emerging Gods (RAMA) as a reflection of the Mother Earths Goddesses (MARA/RAMA) but moved in a vartiery of other directions. In Russian mir (MARA), means peace. Death in the watery stillness below must have been considered to be very peaceful. Mir (MARA) also givers birth to mirror (MARA-) and that was what a watery surface was considered to be, a mirror or a peaceful reflection of what was above.

MEDITATION
The STAR of DAVID

O ne of the ways to defuse the fear trapped images of illusion and to nullify their power is through meditation. The focus of meditation with concentrated effort activates the shimmering light in the third eye and the pulsating ecstasy in the body.

While doing linguistic research in the eighties and early nineties I also did a great deal of meditation. One night after spending the day with friends I had an overwhelming desire to sit and to meditate. I fixed myself into my recliner, the angle of which seemed to set my head buzzing and receded deeply into myself. There was no litany, no mantra, no prayer to recite. Almost immediately the rush began in my body.

Behind the dark screen of my closed eyes, a light began to flicker. It grew more intense as it sparked on and off creating a vertical movement of sparks. Then it was intercepted by two diagonal lines creating a pulsating configuration that began to center itself into loosely extending fingers. As the goose pimples began to pucker my skin, a more intense light began to glow in the center of that emerging construct. The light moved to the edges forming a six pointed star. Right there in the darkness, inside of my head the Star of David was pulsating, expanding, and contracting, brilliant at the center, with a white light changing color at the edges from yellow, to orange, to red. Then the edges of the star softened and the star became one great round light with a darker center like that of an eye in the center of my forehead. Waves of ecstacy followed waves inside and outside of my body.

Many years before I had been told by a psychic that I was protected by the Star of David and here I was heir to it, in the landscape of my mind.

I opened my eyes and I was sitting in the darkness with only the full moon shining through the skylight high above head, round and white, already deep into its journey across the night sky. What did it mean? Where did the Star of David come from? As with everything else that I had encountered, it was much older than what we had been taught and as I was to subsequently learn. Like the SASA dyad, It had ancient links with both the female body and the body of Mother Earth.

During the ancient time of mother centrality the Star of David represented two specific aspects of motherhood. It was the triangle that represented the mother essence. The Star of David consists of two triangles superimposed on each other. One of the triangles, the bottom one represents the triangular shape of the volcanic cone (KANA), the place where Mother Earth creates land, Her greatest offering to life out of Her lavic menstrual blood. Land came first. Without land there would have been no life on Earth. She was the overwhelming singular context of creation. Her volcanic crater (KARATARA) was the creator (KARATARA). Her triangular SHAPE of the volcanic cone of land creation established all of the ancient triads of Goddesses that followed Her, giving birth to the SHAPE of the letter A(ah).

The other triangle of creation is the SHAPE of the female pubis. All mothers were considered to be surrogates to Mother Earth in the creation of smaller (KA) replicas of themselves. The two triangles superimposed one on top of the other, create the Star of David.

RULE EIGHT; ANASTROPHE, PALENDROME, reflection or inversion.

Ironically the name David (DAVADA) is an anastrophe, a reflection of itself. It consists of (DAVA) and (VADA). The (VA) that straddles both syllables deals with both the volcano (VA) on the body of Mother Earth and the vulva (VA) on the body of the individual mother. The (DA) on both ends of David (DAVADA) establishes the 'gift of' (DA) out of two directions, coming and going out of the volcanic body of Mother Earth and out of the body of the individual specific surrogate vulvic mother, the (SASA) of another declination.

When David takes down Goliath with the one third eye in the forehead, he is only sending a message that he is ending the reign of the ancient mothers and their eunuch sons who through their connection to birthing, meditation and mysticism had to be destroyed for the left hemispheric, reasonable, rational, violent, competitive, male dominated world to survive. A similar construct surfaces in Greek when Hercules blinds the one eyed Cyclops. It is the same myth repeated in a different area of the world. It could be joined by the one horned horse, the unicorn. The strength was in the eyes of seeing associated with male sexuality. As male centrality progressed, it all became based on the male sexual eye of seeing that created the fear driven image, pushing it into imagination and then into fantasy and subsequently into the adult fairy talles that became the faith of the fathers.

Hidden in the folds of the triangle is another long sought for explanation that has been shrouded in mystery. The Star of David contains within its ancient mother based structure the SHAPES that define the enigmatic number 666, of the 'beast'. The only reason it has been considered the number of Satan is because it represented the prime metaphor associated with Mother Earth.

666

The most basic internal shape within the Star of David is the hexagon, the six sided form at the center. A hexagon is the six sided shape of the bee cell in which the larva pupate. It is the hidden home of the queen bee laying her endless eggs, creating by herself all of her reality, becoming the metaphor for Mother Earth and lindguistically as the BEE of BEing.

There are two large three sided superimposed triangles creating the Star of David. Two times three equals the first six (6) sides.

The two larger superimposed triangles create six (6) smaller triangular arms of the star.

The two superimposed triangles create a six (6) sided hexagon in the center. It is the shape of the larval bee cell.

All three triangular aspects of the Star of David fit into the ancient mother based hidden bee hive. It was the queen bee in the bee hive that became a metaphoric symbol for the unrelenting creative capacity out of the physical body of Mother Earth.

As male centrality began to emerge on the scene all aspects of creation had to be devined out of the 'hidden' mind of God floating in the ethers.

The 'hidden' hive (HAVA) of the queen bee gave its name to the Hebrew God Jehovah (JA HAVA). In Polish the name for 'hidden' is chova (HAVA).

What had been the actual 'hidden' hive with the bee of being as a metaphoric symbol for the creative capacity of Mother Earth during the time of female centrality, became redefined as the Biblical hero David who killed not only the one eyed Goliath but the triangular construct of Her many faceted bases of power. The Satanic 'beast' was really the unsuspecting industrious queen bee laying her endless eggs metaphortically associating her with the creative capacity of Mother Earth.

THE UNION JACK

Years later when my meditations became deeper and deeper, one night after going through the whole scale on different vowel SOUNDS, I had another series of lines to light up the inner vision of my mind. There was a shimmering of sparkles that lined up into a vertical line. Then a lateral line of light softly emerged and formed a shimmering cross. On top of the shimmering cross two diagonal lines superimposed themselves upon it and an eight pointed star flashed on my inner vision. The arms of the star extended to the edges of my visual inner landscape. I was familiar with the six pointed Star of David but this was something new.

I kept breathing deeply and concentrating on my third eye as what looked like a blazing Union Jack of the British, or the Confederate flag of the United States plastered itself upon the dark screen of my mind. What now?

What I didn't realize at the time is that I was being given specific answers to questions that I hadn't yet formed in my mind. In time they began to make sense as I continued my research into humanity's prehistoric SOUNDS that as contemporary human language are still with us.

TRUTH — The truth will out.

The third eye is the area where truth makes its home. As the illusions of fabricating, lying, acting, pleasing, are stripped away and you stand on the threshold of self realization and truth, you can go into the verbal dance of 'what is truth'. Some will say truth is relative. It is perception through the filter of our minds. Not really. There are some universal agreements. Grass is green. Water is wet. Sky is blue. Where does the word truth derive from? What ancient soul said 'this is true'?

RULE NINE; replace the existing vowel sounds with the (AH) SOUND. Truth (TARATA) becomes an overlapping dyad of (TARA) and (RATA). Tara is the terrain (TARA-), the turf (TARA-) on the body of Mother Earth. (RATA) establishes the activity dealing with return (RATARA-) the circular ratio (RATA) of constant returning of the sun (RA). 'The truth will out', surfaces here. What we are dealing with here is the cyclical passage of time, life, and creation emerging out of the body of Mother Earth.

Another word for the turn around back up, is vert (VARATA). In Spanish verdad is the word for truth. Verdad hides in its folds verde or verdant as green in English. So truth is that which comes back up to the surface as green plants. Was truth considered to be the end of the migratory trek and the newly found green grass in the distant savannah?

Look! 'Grass is green' as an agreement, when they pointed to the 'greener pastures' in the distance, after their six month migratory trek, takes on new meaning. A seed (IS HADA) warmed by the sun and shocked into life by descending sheets of rain, rises back up into the belly of light, up from the body of Mother Earth. The solar wind carries the Kundalini of lifes return to the surface. The water as the conducter of the electrical flow infuses the patient seed with a burst into life. There is nothing that will stop the seed from sprouting. The seed will out, as the truth will out. The process is based on natural law. A seed (IS HADA) deals with 'the gift of' (DA) air (HA) containing in its belly the light of the passing sun and the moisture of the cloud shedding rain.

Lava, leva, lew, love, Levites

The ancient law at the time of female centrality was based on the understanding of natural systems. Law (LAWA) comes out of the same construct as lava, and as lewa (LAVA) for 'left' in Polish.

RULE SIX; PHONOLOGICAL CORRESPONDENCE, sounds that replace each other.

The V and W are often interchangeable. In Polish lewa (LAVA) is the left hand. It was the left handed mothers who defined law out of the natural processes that they experienced around them. The emergence of lava that solidified into land was one of the most important. Mating with the larger brained Neanderthal they may have understood some of the hidden natural processes that we can only guess at.

Based on the (AH) sound, the construct of lava is as ancient as language gets. It was lava as it emerged on the surface out of the volcanic body of Mother Earth that established the truth of law. The emergence of lava began the creation of land and the possibility of life. The shape of that emergence is encoded in the word lava. The phoneme (VA) in lava, deals with the volcano (VALAKANA) out of which it emerged. The angle (LA) deals with the vertical thrust of its ascent, pushed up and out by the ever present tongue (LA) lengua in Latin, and then the angle of its descent to flow across the surface. (KANA) is the volcanic cone (KANA) the maker of smaller substances, in this case land.

It is the primordial activity of land production that helped to define what was true (TARA) on terra (TARA) firma. As the lava cascaded down the flanks on the body of Mother Earth it seemed as if the lava loved (LAVA-) their ancient Mother, to carress Her surface, her skin, as it sped across creating her major off spring, the land upon Her surface.

Since male role in paternity was unknown and it was believed that the blood coagulated in the mothers body for ten lunar months to create the solid replica that emerged from her as a baby, so they also believed that what went on inside of the individual mothers body went on in the same way on the <u>outside</u> of the body of Mother Earth. Her steaming liquid lavic blood hardened into Her baby, the land upon Her surface.

The left (LAFATA) handed mothers, leva (LAVA) in Polish expressed the imperatives of creation in concert with the loving (LAVA-) lavic (LAVA-) fires out of the body of Mother Earth.

The importance of animals surfaces in this cluster of SOUNDS also. In Polish lew (LAVA) is the name for 'lion'. Here we are dealing with the lioness who was as important as the 'bee of being' as a metaphor for Mother Earth. It was understood that the supreme and ultimate killer was Mother Earth Herself. She created everything, maintained them and when they died and decayed she absorbed them back into Her body.

Who was the ultimate killer on those savage, open savannahs? It was the carniverous lioness and her pride, the Polish lew (LAVA). To maintain their cubs they killed and hunted down whatever they could. The feline mothers sMOTHERED their prey with their mouths. Their paws (PAWA-) held the prey in place and surfaces as the name for power (PAWA-). Also in Polish the name for paws is lapa (WAPA) and gives birth to the English word weapon (WAPA-).

The ancient Sphynx sitting astride the desert plateau is a lioness with the head of a pharaoh. In Egyptian iconography it is usual for the human form to have an animal head. The Sphynx is a lioness with a human head and is much more ancient. As a metaphor for the creative and destructive powers of Mother Earth she harkens back to the time of female centrality. It may even go back to before the last glaciation. She represents the power of Mother Earth in many of Her mystical aspects in the emerging male head of state.

The pharaonic chin of the Sphynx has no goatee. It may have links with the hairless and beardless eunuchs who ruled Egypt many millenia ago. As male centralty erupted on the scene, and bearded males took over the power bases of the ancient eunuchs, the eunuchs may have plastered goatees onto their chins to be accepted by the bearded 'band of brothers ' who were taking over.

The whole process may have even more ancient roots and goes

back to the ancient migrations. It was the nanny goat that was one of the animals providing milk for the migrating mothers. In ancient myths milk as a watery liquid and a conductor of electricity, surfaces as being associated with the snake, the carrier of the Kundalini energy.

Among the ancient Hebrews there was a tribe called the Levites (LAVATA). That ancient tribe surfaces with many intetesting characteristics. Its leaders set up a tribal God named Nahash, the serpent or Nahushtan, the God of healing in the desert. The Levites considered themselves to be the sons of the great serpent, Leviathan, or Mother Earth in Her watery aspect.

One of the sources of the word lava are the volcanic fires out of the body of Mother Earth. The other source is the flow of creation out of water, also out of the body of Mother Earth. It echoes water as the Greek conductor of the purifying Kundalini energy of Hercules rerouting the two rivers and flushing out of the Augean stables.

In Hebrew levi, lavo, lavit means to wash in a flowing stream or to pour water over a surface. Water is a conductor of electricity and electricity has its roots in the rays of the sun passing across the surface. Here we have the roots of the Hebrew mikvah (for the males) as the ritual bath and the Christian baptism (for all). It comes out of the understanding that for the Levites the Kundalini serpent energy could be experienced through the contact not with the fiery volcanic lava but a more benign dunking in water.

The Levitic God Leviathan may have originated in the desert as a healer but as male centrality gained momentum he became vilified because he as the guide of the sun had been associated with the body of Mother Earth. The emerging bearded male priesthood went after him in the same way that St George went after all of the snakes in Ireland. He became the demonized Leviathan, the serpent that had to be destroyed.

Yahveh battled the Leviathan, psalm 74

"By the power didst thou cleave the sea monster in two and break the sea serpents head above the water. Thou didst crush Leviathans many heads.'

This reverberates with echoes of the Greeks again with the severed head of Medusa with its many coiling serpents erupting out of her skull. What we are dealing with here is the shift of the Kundalini energy from the birthing breath of the mothers to the davening or ritual rocking back and forth of the fathers.

Since the Leviathan was destroyed by Yahveh, and Medusa by Hercules then the practice of clitorectomies and the removal of the cosmic orgasm must have entered female experience at a very ancient time.

It seems inevitable that the experience of levitation must have come out of the ancient tribe of Levites. Since they crossed paths with the larger brained Neanderthal, could they have gained the lost and mysterious powers that slid those humongous monolithic boulders in place?

Not to be left out, the Nessians were also Hebrew serpent worshippers. The Nessian serpent was called the messiah, the savior. What could his message (MASA-) have been? What was he saving? The word message (MASA-) hides in its linguistic folds the word massage (MASA-). It was the caressing passage of the solar wind across the body of Mother Earth, Her skin that they appreciated, for they loved the massage as much as did their Mother. And what did the Nessian serpent save? Of what was he the savior? It was the sun from being lost within the intestines in the body of Mother Earth after it set into the bloody waters of the Western sea saving them from the perils of the dark night.

The third eye chacra is the step into the possibility of knowledge that is based on what is real and no longer deals with illusion. The body of Mother Earth and the processes inherent in Mother Nature are real and true. All else is illusion and fantasy and has to be dealt with on the level of art. It can be reached through what Jaya Ma tried to impress upon us, 'meditate, meditate, meditate!'

THE SEVENTH CHACRA
THE SAHASRARA CROWN CHACRA
Soft in the head, Consciousness, wisdom, universal identity, thought, violet, OM

For the Hopi and the Tibetans the two bottom chacras and the two top chacras were the same. It would seem that the Egyptians might have felt the same way, for the Uraeus or the cobra exited out of their sixth chacra at the forehead. For thr Hindu the exit in Maha Samadhi is out of the top of the head at the seventh chacra. Gurus and swamis who made the journey out of the top of their heads were said to have a soft spot on the skull where the Kundalini energy made its exit. The derogatory term 'soft in the head' may have its origins out of the ancient adepts who navigated the terrain of the seventh chacra.

Only the very few have had this special trip, for in Hindu the word Maha Samadhi also means death. It is an opening into another level of being. It may be the place where death resides. Or it may be the place where the dream state exists at the same level as consciousness itself. There have been a very few who have reached that state, the prophets, healers, carriers of this energy. Many are called but few are chosen. They could create miracles and manipulate matter. They could bring the dead back to life. Christ was one of those rare people. They could heal and be horse whisperers like the much maligned Rasputin.They could diagnose ailments and prescribe medications like the sleeping prophet Edgar Casey. Nostradamus may have had that opening into that Akashic record where all that is, is stored and exists in the eternal NOW.

Joya MA carried that opening inside of her. She often claimed that she was like a tube through which the energy flowed. To a lesser or greater degree psychics, people with extrasensory perception also are privy to those gifts. It's time that we turned to those people and ask them for the truths that they experience from other levels. Our 'rational' fear driven minds, based on the 'reasonable' left hemisphere have dug us into a technical pit from which there may be no escape.

As the male, fuelled by his solidifying fear, moved away from the body of Mother Earth into the life of the image, the life of the idea, the life of fantasy, the reality based on the rationale, it closed the possibility of connectedness and open-endedness. Rational is that which is rationalized, explained, made explicit, through the use of words, the answer to the why. It is not an experience in itself.

To reason, to be 'rational' comes out of 'ratio' (RATA) which is defined as a 'fixed portion'. To be rational, means to reason with a fixed portion and not to have access to the wisdom of the universe. The circular close ended process has links with the right (RATA) hand of the fathers that replaced in supremacy the left hands of the mothers. The use of ritual (RATA-) belonged to the emerging fathers in their search for the elusive Kundalini experience.

Ancient Hebrew priests wore a chest covering called the 'rational'. Therefore the roots of Western civilization lie in the perception that it evolved not out of the open ended reconnection supplied by the energy of the Earth as Mother but out of the fixed portion of male 'reason' (the over developed left hemisphere of the brain), which unfortunately is not grounded in reality but in fear.

When I lived in Rockland County, New York, I had a singular experience which set me to wondering. My water supply was furnished by a well that sat next to a stream. Every time that we had a rain storm, the storm sewers that had been funneled into my little stream seeped into my well and contaminated my water. At that painful time I never knew that the water was the problem and I was suffering from an array of ailments for which the local doctors could find no remedy. They diagnosed me with chronic fatigue syndrome, fibro myalgia, depression and prescribed a varied assortment of pills.

One night while lying on my back in great pain and trying to meditate, I became aware that my feet were growing cold. Then slowly the cold began creeping up my calves. As the cold crept up my legs another stronger movement was pushing its way out of the bottom of my feet. The thought lept into my panicked mind that I was in the process of dying and that I had better do something about it. But what? I turned to the only option that I had and that was my breath. I started to pant like a dog to get my circulation going. The panting acceletrated into the Bastrika birthing breath which arrested the creeping coldness that was working its way up my legs and sent heat to warm my lifeless feet. After a while, as my body returned to its relatively normal state, I stopped panting and wonder began to spread itself through my mind, as the cold had been spreading up my legs.

All the books and swamis informed me that when you die the energy pops out of the top of your head. Then what happened to me? There was no doubt in my mind that I was on my way out and that the energy of my life was making an exit out of the bottom of my soles. If the Kundalini energy rising up from the body of Mother Earth entered the bottom of my feet, especially the left sole, (the big toe on the left foot turning black, as it did for Vishnu and for me), would it not make the same exit?

Then the myth of Achilles found its way into my brain. Didn't his power reside in his heel? When his heel was punctured the Kundalini energy ran out back down into the body of Mother Earth, not out of the top of his head, but from the bottom of his heel. Curious.

REGRESSION

Past lives?

While in Los Angeles in the late seventhies, I tasted the whole spiritual buffet that the magnificent city had to offer. One of the experiences dealt with being regressed. There were a series of scenarios that I experienced as I lay on that disheveled bed and the regressor lady, with the aid of a mildly hypnotic state, guided me through.

The one that stayed permanently with me happened in an

isolated cave in the desert. Upon entering the black basalt cave through an enormous opening I became aware of the SOUND of running water. To the right of me, on one of the cave walls, was a waterfall. The tumbling white water cascaded down and spread its flow upon large rectangular stone slabs that were lined up in a row. Upon those smooth stone slabs bodies were being prepared for mummification. There were entrails and trails of blood that were being scooped up by the rushing water and deposited into a low lying hole on the left side of the cave.

As I looked at the passing scenario, I realized that I was part of it. There was a solid looking man working on those bodies. His shiny head was bald and he had no other hair on his body. He was very tan with bulging muscular arms and he was wearing a rather bulky blood splattered leather chest covering or apron. There was no doubt to me that he, or I, was a eunuch.

As I gathered up more and more information I often wonderd whether this was the 'rational' of the ancient Hebrew priests, or the apron of the Free Masons? If it was so then what did it mean? Was there a time that the ancient Hebrews practiced mummi-fication? Obviously they must have believed in reincarnation. Mummification was a process of preparing the soul for the jour-ney to the other side, to the side of death. It was a journey similar to the passage through the chacras and a movement out of the top of the head, in Maha Samadhi. Then there is another factor. The much maligned Neanderthal buried their dead in a fetal position, sprinkled with flower petals and red ochre. It would seem that they believed in some sort of rebirth. Was there a connection?

Along with the eunuch, I had other scenes that swam across my mind. I was a little black girl in Africa when men in gold helmets shaped like rams horns swooped down and kidnapped all the children that I was watching and killed me. Then I was a shaman in an American Plains Indian ceremony with tassels at the end of my leather shirt, dancing in a circle and throwing real bones for augury. I was also an old Indian chief laid out on a raft floating down the Colorado River in the Grand Canyon, with my long grey hair trailing in the water behind me, as my tribe wailed their goodbys on the cliffs above me. There were others. What were they? Where did they come from? Some have called them past lives. That only deals with the belief in the process of reincarnation.

In the Epic of Gilgamesh the Sumerian prince took the same journey as the sun and declared that there was no rebirth of the sun (Spanish sol) to which the human soul was to have been attached. So there was no reincarnation and no life after death. This caused a great deal of consternation in the Middle East and the search for immortality began.

The Hindus got out of that context before Gilgamesh made his subterranean sojourns and have based their belief system on reincarnation, karma and the caste system that has lasted to this day. It was a question that I wanted to have answered before I plunged headlong into another 'road less travelled by' holding on to the horse's tail for dear life.

WE DIE TWICE

Then I realized that I had the answer given to me by my mother a year after her death.

One moment I lay on my bed, in my bedroom, back in my apartment in New York City, with my hair up in curlers, wearing my white silk jumpsuit. The next moment without even being aware of it, I had blinked and my mother stood before me at the foot of the bed. She wore the same blue turbin she had asked me to bring to her in the hospital, after they shaved her head and trepanned her skull on a search and destroy mission after the foreign attackers that invaded her brain. The blue turban was a bit askew. She straightened it, not so much to hide her scar, but to hide the baldness with which the operation had shamed her. The turban shifted again for she had little hair with which to hold it in place.

'Mamusiu kochana (dearest) Mamusiu what are you doing here, I thought that you had died'.

She looked down at me with those large sad brown eyes.

"I thought that you had forgotten me." She said in a soft voice with words that seemed to sparkle like a string of lights in the air

JOZEFA SKUZEWSKA REDZISZ (MY MOTHER)

between us.

"Mamusiu, I haven't forgotten you. I don't know where to find you. Where have you been?" The frightened child began to rise in me and my arms and legs began to tremble.

"I am here, where I have always been. I am here." As she answered the blue turban moved forward over her face. She lifted those blessed tender hands to position it more firmly on top of her head. As she did so, I again saw the livid scar on the side of her skull and the memories of her last days flowed over me and through me. Through tears I choked out.

"But we buried you. I saw the Earth strike your coffin. It took so many shovelfuls to cover your coffin while we stood on that hot August day in the pouring rain." I wanted to leap actross the bed and bury my face in her body, smell that wondrous familiar smell and touch her warmth, but a leaden weight locked me to the bed.

"But Mamusiu, We buried you. How can you be here?

"Oh, Basiu, Basiu, you don't understand.We die twice.The first time we die, they bury us as you buried me in the Earth. We die a second time when everyone forgets us."

"Mamusiu, I haven't forgotten you. You took the lights with you when you left me". I reached out to her with one of my hands and the tears blinded me. When I opened my eyes she was gone.

For many years I had relived that experience, lost in the grief for my mother, trying to find a reason to keep going. Now I realized that she had given me an answer to a question that I began to ask many years into the future. But what was it that she had said?

<u>We die twice, the first time when they bury us in the Earth. We die the second time when everyone forgets us.</u>

Immortality exists only as stored pictures in the brains of the people whom we had known, loved and who have passed on. Is that what she was saying to me? I was looking for a larger picture, for something cosmic, eternal, other worldly. She gave me a very practical answer. There is no immortality. We exist only as pictures in other brains. When those brains die off, so do we. And then what?

How about reincarnation? Do we keep recycling forever? Was that system created to keep violent mankind in line? Where did all those regression scenarios come from? Gilgamesh gave us the answer thousands of years ago. There is no reincarnation. The human soul does not take the same journey as the sun, the Spanish sol. Then what happened to me when I sat up in that hotel room in New York City. One minute I was lying peacefully on the bed and the next I sat up except that my body still lay on the bed. Who was that person who had separated from my body? I thought that it was me. Is that where ghosts come from? The body dies. The thinking part stays around wandering and giving people bad dreams.

I always thought that on some level we are a triangular spiral shape that segments itself from that longer helexical spin, with the wide circle on the bottom and the smallest point on top. Our life begins with that enormous spin on the bottom. Then as we age the spin becomes more and more narrow, until it becomes a point at the top and we pop out to some other area. That is why at the lowest spin when we are children time goes by so slowly. Days seem to be like months and evening is way over there, at the end of a year. As we age time begins to speed up. In old age it rushes by at alarming speed because the spin on the top of the spiral is so small.

What happens when the body dies and if that spin is interrupted? Is that the realm of ghost wndering around not knowing where they belong? Is that why most religions decry suicide and make it into a sin? The questions kept spinning in my brain. They gave me little rest.

Under the oaks at Ojai in California with the rain dissipating above the tree canopy above us, Krisha Murti was giving one of his last seminars. He looked spent with dark circles under his eyes and his beautiful face was grey with fatigue. But he answered many questions that were thrown at him. He didn't want to be a guru and he never followed a guru. He carved out his own path. All the questions, in one way or another dealt with people wanting to know how to become self-realized and how to become enlightened. He had one answer that he kept repeating with vaguely controlled patience.

'Watch the way your mind works.'

You don't need a guru. All that you need is to become aware of the activity of your mind. Hilda Charlton advised us that the only area that we need a guru is when we move into the two top chacras. Krishna Murti didn't even go that far. He just kept repeating the same phrase.

'Watch the way your mind works.'

When I was in India I visited the Samadhi of the Mother who had been with Sri Aurobindo. It was situated under an enormous tree. There were many women singing and making flower designs on the large stone slab that marked her tomb. As I grew closer the same stoned physical experience that I had around Joya Ma began to spread itself through me. I didn't know whether it was the tree, the actual place, or the Samadhi of the mother. The male gurus around whom I had meditated never elicited that response in me. Tears may have rolled down my face, but I never got stoned. Was part of being stoned the way that my mind worked? Or was the source of the Kundalini movement beyond my mind?

THE SNAKE (IS NAKA)
(NAKA/KANA, NAGA/GANA, NAHA/HANA)

RULE ELEVEN;The letter S is an emphatic standing for 'it is', remove it from the beginning of words.

Snake becomes (IS NAKE).

RULE NINE; Replace the existing vowels with the (AH) SOUND. (IS NAKE) becomes (IS NAKA). The phoneme (NA) deals with either 'a change from a former state' or 'emergence on the surface' originally dealing with the activity of the nose, smelling and breathing, codifying the shape of the letter (N) in profile. The snake (IS NAKA) as the guide of the sun (IS HANA), creates both possibilities, the sun 'emerging on the surface' with the help of the snake as its guide and creating a 'change from a former state', from the darkness of night into the light of a new day.

The (KA) at the end of snake (IS NAKA) deal with the maker of smaller (KA) things. Everything that rose out of the body of Mother Earth was smaller than She was. The sun (IS HANA) as it emerged on the surFACE with the guidance of the snake (IS NAKA), made plants grow. It worked in concert with the body of Mother Earth in the fashioning of smaller creations.

RULE SIX; PHONOLOGICAL CORRESPONDENCE, SOUNDS made in the same area of the mouth often replace each other.

The Kh of (KANA), Gh of (GANA), and Huh of (HANA) fall into that category.

(KANA) deals with the volcanic cone (KANA) on the body of Mother Earth, the source of all creation, her skin (IS KANA).

(GANA) deals with the process of be-getting, out of the female body of Mother Earth. Gynecology (GANA-) deals with female birthing processes.

(HANA) deals with the 'helping hands' of Mother Earth Her primary helper, the sun (IS HANA).

HAND (IS HANADA) is the (DA) 'gift of' the sun (IS HANA).

RULE EIGHT; ANASTROPHE or PALENDROME, deals with reflection or inversion of SOUNDS or words.

(NAKA/KANA) The snake (IS NAKA) as the solar guide below the surface of Mother Earth, reflects the cone (KANA) of creation above Her surface (NAKA/KANA). A reflective balance between above and below is created.

(NAGA/GANA) The process out of a female body surfacing as gynecology (GANA-) above the surface, is reflected by the (NAGA) below the surface. The Nagas were serpent (IS HARAPA-) worshippers out of Harappa, in ancient India. It expands to include Europe (HARAPA) and the contemporary Sherpa (IS HARAPA). When the snake or serpent energy surfaces, we are dealing with the Kundalini energy doing its work through the body of Mother Earth and through the bodies of individual birthing mothers and through runners, singers and ritual.

(NAHA/HANA) The (NAHA) expands to include the Latin nihilism (NAHA-) of 'nothingness' after the sun (IS HANA) had set into the body of Mother Earth. It deals either with the fall off the edge into the 'nothingness' of the abyss, or with the dead of night after the light of the sun had gone out on the surface of Mother Earth and negated (NAGA-) day light. Day (DAYA) is the (DA) 'gift of' AYA, as light in Persian and dawn in Assyrian.

The universal mythological importance of the snake cannot be overestimated. There is no place on the planet, no moment in time that ancient creation myths do not deal with some aspect of this ubiquitous creature. During the time of female centrality the serpent was considered to be a benign servant, at one with the sun and the body of Mother Earth.

It has to be remembered that <u>the snake was originally a symbol, a metaphor,</u> in spite of the fact that the ancient idea embodied in the snake in time assumed its own physical reality, "The word made flesh" syndrome. In this case the serpentine movement of a symbolic animal was made into a real physical demon.

When the power base on the planet shifted into male central-ity, the actual physical snake because it had been considered to be at one with the body of Mother Earth became as a metaphor, the brunt of a similar vilification and was redefined as the monster, the dragon, gorgon, python, Leviathan, griffin, demon, an exten-sion of the devil, even satan.

It didn't start out that way. Because the snake appears in al-most every creation myth, it has to go back very far in prehistory. It has to go back to the time when our vulnerable ancestors had to deal with a multitude of recurring planetary disasters.

One major cataclysm dealt with a very specific form of plan-etary catastrophe that dealt with the loss of the light of the sun. It could have been an asteroid that thirteen thousand years ago on the North American continent churned up a cloud of dust that created the loss of sunlight and a glacial winter around the globe. The same thing could have occurred closer to home in Africa with a massive volcanic eruption and the storm of sky borne de-bris obliterating the sun and sending the huddling human crea-tures into panic and famine.

Those ancient disasters surface out of the time when the snake became so important. It deals with an extended dark period when the sun ceased to shine down on our stricken ancestors.

It was one thing to lose the sun daily, as night fell across their ancient world. They assumed that the sun would reappear at dawn. In Hebrew the word sana (IS HANA) having its links with the sun (IS HANA) deals with the concept of 'repetition' or 'doing it again' and gave its perception to the word sanity (IS HANA-). The sun (IS HANA) in its habitual passage across the sky was very comforting. It could disappear in the West daily, swallowed into that great flat maw, but it always returned, or was 'born again'. The habitual predictibility of the sun had a link to their sanity.

It was another thing to lose the light of the sun for an extended period of time. They wanted to preclude that from happening. If the sun didn't appear at dawn as the black cloud of dust en-veloped them in darkness, then perhaps the sun got lost in the underground intestines within the body of Mother Earth.

Mother Earth was like all the other mothers, who were Her surrogates in the creation of smaller replicas of themselves. She had the same organs as they had, and was driven by the same needs and processes that they had. Then, they wondered what happened to the predictable, habitual disengorgement of the sun at dawn? Why didn't the sun either become regurgitated out of Her mouth, or pop out of Her vagina in the Eastern sky at dawn?

To create the accursed, extended darkness then it must have seemed to them that the sun got lost along the way in the underground intestinal trails within the body of Mother Earth. For the Bugotu of the South Pacific the word angat (HANAGATA) as 'entrails' establishes itself as dealing with the body of Mother Earth. The tryad beginning with (HANA) is the sun (IS HANA), the (NAGA) deals with the snake (IS NAKA,NAGA) and (GATA) may or may not be a source of the English word gut (GATA). They knew that the sun was the 'helping hands' to their great Mother. Now it was their turn to help Her.

The second major factor that feeds into the emergence of the snake as important at this most ancient time, was that as human beings lost their instinctual certainty due to the intensification of fear, they turned to the creatures around them for guidance.

Not only the bee became a metaphor for being, the ant for the jobs that aunts as nannies performed, the cooperation of the lioness pride in the unrelenting nocturnal hunt, but all the creatures around them were their equals. They had not separated themselves from that expansive crush of life of the African savannah. They looked to the creatures around them to help them with their lives.

Through the panic of darkness that surrounded them, they wondered what creature could help them to guide the sun through all those convoluted intestines within the body of Mother Earth back up to its light. They must have given it a great deal of thought and all the creatures on the savannah came up for consideration.

Animals with four extended appendages and a tail were ruled out because the sticking out appendage angles would get stuck and impede the guide of the sun on its journey through the intestines. Creatures with hair would tickle their great Mother. Birds with their feathers were ruled out because they would get wet and cause a drag on their way through the gut. Fish had sharp fins that could cut the Mothers bowels.

Someone must have had an AHA moment and said.

'How about the snake?' It had no appendages to get in the way. It had no feathers that could drag it down. It had no sharp fins like a fish. It had a smooth scaly skin, a small head with no horns and the intestines would fit it like a glove. It was also in constant contact with the body of Mother Earth. The slithering snake was like a large flat foot on land. Its whole length was in constant contact with the body of Mother Earth.

There was another more immediate respect and affection for the snake. As they squatted down and moved their bowels in the morning sun, the feces that left their bodies coiled down like the lowly snake and created a spiral like cake under their buttocks. They knew that rabbits made droppings and cows made flop pies but through the activity of defecation they had a closer relationship to the snake. As they made 'do', they created a snake like coiling spiral under their bodies. Is it a wonder that the snake not only became the guide of the sun but also became the Kundalini energy coiled at the base of the spine at the sacred, sacral place of the anus (HANASA)? The birthplace (NASA) of the sun (IS HANA)?

As it swam through the waters it created a sinuous form that echoed the coiling shape of the Kundalini energy as it snaked its way up the spine feeding into one of the shapes that emerged as the S shape of 'isness'. Even when wrapped around a tree it hugged the arborial energy of Mother Earth.

With that realization they fantasized that the snake would do its job in guiding the sun out of its labyrinth of darkness. How they got the belief system entrenched for the snake to take its universal position as the guide of the sun, is anyones guess. There must have been a lot of singing, dancing and cajoling. As the pall of debris filling the sky and obscuring the sun began to lift, they rejoiced that the snake was doing its job in guiding the sun back up to its light and began to worship the creature for being such a good guide. The serpentine guide (GADA) of the sun may be one of the most ancient concepts of what eventually became the name for God (GADA). Reading from right to left, (DA) establishes 'the gift of'. The phoneme (GA) deals with 'be-GEtting''. So the sepentine guide as God as the guide (GADA) of the sun, establishes an ancient concept of creation and begetting.

As males, with their dawning knowledge of paternity, began to create their own symbols away from the body of Mother Earth, the sun away from the body of Mother Earth became one of the first and one of the most important deities. Since the sun needed a guide to make its journry up to the light, then the snake became entwined with the journey of the sun.

The sun as a celestial deity in time lost out to the idea, the rational mind locked in the left hemisphere of the brain that was taking over the physical universe of Mother Earth. The idea in the mind was to the physical body, as the sky was to the body of Mother Earth. The next movement of male deities was into the mind and into the sky as the 'hidden' Jehovah God of the Hebrews, leaving Mother Earth and the individual mothers behind.

That began the original journey of snake worship associating it with the journey of the sun back up to the light. As the sun sank into the waters of the Western sky they urged the snake to get ahead of the sinking sun and then guide it through the dark night to be reborn at dawn. The 'dark night of the soul' takes on a different meaning if you introduce the Spanish sol (IS HALA) as the sun and its relationship to the human soul (IS HALA).

AT ONE
atone

As the guide of the sun, the snake became at one with the sun. At this time the sun was at one with the body of Mother Earth. So the sun, snake and Mother Earth were originally considered as one unit of cooperative creation. Because the snake could find its way through the darkened subterranean intestines it was considered to be very smart. This was before the separation myths and a shift into male centrality away from the body of Mother Earth entered the scene.

Because the snake guided the sun to be reborn at dawn, it also became the symbol for the movement of the solar wind up from the Earth along the ley lines and then making an entrance into the human body through the bottom of the soles.

The snake became the symbolic movement of the Kundaini energy, not only slithering through the body of Mother Earth as the guide of the sun but also as the guide of what was also the solar wind through the bodies of all living creatures.

It came to represent the two serpentine streams that lay coiled three and a half times at the base of the spine. One coil dealt with the sun and the other with the moon, the Ida Pingali of the Tantrists. They must have become aware that when a massive asteroid or volcanic eruption spread its rubble against the sky and obscured the sun during the day, it also obscured the moon during the night. Both streams of creative celestial power had to be given their due.

Since the energy of the sun as the solar wind moved up through the mantle on the body of Mother Earth during the day, they also postulated that the lunar energy of the moon must have done the same thing at night. They settled on a dual stream; the solar energy and the lunar energy, the Ida and the Pingali coiling upwards through the chacras, together carrying the seeds of evolutionary change.

On the body of Mother Earth those streams surfaced along the pre historically chartered ley lines. Within the human body they surfaced at the base of the spine coiling around the stem of the spinal column burning out the entrapped fear that had found its home there. It is the two snakes for the Tantrists and the two snakes for the Greeks as the Caduceus that came to exemplify the serpentine process of change and healing. For the Chinese the s'hen (IS HANA) is the double meandering pattern of rising energy that has its links with the sun (IS HANA). The Egyptians defined the letter (H) as a hank (HANAKA), a double twisting up the spine associated not only with the snake (IS NAKA) but with the ritual officiator over the rites of the setting sun, the eunuch (HANAKA), uncle (HANAKALA) weeping and wailing, wishing the snake luck on its journey as the solar guide.

It was the Greek God Helios of the sun that emerged as the healer. The lunar God of the ancient mothers represented as one of the curving snakes, had been scrapped along with female centrality but still remains on the medical staff of the Caduceus.

To heal (HALA) deals with the solar (IS HALA-) wind that emerged at an angle (LA) out of the side of the body of Mother Earth and then travelled across Her belly of air (HA) above Her surFACE.

As the Tantrists dealt with the snake energy lying coiled three and a half times at the base of the spine ready to uncoil and do its job of transformation, so the Fon of Africa believed that the snake gathered up the body of Mother Earth in its coils and gave men a place to live. There were 3500 coils above the ground and 3500 coils below ground. An EVEN distribution of balance surfaces for the Fon. The three and a half coils of the Tantric Ida and Pingali within the human body seem to echo the 3500 coils of the Fon above and below the body of Mother Earth. Or is it a coincidence? Both add up to the number seven (IS HAVANA) or, IS EVEN). The same concept surfaces in the Egyptian mastabas with seven steps under the ground and seven steps above.

With these numbers there occurs a shift from female centrality and the snake as a symbol for the process of transformation for the Tantrists and the emergence of male centrality based on the place to live and the territorial demands of the Fon.

The snake was more than the symbolic guide of the sun and the ancient moon. On the most expansive level it represented the connection between Mother Earth and Her helping hands, the sun. On the human level it came to define two processes. One dealt with the coiling serpentine energy of the Kundalini as it was perceived to weave its way up the spine. The other became a universal symbol for the vehicle of connection between the two hemispheres of the brain to create a connection, a balance, the IS EVEN concept locked in the number seven (IS EVEN). For some it was a rainbow. For others it was a ladder. It is the much neglected corpus collosum for contemporary humanity.

The Australian Aborigines believe that their shamans find rock crystals in pools where the rainbow serpent lives and fills their bodies with splinters of light. It is said that the shaman uses the rainbow as a bridge of passage to be at one with the flow. (A shaman is a she man or (IS HAMANA) having links with what is truly human (HAMANA), without the illusions of fantasy locked in as infantile panic stricken habits.

A rainbow is a symbol for the bridge, a connection between the two hemispheres of the brain. When the two hemispheres are balanced then you have an EVEN (HAVANA) distribution of energy based on compassion and reason. Libra with her scales of destiny balanced, surfaces here. At the time that these concepts were becoming codified the ancient mothers were obsessed by the concept of evenness and balance.

One of the original perceptions of evenness may have been observed as the sun rose in the Eastern sky at the equator and then passed overhead halving the sky into two even parts. One half belonged to the South and the other half belonged to the North. To halve (HA(LA)VA) is to have (HAVA). The (LA) as the tongue pushing the sun out of the mouth of Mother Earth, regurgitating it at dawn, plays the same linguistic construct as in word (WARADA) and world (WARA(LA)DA) and Avalon (HAVA (LA) NA) of Avon (HAVANA).

Since the sun was the greatest helper to Mother Earth then that halving of the belly of air above them took on an air of great significance. It created a predictable balance in their ancient world.

This same preoccupation dealing with balance existed in ancient Egypt, for the pharaohs were obliged to keep all things evenly balanced with the River Nile flowing as prescribed, creating universal balance and peace. It must have been perceived that they had the energy of the two polarities (SASA) balanced within them.

Not only did the internal Kunalini flow create a balance between the two hemispheres of the brain but it also created an opening into the total flow of the universe.

It also ushered in the possibility of authority and power. Along with the Uraeus of the Egyptians as a cobra arching as the third eye from the forehead of Isis, the giver of life, the ultimate Goddess of Creation, is also depicted her as wearing a throne on top of her head. She as Mother Earth was the ultimate ruler. Ruler had two meanings like rock and stone. the RU of Mothers blood; ruddy, ruby, red created the leader, the ruler of our ancient clan. It was also the measurer, the ruler associated with the moon and menstruation.

The throne is the seat of power and evolved out of the perception that the one who sat on the seat of power was a SEER, one who had internal vision, in whom the movement of the Kundalini energy had been awakened. Therefore, you had to SEE with the vision of the third eye, the eye of truth, in order to be able to rule. Power came to be expressed as the seat of the SEER. It surfaces today in Rome with the pope, not necessarily with the throne on his head, but without experiencing it, representing the Seat of the holy SEE.

In Malta, the temple of Gigantia has a drawing of a snake on the back of a throne of stone. It extends the perception that to rule you had to have the Kundalini energy awakened in you. You had to SEE with an internal vision of the third eye. You had to be a SEER.

A throne (TARANA) originally emerged out of (RANA) the 'wound of dawn' in Polish on the body of Mother Earth out of Her terrain (TARANA) of natural law. As male centrality gained momentum the throne (TARANA) of power became the tyranny (TARANA) by the Alpha male.

The Sioux Indians of North America have a spirit named Wakan (WAKANA) which means both 'wizard' and 'serpent'. To have the serpentine Kundaini energy awaken in you, you can't continue sleepwalking. You have to wake up. You have to be awakened (WAKANA-) to what is real.

Among the Dahomey of Africa, the Mother creatress Mawu is supported by a great serpent. The name Mawu deals with Mother Earth in Her aspect as water. MA is the general name for Mother Earth. The syllable (Wu) is Her specific aspect as water.

RULE EIGHT; ANASTROPHE, PALENDROME or reflection.

When you use the process of reflection then MAWU becomes WUMA and with the addition of the (N) of 'change from a former state', at the end, you get WUMAN, or woman. Therefore for the Dahomey, the 'mother creatress' supported by a great serpent was not only the Kundalini blessed birthing mother, who with her unfolding ecstatic breath created life out of her body.

The Maori of New Zealand believe that the rainbow serpents go to a dangerous place where fear is stimulated and empty the body of that which we call soul and fill the body with spiritual matter. One way for the Kundalini energy, symbolized by the serpents, has to be stimulated by the guru, is in order for the habitual fears that have been locked in the chacras can be faced and released. A similar process existed in the ancient abaton.

When I came across this perception of the Maori, I understood what Joya MA had done with me concerning THE BETRAYAL. She took me to that place where my anguish was stored (the dangerous place where fear is stimulated) and with her powers released it, freeing me from my guilt, shame and sadness.

Among the Dogon of Africa, for whom the ram was of primary importance, as it was for many herding nomads, they fused their love for the ram with the spiritual energy of the snake and used the snake-ram combination as a metaphoric creature of passage across the two hemispheres of the brain. Their Goddess Amma representing their snake-ram, turned into a four colored rainbow.

Passage could only be made when a balance was achieved. We are in male centrality, for not only is the ram a male sheep, but the number four as a square, evolved as a male symbol.

The Goddess Amma is an anastrophe. In her name is the AM/ MA or a reflection, the equal reflective distribution of the passage of the heavenly bodies above and below the body of Mother Earth.

Amma (HAMA) is also the blood of the mother dealing with the sun in one of its underground sojourns through the body of Mother Earth.

For the Pitjandara tribe of Ayers Rock in Australia, the tjurunga, a symbolic icon, made of stone or wood, represents the 'other body', as are trees, water holes, caves, ceremonial grounds, animals and all are the offering of the snake. It is the snake that lives in the water that in some Australian languages has a similar root to 'milk' and 'women'. It was for an extra supply of milk that the ancient mothers followed the herbivore migrations across the continent of Africa.

Sa in ancient Egypt was called 'the sacred blood of Isis' who was considered to be the Goddess of creation and transformation. Sa to the Hebrews and Hindus was not only blood but the carrier of intelligence and spirit. In Latin, blood is sanguis (IS HANAGASA) and emerged in French as sangre (IS HANAGARA). Both words contain the (NAGA) or snake (IS NAKA, NAGA) in them, with liquid blood as the carrier of the Kundalini life force.

It was perceived that only actual menstrual blood created life and therefore not only was blood considered sacred but carried the serpentine spiral flow through the body. The Hebrews bled their animals (kashered, kosher (KASA-) them in order to ingest the holy liquid. The Hindu soma (IS HAMA), the blood (SA) of the mother (MA) may have had the same properties. In Greek ema (HAMA) is the name for blood.

In the Babylonian myth, the Goddess Kadi (KADA) was the most ancient serpent with a woman's head and breasts (intelligence and milk). The Hebrew word for temple prostitute was Kadesha (KADASA) the holy one, associated with the serpent energy carried by the blood (SA). In India Kudru (KADARA) the mother of all Nagas or serpents, gave immortality to the people through the drinking of menstrual blood.

In ancient Greece, Pythia the woman who brought forth the oracle of divine wisdom, sat on a three legged stool around whose legs was coiled a python. The snake was defined as the seat of wisdom (it knew how to guide the sun to be 'born again' at dawn). It dealt with the internal flow of the solar wind of the Kundalini energy, the shape of the internal flow of the python, the activator of timelessness (it all happens in the NOW), and the possibility of prophecy. Pythia was defined as a sacred oracle prophetess during female centrality and as a witch during male centrality. Her subsequent descendents as witches were universally burned at the stake. Shamans, and homosexuals are still villified.

The Egyptian Mother Goddess Isis is protected by the seven serpents of Buto. The Hindu Lord Buddha is associated with the snake who spreads his seven hoods over Buddha's head at birth. When the number seven is associated with the snake we are dealing with the chacras and the process of transformation.

According to the Vedas (Indian truths), suns are serpents who have sloughed off their reptilian skins and while guiding the sun through the underground channels within the body of Mother Earth, have become transformed, ie. born again.

The seven serpents of Buto over the head of Isis and the seven hoods of the snake over Buddhas head deal with the seven chacras that have to have the Kundalini energy burn her way through them. When that occurs, the adept stands transformed, no longer attached to any material possession. He takes his begging bowl and pursues a life of renunciation. Not a Western ideal.

The seven heads of the snake are the seven chacras that have to be faced and the fears trapped there have to be cleaned out before an adept can become self-realized. Seven (IS EVEN) creates not only a balance in the brain but is also the number for 'separation'. You separate yourself from your panic stricken habitual self and if you burn through all seven of your chacras, you then stand on the thresh hold of eternity and the ultimate separation into Maha Samadhi (death in Hindu).

This takes the job of the ancient snake as the guide to the sun and expands it into the job of transformation. The original most ancient transformation dealt with the sun sinking into the bloody waters in the Western horizon after Mother Earth ate it and then the blood of the sun coagulated into two major entities; the land on the surface out of Mother Earths lavic menstrual blood and the integral round flat disc of the sun that rose pale and wan at dawn. Mother Earth transformed the liquid blood into a solid mass either as land on Her surFACE, or the round disc of the sun in the Eastern sky.

In ancient Greece, heroes were worshipped in the form of bearded snakes, a concept which went back to pharoanic Egypt and the many shifts that that ancient civilization embodied. When an animal sufaces with a human head we are in female centrality. When the shift is made with the human body having an animal head, we are in male centrality.

Egyptian Queens like Hatshepsut and Cleopatra were called 'serpents of the Nile' and wore goatees. Ancient snakes also had goatees and were symbolically bearded. In one direction it takes us back to the importance of the nanny goat as the provider of milk and ultimately a seat of power at the time of the very ancient migrations. Then in another direction, at a very ancient time as the bald eunuchs assumed power to compete with the heteosexual band of brothers, they must have plasteed their naked chins with goat hair.

The goatee also surfaces on the chins of all the Egyptian pharoahs. What it means is that at the most ancient time Egyptian pharoahs had no hair on their bodies. They were bald. Who else was bald? Obviously the eunuchs. As the power bases shifted due to the emergence of male centrality, to prove their right to be rulers, the subsequent male pharaonic rulers plastered a goatee on their chins. The Sphynx emerged out of that ancient prehistoric time, for there is no sign of a goatee on her chin.

The members of the Zoa tribe of the Amazon basin, have a hole in their bottom lip through which they push a piece of wood making it look like a goatee. They relate ancient stories told by the elders that they dispersed after a great flood overran their distant home. Since the flood story surfaces throughout the ancient Middle Eastern mythological world, it may have occurred when eight thousand years ago the Meditteranean Sea crashed through the Bosphorus and created the Black Sea, obliterating everything that it submerged.

The Zoa are a peaceful group living close to nature in their jungle home with the women having four husbands. The four husbands tell their own story and harken back to a transitional time between the centrality of women and the centrality of men. One husband through intercourse made the babies. Another one, without penetration, created the sensual life of the mother, a custom that they shared with the Gypsies. The youngest husband was taught by his older female teacher how to pleasure his partner. The last one as he aged was cared for by the tribe, as were all the children.

The women wear a halo of downy white feathers around their heads. When a woman becomes pregnant all the men also wear the halo of white feathers around their heads. Feathers representing the upward flow associated with birds represent the creative aspect of the rising Kundalini energy. As the uplifting flight of birds the story surfaces all over the world.

The creative aspect of the Kundalini energy also surfaces in Brittany, at Stone Mare. The Druids invoked the 'serpent of the rock' to cure barrenness in women. If the Kundalini energy could be invoked through the use of the 'rock' then the drumming circle at Stonehenge cannot be that far behind.

In the New World, the same belief system surfaces for the Hopi Indians who danced the snake dance to insure the fertility of their corn.

In Brazil, the Maloka Indians of the Mato Grosso region believe that when people die, they walk over the backs of snakes to the village of the dead. The Kundalini serpent energy was used as a bridge into immortality and the snake as its vehicle of passage.

In the Mahabharata, the epic poem of India, the hero seeks immortality in the underworld called the City of Serpents, the descent into the underworld (where the fear driven images are stored) to the source of the flow, to the place where you can fall no further. It is the beginning of the journey back up to the light.

In Babylonian myth and iconography, the Goddess Tiamat, in the form of a great serpent, offered man the food of immortality. (It was considered that transformation could come only through the Kundalini serpent energy inherent in the Mother).

Ninhursag, the Akkadian Goddess of Creation was perceived as the mistress of serpents. The ancient Akkadian word for 'priestess', was 'snake charmer'. The Akkadian Goddess of Creation had the Kundalini energy at her fingertips.

Out of early Sumeria and Babylon come serpents called the 'lord or lady of life'. The masculine name of lord (LARADA) is the 'gift of' (DA), and (LARA), the left handed mother.

In ancient Crete, serpents had the secret to restore life to the dead. Polyidos brought Glaucas, the Minoan prince back to life because he knew the secret of the serpents. He understood the role of the Kundalini energy having risen to the seventh chacra.

Christ performed the same miracle in Galilee on Lazarus restoring him to his life by bringing him back from the dead.

Melancus had his ears lickd by snakes and understood the language of birds. The Kundalini energy opened up the vistas to the communication with other ceatures.

The Napishtim (Noah) became immortal, shed his old diseased skin like a snake and emerged from it reborn, because he received the elixir of immortality from Sheba. Noah (NAHA/HANA) is the Biblical metaphor for the sun (IS HANA) in its transformative state under skin of Mother Earth (HANA/NAHA)

Egyptian, Greek and Roman priests carried snakes in their rituals. Temples of Cambodia and China contain large avenues guarded by arched and ever vigilant statues of serpents.

In the Andes, at the Chavin de Haunter, there is a snake carved over the entrance.

Etruscan female deities have been discovered as figurines holding coiling snakes around their arms and their hands (energy of healing).

In Baume Latronne cave, where the Garde River flows into the Rhone above Taracon, there is a painting of a serpent with the head of a bear. (Very ancient, the creature with a human head).

The lioness emerged as the most powerful animal in Africa. The bear was perceived to be the most powerful animal in Europe. Because it hibernated (HABA-), it became associated with the Kundalini serpent energy of Nirva Kalpa Samadhi.

When the sun guided by the snake slid through the underground tunnels within the body of Mother Earth, it was perceived to hibernate, to go through a coma like state, the state of temporary or Nirva Kalpa Samadhi. It is the same process that when the Kundalini energy reaches the lotus chacra, it puts you into a state of coma like trance, akin to a state of hibernation. Your breath becomes suspended and your heart beats with an imperceptible beat. You are on the thresh hold of passage. One foot is on this side of the divide and the other has already crossed over.

The word divide (DAVADA) establishes its links with David (DAVADA) the Hebrew salayer of Goliath establishing in his name the even balance of the seer who needed the internal light to glow in order to rule. He in his olderst manifestation encodes in his name the knowledge of the Kundalini energy of passage. For the Hebrews haba meant 'after life' and olam haba dealt with 'the world to come'. It was the process of the transformative hibernative (HABA-) coma that carried the adepts into the other world.

The bear with its physical power and yearly hibernation is an apt creature to represent the Kundalini energy in ancient Europe (HARAPA) of the serpent (IS HARAPA-).

The destruction of 'Paganism' of ancient Europe dealt with the symbolic destruction of the lowly serpent, actually representing the Kundalini energy that was experienced both through the ley lines on the body of Mother Earth through the experience of individual birthing mothers, long distance runners singers and ritual.

It seems that for many Europeans being buried alive was the worst prognosis. It may have been that more people moved into the temporary hibernative state (Nirva Kalpa Samadhi), than was misunderstood at the time. The death of Christ on the cross and then his rebirth in the cave may have come out of that ancient experience.

As males began to understand their role in procreation they established their own deities away from the body of Mother Earth. They somehow had to deal with the power inherent in the lowly snake who as the solar guide was so intimately associated with the sun and the body of Mother Earth. They dealt with the SHAPE of the movement of the Kundalini energy upward, up and out of the ley lines on the body of Mother Earth and up the spine coiling upward through the chacras in the human body. In both cases the movement was obviously up toward the light.

The emerging power of the males had an AHA moment. What creature spun its way upward on the invisible thermal currents at dawn? Obviously the large feather covered predatory birds like eagles, hawks, falcons, condors, vultures, all spun their way up to the heavens at dawn. They likened the movement upward of the soaring birds to the upward coiling of the Kundalini energy. But they had a problem. What to do with the snake. They needed the snake to keep the sun from losing its way and get stuck in the bowels within the body of Mother Earth. Goose pimples must have flooded their bodies at the next inspiration, as the lowly snake grew wings and feathers and emerged as the feathered serpent. Facts didn't get in their way as they tried to explain their new male sourced mythological reality. Whenever you have metaphorical flying raptors swooping down on some aspect of the snake you are dealing with the patriarchy killing the matriarchy. You are also dealing with confusion, with obfuscation, with the mist of the mister and the fallacy of the phallus. What also surfaces here is the bird feather (FATARA) as it becomes associated with father (FATARA) as it is still expressed by the Ibu of the Amazon Basin. The (FATARA) becomes (FATA) of fate (FATA) and (TARA) the terrain (TARA-) on the body of Mother Earth.

After a series of major planetary catastrophies, as displaced people settled in what subsequently became the 'New World', they came up with new power bases and the plumed or feathered serpent emerged supreme.

The Zuni Indians carry the image of Koloowisi (KALAWASA) the plumed serpent. Many of the Indian tribes have chiefs wearing feathered head-dresses. Courageous acts of young males were rewarded with feathers stuck in a head band. It seems like a feathered down version of the Egyptian Uraeus emerging out of the forehead in the shape of a cobra. The saying' A feather in your cap' harkens back to that ancient concept of accomplishment.

In Yukatan, Gukumatz, the plumed serpent Kul-kul-kan (KALA-KALA-KANA) was the lord of the wind and water. Even though the plumed serpent was redefined as representing male energy, the wind and water came out of the body of Mother Earth, as did his name. The letter (K) comes out of the body of Mother Earth making smaller aspects of Herself. Kul (KALA) is feather. Kan (KANA) is the cone (KANA) of creation, the volcanic cone shaped crater out of which She gave birth to smaller aspects of Herself; lava, land, rubble, smoke, ashes, boulders and other flying debris.

In Mexico, Quetzalcoatl, the plumed serpent of the Toltec, Aztec contained a multileveled mother connection. He was not only represented by a serpent, soared lightly upward like a bird, but had a precious twin named Quetzal, who not only established the concept of twinning and reflection but it also is the name for 'dog'. The dog as a familiar creature surfaces in many of the ancient myths. Like a devoted pet and companion, it dogged human footsteps like a habit (HABATA). Once a habit was established through a filter of panic during humanity's helpless infancy, like the dog it couldn't be shaken. The dog in one of its many manifestations became a symbol for the dogging of human footsteps.

In Egypt the same concept took on a different entity. For one of the seven souls given to a child at birth was the Khaibit (HABATA, KABATA) or the shadow. A shadow could not be shaken and dogged the human creature like a habit (HABATA), or like the dog.

In Hebrew a Seraph (IS HARAFA, HARAPA) is a word that is used to define the 'divine fiery serpent' (IS HARAPA-) who became an angel. The Seraphim were serpent spirits, creatures of the light carrying the spiral Kundalini energy upward. Instead of using actual birds to create the spiral Kundalini ascent, the ancient

Hebrews stayed with the human form but gave it wings. They created angels, who may not have had their bodies covered with feathers, as they had done in the 'new world' but they grew bird wings to carry them upward on the invisible internal thermal energies. Since the Bible claimed that "man had been created in the image of God", then the ancient Hebrews had to stay with the human form with wings and not turn to birds to make the heavenly ascent.

It was the God (Kundalini) serpent energy in human beings soaring upward along the seven chacras that gave birth to the angels with their angled wings. Here we have the answer to the fourteen angels that watch over babies. For it is the two streams of the Kundalini energy as the coiling upward snakes of the Ida and Pingali, the seven solar and lunar currents that not only protect the sleeping babies but define the fourteen Hebraic angels.

In another direction, the angels split into two parts. One becomes the Seraphim (IS HARAPA-) as the serpent (IS HARAPA-) of light. The other becomes the Seraphim (IS HARAPA-) the serpent (IS HARAPA-) of darkness. We are still dealing with the sun snake combination above the body of Mother Earth as light and the sun snake combination below the body of Mother Earth as darkness. With the growth of human numbers, judgment enters the picture. The light of the sun above the plane becomes 'the good' and became associated with males. The darkness of the sun below the plane becomes associated with the mothers and emerges as 'the evil'. In time the evil becomes the devil, or the (D) the 'gift of' the evil.

The new battle emerges between the good and the evil sanctioned by the mind of God in the sky. The angels also take sides. One represents the 'good' sitting on the left shoulder and one representing the 'evil' sitting on the right shoulder. 'The devil made me do it' becomes very clear, as the 'gift of; (D) evil . We're getting closer to the actual problem that the bifurcated two hemispheres of the brain represent.

On the actual physical plane as males begin their destruction of the many snake and serpent deities representing the female Kundalini essence, the carnage expands to include all aspects of Mother Earth, the sea, Her ground of being and even the belly of air above Her. The mythical heroes in every culture put on their animal skins, feather caps, shields, take up their spears, lances, knives, arrows, javelins and jumping on their steeds, do battle against the symbolic snake, serpent, gorgon, dragon, demon or monster of any and every kind.

The ancient power based in the panting breath of ecstasy of the birthing mother symbolized by the serpent, had to be destroyed for the new male power base to emerge.

A mythological carnage swept the planet and spilled into the real world as women became the recipients of a recurrent wave of abuse, violence, rape and clitorectomies.

The young pubescent male shoved out of the family group at puberty as the heroic dragon slayer, became the emissary of the evolving patriarchies paving the way for the emergence of the father God in the sky. The search for the holy grail, the golden fleece and all the metaphors for the male ritual search for the experience of the Kundalini energy, begin to fill the pages of male history, his story.

A recognizable Greek solar God Apollo kills the Dionysian python, the voice out of the mouth of Mother Earth. The place where he commits the murder becomes sacred, the actual physical home of the Oracle of Delphi.

Python (the great serpent) was born of Hera (HARA) without the aid of Zeus. This establishes the reality that <u>the birthing breath that gave rise to mysticism</u> (MASATA) <u>could only be experienced by women</u>. Ma is the universal name for the mother except in Japan. For the Japanese the personal mother is called HA HA of the panting breath.

Men, even Gods like Zeus, were not part of that initial ecstatic experience. As such with the emergence of male centrality, it had to be scrapped.

It also establishes the fact that the 'great serpent' representing the Kundalini energy was native to, or born out of the mothers belly. In Hebrew 'hara' means either 'pregnant belly' or 'gestating mountain' (out of which the sun was born). In Japanese 'hara' also means belly as in hara kiri or disembowelment. On a strange, bizarre level both words, out of two disparate cultures mean the same thing, the evacuation out of the belly. In Hebrew, one gets a baby out of an individual mother's belly, or the sun out of the mountainous bellies on the body of Mother Earth. In Japanese one gets the actual bowels. In Maori, who left Africa fifty thousand years ago, maHARA stands for 'intestines.'

Hera working by herself deals with the most primal form of birthing, female out of female as the process of cell separation, mothers creating endless daughters; cloning, mitosis, parthogenesis. The expanding universe. No Big Bang of the male orgasm here.

The concept emerges out of the most ancient human perception of creation. Mother Earth giving birth to Herself (in the creation on land on her surface) out of Herself, by Herself, out of Her internal belly. Virgin birth in action.

In the Epic of Gilgamesh, the prince on his journey to find whether the soul takes the same path to immortality as the sun, slays the Goddess Kur. She too represents the female underground serpentine energy. Ku in Sanskrit defines the female principle out of the body of Mother Earth. It is the first syllable of the Kundalini energy. In Polish Kurva is a bitch and the most heinous epitaph that could be thrown against a woman the world over. Here the dogged dog as a bitch surfaces tying it to the immolating process of the Kundalini energy.

The Chaldean myth of Marduk. Armed with a thousand lightning bolts he slays Tiamat, the ancient Goddess as serpent. Originally both Marduk and Tiamat were female as the Ma in Marduk and (MATA) in Tiamat (TAYAMATA) reveal out of their ancient linguistic roots.

The Minoan Cretan hero Perseus cuts off the head of the Gorgon, the enraged and abused Medusa with snakes as her hair. Her Kundalini energy running rampant, emerging out of the lotus chacra out of the top of her head.

Hittite storm Gods fought the great serpent Illuyanka and killed her.

Odysseus fought and killed the whirlpool, the symbol of the spiral or Kundalini energy in water. All aspects of the coiling, spiral serpentine energy experienced by birthing mothers had to be symbolically destroyed.

Hebrew Tohem (TAHAMA) as the sea monster is killed by Gods

fiery chariot. The (-HAMA) of 'mother's blood', surfaces here.

In the Greek myth, Hercules strangled two serpents with his bare hands while still in his cradle.(With that act he destroyed the possibility of using the double helix of female serpent energy as a vehicle for transformation and had to go through his own heroic labors). It may also mean that with the destruction of the double helexical energy he avoided his own castration.

For the Greeks Hercules defined the change from the use of the female Kundalini energy, to the use of the male ritual for transformation and reconnection, based on conscious external will to recreate the universe. With it he sows the seeds of science and goes on to kill the hydra.

In Hinduism, Krishna was the hydra headed snake. In the Bhavagad Gita, Arjuna had a vision of Krishna and proclaims;
    "…Oh my God, I see all Gods within your body,
    Each in his own degree, the multitude of creatures,
    See Lord Brahma, throned upon the lotus,
    See all the sages, and the holy serpents."
The madness expands in ever widening circles as in Ireland St George slays the metaphoric dragon ie the pagan matriarchy. St Patrick does him one better and actually physically kills off all the poor innocent snakes in Ireland.

Beowolf the Old English hero slays the son of the swamp dragon and the swamp dragon Herself. Here we have the ancient mother and her castrated son both as carriers of the Kundalini energy being destroyed.

Teutonic Siegfried also destroys the dragon. Since there were only symbolical dragons in the fantasy filled minds of the emerging male centralists then it is an expanding madness that like a virus swept the world.

After the shifts from female to male centrality had become so-lidified, the rational Greeks came up with the Phoenix who represents the process of male transformation as an internal immolation and a rebirth without the use of the internal energy flow symbolized by the serpent. The Phoenix enters Greek mythology as all bird, all male, all idea, emerging out of his own ashes. It represents Zeus creating reality out of his head in the form of Athena and Adam creating Eve out of his rib.

Ashes became a symbol of the residue of the internal fire that burns out the nadis (synapses-nerve endings) of the Tantrists. The ash tree was the symbol of life in the Icelandic myths. African natives use ash to smear their bodies. Hindu babas use it as vibuti for healing. Werner Erhart of EST shared with his students the perception that anger, rage of any form, leaves a residue of ash within the body that clogs up its physical and psychological workings.

There was an understood danger in flying too close to the sun, as the myth of Icarus proclaims. He melted his wings which were made of wax, the mother bee substance and fell back down to Earth. The myth establishes a warning. The flight to the sun has to be made CONSCIOUSLY, otherwise it may be the cause of an internal immolation. The unconscious movement of the Kundalini energy may be at the base of disintegration and the emergence of voices and visions. It can be immensely traumatic as has been documented by the ravings of Biblical prophets, saints, schitzophrenics and contemporary babas; St John, Baba Muktananda, Baba Vivekananda, and Rama Krishna.

It is the facing of the internal fears that is most perilous for human beings, especially image driven males. The Kundalini energy as a process of healing and reconnection forces the facing of fear. The awakened spiral movement within has to burn out the content. The images accompanied by fear as obsessions (HABA-) are locked in the mind. The whole internal moving picture landscape has to be made blank. Everything has to be learned anew without the baggage of habit. To be 'born again', on the level of a transformed human being, takes on new meaning.

The snake in the myth of the Garden of Eden, not unlike the Neanderthal creature, has been given a bad rap. A small clue surfaces in the name of the 'garden' before the poor snake can take its proper place. Eden (HADANA) comes from the same root as hedonism (HADANA-). It has close links with the lost city of Sodom (IS HADAMA) of Sodom and Gomorrah. Hidden in the linguistic folds of Chassidim (HA (SA)DAMA) is its source with Sodom (IS HADAMA). It was a Hebrew sect dealing with a merit system and the reward of going to heaven. Hedonism deals with pleasure. Whose pleasure were the ancient Hebraic rabbis nullifying? The myth tells its own story.

The poor snake is no longer the worshipped symbol of the ecstatic birthing breath out of female centrality, but a demon who as the sacred Mother Earth Kundalini energy will usher in the 'fall of man'. Twisting himself around the tree, in one of his most ancient manifestations, he goes after Eve, not Adam, but Eve. He knows that he can have his way with Eve because she is the compliant one. Adam had a first wife named Lilith (LALATA) who was happy and sang, or lalated (LALATA-) all the time. She knew the birthing breath and would not give it up either through a clitorectomy or by not having satisfacion during the sex act. In Finnish her singing talent pops up out of the same root, as laulaa (LALA) which defines 'singing'.

The snake was not only smart but insidious. Hidden within him is the ancient energy of serpentine joy associated with the birthing ecstasy of the mother that he symbolized. He tempts Eve with an apple, some say pomegranate. The apple halved displays five pits, the pentagram or the shape of a five pointed star.

At the time of mother centrality the triangle reigned supreme., representing both the triangular volcanic come as the source of creation on the body of Mother Earth and the triangular vulvic patch on the individual mother's body. With male role in procreation becoming realized the square assumed its symbolic male role. Women struggling to get their power back came up with the five pointed star. Because it was associated with women along with the number thirteen, the lunar flow, and the snake, it became vilified and associated with Satan.

The same shift in perception deals with the original name of Mary (MARA). She was the aspect of Mother Earth as water, the marine environment. As mothers were trying to get their power back they tried to reverse the shift from RAMA back to MARA and the emergence of Rama as a universal name for ruler. In Christianity Mother Mary (MARA) assumes her ancient place of ruler, Mother of God;

'Hail Mary full of grace, the Lord is with thee,
Holy Mary, Mother of God'

The snake was really trying to get Eve to get her power back through the subtle eating of the apple containing the pentagram of five pits. He was trying to say to her,

"Dear you don't seem to know what you have given up or lost. I'm here to give it back to you. I know that your boss admonished you not to eat this apple because it contains all of the joyful qualities of power that you have given up. Here take a bite and you'll see what I mean".

Eve takes a bite of the Kundalini energy and likes it so much that she shares it with Adam. He hasn't gone through all of the heroic trials that male adepts have to perform and either flies too close to the sun like Icarus, or self immolates like the Phoenix. In either case their boss throws them out of the Garden of Eden. What is the ancient tree of knowledge that they have trespassed against? <u>It is the singular and universal knowledge of the Kundalini energy that only the birthing mother can naturally experience.</u>

The snake represents the Kundalini energy and what he tries to do with Eve, is give back to her the mystical birthing experience. The new male centrality will have none of that. It is out of the mystical birthing experience and the trance state that it creates, that all the subsequent powers emerged; the knowledge of immortality, the seat of power, the ability to rule, the capacity to heal, the capacity to bring back the dead, perform miracles, establish fertility, manipulate the stuff of matter, defuse panic stricken fear, create the passion of intimacy, understand the language of birds and all the rest of the stuff that exists in the Akashik record.

The ruler comes out of the double meaning of the word. To rule deals with (RU-) the color of the motherts blood as russet, ruby red, ruddy. It was with the passage of her blood that she became a potential mother and a ruler. The other ruler deals with the moon and its passage across the sky. As a ruler, the moon measured the monthly flow of menstrual blood out of female bodies. It is also the counter (KANATA-) of time associated with the female cunt (KANATA). It echoes the same concept as the Greek 'meter', for mother. Ruler relects itself (RALARA) (RALA) and (LARA) (LALA) is that which is real (RALA) and (LARA) is she left handed Mother that created the reality. It emerged with migrating humanity in Russia as the home of the RUS or Vikings and to this day use red as its color.

When Hermes beomes the 'messenger of the Gods' all that it means is, that he is bringing HER the message as menses, or menstruation and it came from heaven, from the moon. With male centrality the original meaning was lost and the moon became redefined and demoted as one of the celestial deities.

The Hebrew rabbis had to stay in the left hemisphere and remain 'rational'. They had to restrain and nullify the powers of the ancient mothers. Fearing like Zeus with Hera, that they were irrelevant in that singular act of creation, they had to create their own power bases in the hidden mind of God in the sky and on the closed circle of 'rational' thought.

Something else peeps through and cannot be stilled. At the time that all of this was happening there were two human creatures on the planet existing in similar places for many thousands of years. One was the Homo Sapiens. The other was the Neanderthal. What perceptions did they share in all of this? But first the eunuch uncle.

EUNUCH (HANAKA)
UNCLE (HANAKALA)

T he crux of all of this was the construction of the ancient human family (FAMALA). It was based on the female (FAMALA) matriarch and her relatives, not unlike the elephant herd. The overlapping dyads of (FAMA) and (MALA) contain the (MA) of the mother at the center. In Polish (MALA) means 'the small individual she'. The (FA) of (FAMA) deals with the fingers of the hand that do most of the work of mothering (MA).

They expand to include the body of Mother Earth (MA). The (FA) of the four or five fingers of fire in the Eastern sky deal with the shape of the rays of the sun at dawn breaking through the pall of night and acting like the helping hands of Mother Earth. She was the large all inclusive familial context.

When all of these concepts were being codified into SOUNDS and letters, the male role in procreation was unknown. Mating at one end of the year didn't seem to have any relationship with having a baby ten lunar months later. Clusters of women and their children had no one to protect them. Fatherhood was unknown. Sexual cues were changing. There was much violence. Rape was the order of the day. Children were kidnapped. Mothers were killed.

One of those AHA moments entered the scene. The ancient mothers came upon a plan. They had sons. The sons became violent when they reached puberty and had to be shoved out of the familial clan. Somehow they knew that castrated male creatures became docile and young boys could be used to protect the family. So they castrated their first born sons to become the uncles (HANAKALA) to their subsequent sister's children. The eunuch (HANAKA) uncle (HANAKALA) established much of what became our subsequent, if hidden global human history.

In the word for eunuch (HANAKA) we have the overlapping

dyads of (HANA) and (NAKA) the sun (IS HANA) and the snake (IS NAKA). There in lies the tale.

Human beings were so greatful that the sun rose in the Eastern sky every day at dawn, that they gathered together at the foot of the mountains and like the birds joined the racket and sang their hallelujahs to awaken the sleeping sun.

In Swahili the word ALFA GIRI gives us a clue as to how all of this occurred. The Swahili Alfa (HALAFA) shares the same roots as the Greek Alpha (HALAFA), or that which came first. To light the day, the sun came first. In Bemba '-sanika' (IS HANAKA) means 'to make light'. The eunuch (HANAKA) the first born castrated son at his mothers side was associated with that ancient ritual of greeting the sun.

The elephant (HALAFA-) matriarch sensed the falling rains in the distant savannahs and began the ancient migration to 'greener pastures'. She was the first creature to show the rest of the herbivores the direction toward the showers in the distance. The falling sHOWers showed her HOW to proceed. The Swahili ALFA, (HALA-) the Greek ALPHA (HALA-), the African elephant (HALA) all contain the Spanish sol (IS HALA-), or Greek eelyos (HALA-) of the sun. There was no doubt about it, after the dark night, the blessed sun came first. But there was a wrinkle here. Something came before the sun.

It was the glow of light that spread its radiance upon the sleeping body of Mother Earth. That is when the birds began their avian symphony, when primates screeched their welcome, when human beings sang (IS HANAGA) their hallelujahs. They knew that when the glow started to spread its promise against the Eastern sky, they had to help the sun on its journey up toward its light. Where did all of this happen? At the foot of the gestating mountains, out of whose peaks the sun emerged triumphant. For Giri (GARA) out of Alfa Giri comes out of the same linguistic root as mountain or gura (GARA)) in Polish. (GA) is the begetter of the sun (RA).

So Alfa Giri deals with the glow in the Eastern sky before the sun made its appearance out of the gestating mountainous bellies on the body of Mother Earth. The same concept is echoed in the Hebrew word hara for 'mountain'. (HA) as the belly of air above the body of Mother Earth. (RA) is the sun that sails through that belly of air (HARA).

RULE SIX; PHONOLOGICAL CORRESPONDEBCE sounds made in the same area of the mouth are often interchangeable.

The (GA) of giri (GARA) and the (HA) of the Hebrew hara are interchangeable.

The greeting to the sun never varied. It was a ritual that could not be overlooked. Because it emerged out of the mountains at dawn, the mountains were considerd to be sacred. The mountains were considered to be the mouths out of which Mother Earth regurgitated the sun or later on, the vulva at the rim, out of which the sun was evicted. The word reGURgitate gives us a clue. You don't vomit out of the mountain unless the mountain is a mouth of birthing on the surFACE of Mother Earth.

In the Bemba creation myth Mother Earth vomited the sun, moon, stars and nine living creatures. She vomited all into being. The fact that nine living creatures are mentioned deals with the solar nine months of geatation that was replacing the ten lunar months associated with mother centrality. Similar process surfaces in a Greek myth as Cronos, the God of time, who vomited 'stones' as a set up for Zeus (SASA). When stones enter the creation myths you know that you are dealing with the role that stones played in becoming stoned and the myth has links with the Kundalini energy.

The familial construct of the mothers and their eunuch (HANAKA) sons officiated over the ancient rites of the rising sun. They also thanked the snake (IS NAKA) for guiding the sun (IS HANA) to be born at dawn.

At the end of the day they performed a similar rite to the sun but it consisted of wailing at the wake in the Western sky and the wall of water into which the sun was swallowed. They lamented over the loss of the suns light. It was not only perilous for them to face the dark night but they wailed for the sun and the great loss that it must have felt, to lose its rays of light.

The loss of the suns rays was likened not only to the loss of hair, as in the Samson story, but to the loss of the male genitalia due to castration. As such, the mothers continued to welcome the sun at dawn. The wailing at the Western wall at the death of the sun and its rays of light was taken over by the eunuch (HANAKA) uncles (HANAKALA)and the emerging priesthood.

As human families expanded, in time there emerged a powerful group of castrated uncles, homosexual males, transvestites who created a powerful priesthood that exists to this day. The Yin Yang of the Chinese tells the same story. Yang (HAYANAGA) contains the (NAGA) of the snake (NAGA, NAKA) as related to the male eunuch (HANAKA) uncles.

The castrated males had their testicles removed and as such they lost their male essence evolving with the female essence of the mother. The homosexual males fused with the female energy before birth emerged with the same result. The transvestites created the theatrical costume based drama that exists in religion to this day.

There were two bases that began to vie for power. One was the eunuch priesthood. The other was the hetertosexual males, the bearded 'gang of brothers', who circled the periphery of the familial herd that had to be defended by the eunuch uncles.

It must have been an immensely successful social construct. Unkind, but deeply rooted in the fabric of prehistory. It has been kept silent and secretive during much of his story of mankind.

CASTRATION

T he word for castration surfaces in many languages of the world. As a symbol of liberation from a violent male hierarchy the word lib means to castrate. It also means that Libra with her balanced scales, deals with liberaty and liberty meant freedom on the level of balance between the two hemispheres of the brain.

In Amharic sank (IS HANAKA) means 'even'. So the castrated first born son as the eunuch (HANAKA) was considered to be balanced, to be 'even'.

In Chinese yange (HAYA NAGA) of the Yin Yang (HAYANAGA) also means castration, with the snake (IS NAKA, NAGA) under the plane of Mother Earth. But more closely, AYA (HAYA) in Perian means light, In Assyrian AYA (HAYA) means dawn, relating it to the sun.

Castrate (KASATARATA) hides in its linguistic overlaps a variety of clues. (KASA, SATA, TARA, RATA).

(KASA) bears a marked resemblance to the female coos (KASA), which the process of castration emulated.

(SATA) surfaces as satya (SATA) in Sanskrit for 'being'.

(TARA) deals with the terrain (TARA-), the body of Mother Earth.

(RATA) deals with the ritual (RATA-) that creates the ratio (RATA) of return (RATA-) back into balance.

In Amharic Mokkata (MAKATA) means to castrate, the cutting (KATA-) done in the service of the mother (MA), the ultimate maker (MAKA-) of smaller (KA) things. Another name for castration in Amharic is sanga (IS HANAGA) also containing with in its linguistic folds the sun (IS HANA) and the snake (IS NAKA,NAGA) and the eunuch (HANAKA/HANAGA) uncle (HANAKALA). It doesn't end there, for castration in Amharic also surfaces in sallaba (IS HALABA). A eunuch is salab (IS HALABA). The BA on the end deals with the 'two in one' concept encoded in the letter B, of the solar (IS HALA-) disc rising and setting, above and below the plane of Mother Earth. Mother Earth, like the eunuch, was also considered the all encompassing androgyny. LABA surfaces in Latin as labios (LABA-) or lips. Were lips used to sever the male genitalia?

Out of Bemba there are two words that define castration; tungula (TANAGALA) and mutungu (MATANAGA). Both contain the snake (IS NAKA, NAGA) in them. Tungula also contains (TANA) which deals with holding with the ten (TANA) fingers. And (GALA) usually deals with the moon in its capacity as the bringer of milk. The sun dealt with red blood. The moon dealt with white milk. Tungulula (TANAGALALA) is the name for 'guide' or 'shower of the way'. With the (LALA) on the end of Tungulula, as they migrated across the savannahs of Africa the 'guide' or 'shower of the way' may have kept them together through singing (IS HANAGA-).

The Enoch (HANAKA) of the Bible seduces women as do the angels. God becomes angry. Flood wipes away Enochs children and he went to heaven with God. Who was Enoch (HANAKA)? How was he related to the castrated eunuchs (HANAKA-) who officiated over the rites of the setting sun? Were the angels (HANAGALA) as Seraphim, echoing the same root as uncle (HANAKALA) part of that ancient construct?

In Sanskrit the name for the 'world' is angi (HANAGA), the sun (IS HANA) above the plane and the snake (IS NAKA, NAGA) below the plane. With the addition of the RA of the sun, the angi of the 'world' in Sanskrit becomes ang(r)y (HANAGARA) in English. Taking it back to the first chacra, the world and anger are defined by hunger (HANAGARA).

The first born son in Amharic is angaffa (HANAGAFA) destined to become a eunuch (HANAKA) and the keeper of the sun-snake ritual as the helper with his five fingers (FA).

In Basque a boys name is inaki (HANAKA). It establishes the same concept. Some linguists have claimed that Basque is not part of the Indo-European group of languages. These ancient words bear witness to the realization that Basque stretches even further back in time to Africa.

In the Epic of Gilgamesh, the prince's friend is Enkidu (HANAKADA). It is the 'gift of' (DA), of (ENKIDU), (HANAKA). He has long arms, is hairy and eats herbs. Sounds like the Neanderthal. He surfaces later in European myth as Lug. There seems to be a link with the eunuch (HANAKA) uncle (HANAKALA) and Enkidu (HANAKADA) in the Epic of Gilgamesh.

Does that mean that the castration of first born sons occurred among the Neanderthal and that they also invented speech? Scientists have recently discovered that the voice box of the Neandethal sat high up in the thoracic cavity and could not make vowel sounds. Did not the original Hebrew written language emerge without vowel sounds? Did not the ancient Jews write from right to left, as if written by the left hand of the mothers?

The whole picture of the Neanderthal has to be dealt with. They lived in the similar area of the world as did the Homo Sapiens for thousands of years. Then they disappeared. Not quite. Some facts we have become aware of.

The Neanderthal brain was larger than the brain of the Homo Sapiens, our violent male ancestor. Not only was it larger but the skull was elongated in the back and the forehead was flatter. The elongated shape and the flat forehead surface in the royal drawings and sculptures on pharaonic Egyptian walls. Ancient mothers all over the world have flattened the foreheads of their children. They were mimicking a group of people that they considered to be smarter and in some way superior. You don't mimick someone who is inferior and dumber.

Were the ancient Levites part of the Neanderthal construct? They were left handed, in Polish "leva" means left hand. They worshipped the Leviathan or serpent associated with the ancient mothers. If they were superior as some aspects of the discovery indicates, then what were their special powers? Could they have been the ones to levitate those ancient massive stones into place?

What did the larger brain of the Neanderthal contain? Was it the balance between the two hemispheres of the brain that made them not only superior but balanced and compassionate? They did care for their wounded and old. Remains have been found of healing limbs that needed care. They buried their dead with flowers assuming that they would be reborn to an afterlife. The Neanderthal believed in reincarnation. Did they come from a much more ancient time? Were they the tattered remains of a civilization that had been destroyed by a catastrophic ice age? Did they survive in those icy European caverns while painting animal pictures on those cave walls of a time when the verdant savannah was their home? As more bones surface, more will become known.

There are further clues. In a cave in Carmel Israel there have been found layers that indicate that the Neanderthal and the Homo Sapiens lived there at the same time. Why wouldn't they have mated? The human creature cannot mate with chimpanzees, not even the Bonobo, but the Neanderthal looks like an easy contestant for rape and cohabitation. It may be why the ancient mothers needed the eunuch sons to protect their families. It may have been that all of this comes out of Neanderthal sensibility. The violent Homo Sapien was to the Neanderthal like the males were to the females, the white race has been to the colored races, like the European settlers were to the indigenous Indians, like the Africaners were to the black natives, like the Australians were to the Aborigines, like tsars were to the serfs, like dictators were to the masses, like contemporary corporations are to the workers. The strong in power swallow the weaker, eat or be eaten of the first chacra. It may be that on the anthropological level, the homo-sapien had a double input. One was through the violent male chimpanzee, then the Home Sapiens and then the ruling class of mankind. The other was the Bonobo, the Neandethal and the compassionate but dwindling members of the human family.

HEBREW (HABARA)

There is a series of linguistic clues that have to be dealt with. They surface with the name of an ancient tribe of Jews. The word is Hebrew (HABARA). Hebe (HABA) is the virgin aspect of Hera, the Greek triad of the mother Goddesses of creation. Not only was Mother Earth the ancient virgin, giving birth to Herself, by Herself, out of Herself, but the sun as the virgin Hebe (HABA) was also considered as having come first, untouched and untainted by reality.

Hebe (HABA) is a derogatory name for Hebrews (HABA-).

In its most ancient manifestation HABA is an ancient name of the sun in its 'two in one' role (BA) of rising and setting. It is the original linguistic source for the concept of habit (HABA-).

The next surprise is the word hybrid (HABARADA) or 'the gift of' (DA) the Hebrew (HABARA). In Polish there is a flower called chaber (HABARA) and it is a batchelors button. Were not the single male eunuchs out of necessity batchelors? The word single (IS HANAGALA) is exactly of the same linguistic construct as uncle (HANAGALA) who as the castrated male was also a batchelor.

The single hooved ungulates (HANAGALA-) join this parade. Split hooves were considered to be the symbol of the devil, echoing the split buttochs on the mother's body out of which life issued forth on the planet. The African country of Senegal (IS HANAGALA) echoes with the same linguistic construct as does Angola (HANAGALA) and Anglia(HANAGALA) (England).

One of the primary linguistically documented prehistoric dispersals around the planet after a major planetary catastrophe and the loss of sunlight for an extended length of time, dealt with the dissemination of the snake as the guide of the sun. The snake, in one form or another, surfaces in all of the mythologies of the world. Therefore the snake must have had its origin out of a single area and that was along the eastern rift of the African continent and then at the Sahara desert.

Due to changes in the monsoon patterns, the verdant Sahara became a sandy wasteland. They were smart enough to know where to find greener pastures. Some journeyed out of the jungles of Angola (HANAGALA). Others went East to the Nile Valley, where there was an annual flood. Others kept trudging to and from Senegal (IS HANAGALA), where they have had their own circles of stone. A whole crowd skipped over the Meditteranean Sea onto the peninsula of Iberia (HABARA). Sounds familiar? Still others kept going North into France, Brittany and England, (old Anglia (HANAGALA). The one thing that these names have in common is that the eunuch (HANAKA) uncle (HANAKALA) was the 'shower of the way', the 'guide' who not only named the new lands but settled there. As far north as Siberia (IS HABARA) bears linquistic links with Hebrew(HABARA).

After one of the great dispersals as far as the British Isles, their new found land as Anglia (HANAGALA) and Scotland, the family of Sinclair (IS HANAKALA-) surfaced with the name of the single eunuch uncle (HANAKALA) and the single hooved herbivore that may have had their ancient roots in Senegal and Angola.

The name Anglia (HANAGALA) came out of the angle (HANAGALA) that the sun was perceived to set in the Western sky as it fell off the edge off the flat surFACE of Mother Earth giving birth to the SHAPE of the number seven which emerged as the number for the concept of 'separation' and death.

It is not an accident that the British Isles were considered to be the end of the world, the ultimate terminus or 'separation' at this specific ancient time. The eunuch uncles wailed with grief as the sun sank (IS HANAKA) down into its waterty wall of death. They named their land of wailing at the Western waters, Wales.

In Spain on the Iberian peninsula, haber (HABARA) means 'to have' and saber (IS HABARA) means 'to know' What was it that the ancient Hebrews 'had' and 'knew' that set them apart to become the chosen?

To hibernate (HABARA-) is to go into a state akin to Nirvi Kalpa Samadhi.

The ancient Greeks in love with their Pantheon of Gods must have felt that the Hebrews, who claimed to have been made in the image of a single God, must have had a lot of nerve and were very arrogant. They attached the word hubris (HABARASA) as one of the outstanding qualities of their strutting neighbors. The 'bris' at the end of hubris gives it away as the barbaric ceremony of circumcision that the Jews practiced. Then in the language of Bemba 'to suck' is onka (HANAKA), the ancient castration ceremony that evolved into the less destructive surgery of circumcision. A special rabbi , (moyil), sucked the blood from the violated penis. In Finnish the word 'to suck', is imed (HAMADA) hiding in its linguistic folds the 'gift of' (DA) (HAMA), or blood.

To remove part of the penis is to abbreviate (HABARA-) it, to make it smaller. When the two very similar, but possibly not identical human groups mated, the mothers may have had ptoblems giving birth. To miscarry is to abort (HABARA-).

As they dispersed due to climactic disasters some went North to the area around Portugal on the Iberian (HABARA-) penincula. The skeletal remains of a boy having both the characteristics of a Neanderthal and the Homo Sapien have been discovered in Portugal.

The concept of hybrid (HABARADA) stretches to cover more bases. The zebra (IS HABARA) with its double pattern of stripes may very well have been thought of as a hybrid (HABARADA), a fusion of both black and white patterns.

There must have been a humongous catastrophic event that sent our ancient ancestors to the far corners of the Earth. Peoples who have the eunuch (HANAKA) name hidden in their linguistic folds have surfaced all over the world. In most cases the consonants carrying the sound and meaning stay relatively constant. The vowels on the other hand carrying the melody have a tendency to shift around with the performer.

Anak (HANAKA) Krakatoa surfaces as the son (IS HANA) of Krakatoa, the mother volcano in Indonesia off the coast of Asia.

Like Beowolf killing the marsh monster and her eunuch son, Anak (HANAKA) surfaces as the son of the ultimate creative source as the volcano on the body of Mother Earth. If surrogate mothers on the planetary plane could have a eunuch son as their protectors, then so could Mother Earth.

In Cambodia Ankor (HANAKA-) Wat, carries in its name the sun (IS HANA) snake (IS NAKA) construct. The massive temples with the heads of snakes pointing upwards to the sun, maintain their linguistic relationship with the ancient eunuch (HANAKA).

Tihuanako (-HANAKA) of Inca (HANAKA) on the South American continent in the country of Peru, is composed of massive stone constructions with sculptured heads and faces of many of the races on the planet. Much of linear history has to be rewritten. Ancient human beings travelled far and wide. They used the wide expanses of water and the specific ley lines as their highways. They were also 'guided' by the ever present and growing in importance, eunuch (HANAKA) uncles (HANAKALA).

Kara Hunge (HANAGA) north of Africa in Armenia, is perhaps more than seventy five hundred years old. Enormous H shaped blocks of stone remain that have been cut precisely the same. Was the ancient knowledge of stone construction and levitation contained in the larger Neanderthal brains?

Henge (HANAGA) is a circle. In England, ANGLIA (HANAGALA) Stone Henge still exists as a circle of stones. Those similar circles of stone also surface in Senegal (IS HANA GALA). When drummers sat inside a circle of stones they created an Alpha state of resonance that left them stoned. It was a ceremony which included the use of the activation of the Kundalini energy as the male ritual of transformation. They considered it as a 'spiritual' experience and it became associated with the emerging male God.

A group of male Hebrews went South to Lemba in South Eastern Africa. They carried an enormous drum with them called Lgoma (LAGAMA) Lugundu (LAGANADA). Some have maintained that the massive drum that they carried on their shoulders may have been the Arc of the Covenant. Since it was the activity of drumming in a closed stone circle that created the Alpha state of transformation in Senegal and Stone Henge, it would make sense. The Lemba people practice some of the ancient Hebrew customs and claim to be descendents of the Jews. In the word Lugundu (LAGANADA) there surfaces (GANADA), with the change of the (GA) to a (KA), you emerge with (KANADA) and establish ancient links with the Kundalini energy and the Goddess Kunda (KANADA) out of India and Canada (KANADA) in North America. Another clue that surfaces is that the drum was not allowed to touch the ground. Why? Because the ground was sacred and belonged to the ancient mothers. Same concept as 'the gurus feet are holy.'

Seneca (IS HANAKA) on the North American continent is the name of American Indians.

Anuket (HANAKATA) Yoni, in Egypt, known as the 'the clasper', the source of the Nile, male and female androgyny, known as 'the one' (HANA).

AN-KI (HANAKA) Sumerian original sisters, representing heaven, or the sun (IS HANA) and Earth with the snake (IS NAKA) working its way through the underground maze. During the turn into male centrality and the emergence of separation myths, things could not go on until heaven and Earth became separated, so that males could create their own sky gods.

Enki (HANAKA) Sumerian 'Brotherhood of the Snake' creates a movement into male centrality.

Ananaki (HANANAKA), Iraq Sumerian 'winged spirits'. The winged serpent had his day in the very 'old world' as part of the emerging angels (HANAGALA). The benevolent eunuch (HANAKA), uncle (HANAKALA) has had the name avuncular attached to him.

Nihongi (-HANAGA) Japanese myth, heaven and Earth not yet separated. The Yin and the Yang (HAYANAGA) not yet divided. They formed a chaotic egg like mass associated with the fecundity of birds. Males fighting for their own place in the sun.

Enigoro (HANAGARA) Iriquois Indians of North America in their creation myth believed that the source of creation was male

twins, the first brothers. One was light (the sun above the surface) the other was dark (the hidden sun below the surface). One
was good the other was bad. A similar myth emerges in Egypt
of the two brothers, the risen sun Osiris and the setting sun Set,
vying for power with male centrality religion as a source of judgment, not transformation, enters the picture.

Also out of Egypt the Ankh (HANAKA) was the self begotten, self produced virgin, who gave birth to the sun (IS HANA).
Mother Earth surfaces as not only a virgin but also as the ultimate androgyny and as the ubiquitous partner of the snake (IS
NAKA) worshipping eunuch (HANAKA).

Angels (HANAGALA) There exists a linguistic bridge between
the eunuch uncles and the angels that sprouted wings and took
to the skies. It exists in Finnish as enkeli (HANAKALA) which
is the name for angel (HANAGALA) and contains within its linguistic structure both the sun (IS HANA), the snake (IS NAKA,
NAGA) and milk (GALA). The Biblical angels (HANAGALA)
were spirits of the sun who were also eunuchs (HANAKA). In
Finnish henki (HANAKA) means 'spirit'.

Ironically it was at the foot, or the ankle (HANAKALA) that
the Kundalini energy entered the human body. Since the solar
wind was guided by the snake then the eunuch uncle surfaces here
also. Achilles had trouble with his heel or ankle (HANAKALA)
where his power resided. When the heel was pierceced and compromised, it led to his downfall.

Tohonga (-HANAGA) Maori medicine man, establishes the
shaman as the sun-snake healer on the far reaches of the Southern
Hemisphere populated more than fifty thousand years ago.

Hank (HANAKA) as the name for the letter H, are the Egyptian
solar and lunar energies intertwined.

S'hen (IS HANA) is the Chinese rising energy forming a double
meander pattern. Both the Egyptian and Chinese Kundalini energies of the sun and moon echo the Ida Pingali of the Tantristas.

Shi Huang Di (IS HANAGA DA) The first Chinese emperor,
created a unified China, born of a virgin, sculptured an empire
under the Chinese Earth with an army of terra cotta soldiers

and hidden in his name is the (DA) the 'gift of' the eunuch (HANAKA).

Anukas (HANAKASA) is the Lithuanian grandchild, if a first born son had been destined to beome a eunuch. Much of primogeniture, and the power of the birst born son, especially in Britain, emerges out of this ancient convoluted concept.

Unktahe (HANAKA-) In Central America, Mexican Indians are the masters of magic, dreams, witchcraft, and as the shamans, manipulators of matter.

In the South Pacific Islands, for the Bugotu natives angat (HANAGA-) are 'entrails'. The sun (IS HANA) guided by the snake (IS NAKA, NAGA) had to pass through the entrails or intestines within the body of Mother Earth to be 'born again' at dawn.

Huna Ku (HANAKA) Maya 'end of the world'. It looks like it deals with some aspect of the sun (IS HANA) and the snake (IS NAKA, NAGA) combo.

BRAT (BARATA)
BROTHER (BARATA-)
BRITAIN (BARATA-)

Brat (BARATA) as brother in Polish, contains two dyads. (BARA) and (RATA). BARA establishes the concept of (B) as 'two in one' and (RA) establishes the sun. RATA is the ratio (RATA) of the circular journey of the sun above and below the body of Mother Earth. So Brat (BARATA) establishes the dependable journey of the sun in a circle round and round the body of Mother Earth. It not only establishes the concept of habit but of predictability which led to sanity (IS HANA-).

The sun snake combination may have created the eunuch but it was the first born son that was saddled with the consequences of becoming the protective uncle and older brother. Avuncular (HAVANAKALARA) which means both uncle and benevolent contains with it so many possibilies that it boggles the mind. It contains the snake (IS NAKA). It also contains (HAVANA) the ancient place and destination for the journey of transformation into death, the heaven (HAVANA), the Avon (HAVANA) as the passage across the great divide of the Atlantic Ocean, based on the even (HAVANA) distribution of life and death and the equal balance of the two hemispheres of the brain. (LARA) deals with left handedness.

In Polish brat (BARATA) means brother (BARATARA), the doer (-er), the helper of the family. Also in Polish bratek (BARATAKA) means 'small brother' as the letter (K) at the end establishes.

RULE EIGHTEEN; HOMOPHONES, puns actoss languages.

A bratek, also in Polish is the name of a flower. That flower surfaces in English as Pansy. Pansy is a derogayory term for a male homosexual. Pansy (PANASA) has the same linguistic structure as penis (PANASA). The small 'he' as the little brother may have been part of the eunuch brotherhood, the abbreviated one.

In Finnish synkaa (IS HANAKA) is 'sinister', or 'somber'. Sinister is one of the names for being left handed. Across linguistic divides in Polish the word synkaa or synek (IS HANAKA) means the 'small son'. The (K) at the end also gives it away.

For the Arawako natives of Columbia, who live isolated in their jungle covered mountain homes come down to the Columbian cities to warn people that they are destroying the sacred body of Mother Earth. They blame the problems on the 'evil younger brother'. Their high priest is called a mamo. The construction of their society has ancient links with Africa. The evil younger brother was the pubescent male that was thrown out of the clan at puberty to create the marauding 'band of brothers' at the periphery. The high priest as mamo (MAMA) sounds like the eunuch, the castrated first born son who became the mimic (MAMA-) of the mother. The Arawako Indians worship the body of Mother Earth, her springs, caves and mountains. They emerge out of their mountain homes to warn humanity that we are killing Mother Earth.

In Basque on the Iberian Peninsula the name for a boy is mutila (MATALA). The verb to mutilate (MATALA-) leaps to mind but it can go in another direction. In Polish the name for a butterfly is motyl (MATALA). In Spanish also on the Iberian Peninsula the name for a butterfly is mariposa, having its links with mara, Mother Earth in her marine aspect as water. Mariposa is also a derogatory name for a male homosexual related to the small brother who was the one with an abbreviated genitalia.

The (MATA) in MATALA deals both with the mouth (MATA) as the killer (MATA) and (TALA) is the tail (TALA). Was the penis considerd a tail along with being another finger, phallus (FALASA) as palec (PALASA), or finger, in Polish? These concepts emerged out of that distant time when male role in paternity was unknown. He may not have been part of the reproductive fringe but in Lithuanian as Burtinin (BARATA-) Sas (SASA) he was known as a 'sorcerer' and 'magician'. The Burtinin Sas establishes him as a brother (BARATA-) brat (BARATA) in Polish. With the (SASA) on the end of his name it establishes him as a seer, one in whom the two hemispheres of the brain were balanced, containing both the energy (SA) of his personal mother and the energy (SA) of Mother Earth.

In France he was known as brut (BARATA) the dry one, the one who could not reproduce. The same moniker surfaces in English as the brute (BARATA), the Enkidu of the Gilgamesh myth and the Lug of the European Neanderthal. As the Finnish henki (HANAKA) he was associated with the sun (IS HANA) snake (IS NAKA) Kundalini combination, as the 'spirit of life'.

During one of the great North African dispersals, some of the brothers who went West to Anglia, the angle of descent for the setting sun renamed it Britain (BARATA-), or the home of the ancient Brat, (BARATA), the brother (BARATA-) of the ever present eunuch uncle.

With that realization I began to understamd the meaning of the British (BARATA-) Union Jack flashing in the darkened landscape of my meditating mind. It represented the eight pointed star that became associated with the Brits (BARA-). As they meditated, they must have experienced the same eight pointed star flashing in their third eye. They created the eight pointed star of the four diagonal lines as a symbol to exemplify their ecstatic experience in a new found land, at the edge of the world, in Anglia (HANAGALA).

Within the folds of the word vibrate (VABARATA) we have the brat (BARATA) connected to the (VA) of the Mother energy. When a shaman enters the trance state he not only vibrates but thrashes around as the Kundalini energy overwhelmes his body.

For the Tibetans the eight points surface in their wheel, a symbol on their flag associating it with the chacras but having more ancient antecedents. The Tibetans were the only country on the planet that while understanding the rush of male violence at puberty, didn't castrate them, didn't create armies and send them off to be killed in war, but put them into monesteries and using many forms of ritual, raised the Kundalini energy within them.

This gave the monks great pleasure and a link with the ecstasy of the birthing mothers. Instead of rushing around the world chasing the golden fleece, the holy grail and all the other male ritual symbols of transformative power, they chanted their way into transformation. It is no wonder that the authoritarian, single focused left hemispheric Chinese rulers, understanding the process of fear defusion and peace, want to get rid of them.

WISH FULFILLMENT

Personal results of the Kunalini experience.

S ince I was a very small child in Poland, I often wondered why men were in charge and why women were so badly treated. It was my mother who was the sensible one. My father was always doing battle with someone, real or imagined. As I grew older, at the age of nine emigrating to the United States, because I was a very pretty child and an even prettier young woman, I became the recipient of much unwanted sexual attention.

I also became aware that women were universally abused and considered second class citizens. It rankeled me that I had to prove that I had a brain along with a female body and good looks. Smarting under a patina of charm, one overriding question plagued me. How did this happen? How did all of this universal injustice against women come into being?

Mothers were at the center of most animal configurations. How did human mothers become peripheral? It wasn't fair. I wanted desperately to know how that context which had been mother centrered in most creatures, shifted to father centrality and his perception of reality which was based on the rational 'ideal' and not necessarily on the experience of the 'real'?

Trying to find the answers to a question that never gave me any peace, I poured over books, did a lot of listening, a lot of talking and arguing, took many courses, got a Batchelors in Philosophy from Hunter College and still no answers seemed to satisfy my questing brain. I desperately wanted to find an answer.

In my life, I experienced that wish fulfillment works on many levels. You have to be very clear what you want. Then you have to ask the universe to get it for you. 'Seek and you shall find, ask and it shall be answered'. It may be a Biblical saying related to God, but it works on a simple pragmatic level.

When I was building my studio in Rockland County, I needed some shutters. Money was never in plentiful supply, so I had to improvise. Garage sales and dumpsters became my friends. In the following weeks after I asked the universe to help me, the mass of shutters that fell into my eager arms was overwhelming. I found them lying by the road side, leaning on deserted fences, for sale at thrift shops and flea markets. One end of day, while a garage sale was wrapping up its remaining treasures, I found dozens of wainscoat shutters that they were too happy to get rid of. Those shutters in time encircled my living room.

There was a process at work here that I had begun to understand. It dealt with a true desire and true clarity. The answers to my need for shutters was easy. Then how did it happen that I got the answrrs to some of the questions that overwhelmed my mind? At the time it seemed that I was riding the horse backwards, but in retrospect all those detours along the way had been filled with answers to my singular quest. Like a magnet I was pulled in the direction that would give me the answers for which I had been so desperstely searching. Along the way I studied Theatre and Communication at Columbia University, which led to a Masters Degree and exposed me to linguistics and phonetics.

It happened in the late sixties. For a friend of mine, Ingrid Weckerle who left on a sabbatical, I embarked on teaching all aspects of English to a class of girls at Hunter College High School. When she came back. My job ended. Then I held a position at the Theatre Arts department of Columbia University. My job at the department ended as rebelling students at odds with the Vietnam war, occupied the library and the Theatre Arts Department lost its funding. My job ended.

Greta Walker helped me to get a job at radio station WRVR under the Riverside Church, initially announcing classical music, then as an on the air interviewer. The station which was losing its funding from the Rockefeller Foundation, switched over to Jazz. Along with Artie Shaw and other talk show hosts, I lost my job.

Then I got a job on cable television interviewing contemporary authors for which I didn't receive any salary. After meeting with Anais Nin, Maya Angelou, and many others, it became too expensive to toodle up to 125th street and Lenox Avenue where the cable station studio was situated. I soon quit.

Then one late summer day, as I was walking up Sixty Eighth Street and Columbus Avenue in New York City, I came across a friend, Aileen Hussung, who was talking to a red haired, white faced little man named David Kitchen, who when he heard my last name, Hammerstein, asked me if I would ever be interested in playing Maria in the 'Sound of Music'. I said Why not. I was forty seven but looked younger. Mary Martin played Maria when she was forty-nine.

I marked time in place collecting unemployment insurance and trying out for auditions and cattle calls. Then one day in the late fall I got a long distance call from El Paso, Texas. It was David Kitchen. He was putting together a Christmas show at the Adobe Horseshoe Dinner Theatre, featuring 'The Sound of Music' and he didn't have a Maria. Would I be interested in playing her? I said yes, the plane tickets arrived and I flew to Texas. After a very successful run, with actual Catholic nuns bringing children across the border from Mexico to see the show and kissing my hands, thinking that I was a real nun, the show ended. I was out of another job.

When I was still doing shows on Broadway, and the Milliken Industrials that had been spin off of the Broadway shows, I had met Valerie Harper. We became fast friends. She had gone to Hollywood and became a celebrity on the Mary Tyler Moore Show, and then became a star in her own right in Rhoda. We stayed in touch and Valerie invited me to come and stay with her husband Dick in Westwood after my show closed in El Paso. This I did and a few days after my arrival I joined Valerie and Dick at an EST seminar. Half way through the seminar I realized what Werner was doing and signed up to go on staff.

In many ways Wertner Erhart was the most intellectually brilliant man that I had ever met. He somehow put together the psychological concepts of the West and the 'spiritual' understanding of the East.

He also had exquisite taste and knew how to entertain the people who worked for him. Periodically he would have communication workshops in San Francisco where all the people whom he employed around the country would assemble and share their experiences. It was there that I became aware of Baba Muktananda, the Dalai Lama, Buckminster Fuller and others. It was an exciting time. We worked sixteen hours a day for what worked out to be about a dollar seventy cents an hour. It didn't matter. We were going to change the world with our newly found 'choice', 'clarity' and 'awareness'. But the EST world was beginning to show some fault lines. Cracks were beginning to show when I learned that 'stats' (statistics) were all that mattered. The EST game was a male game and we became aware that women were playing checkers on a chess board. It was mechanical, end result oriented in a male defined world and lacked human emotion. After a great deal of soul searching, I quit. Werner had exposed us to the manipulations and lies that were stored in language and to the mysteries that were still stored in the Eastern religions. It was becoming apparent to me that the roots of my search existed somewhere in THE WORD which covered both bases; language and religion.

While on staff with EST in Santa Monica, I had rented an apartment first in Westwood and then in Venice and flew back to Rockland County to rent my house and to get my furniture. On the airplane on the seat next to me lay a magazine with a cover that said, Baba Muktananda the guru of the Catskills. Since I had met Baba at one of Werners communication workshops, I decided to take a trip to the Catskills. At the time I was also searching for a conveyance that would take my three thousand pounds of furniture to the West Coast. The moving company eatimates for the move were exhorbitant.

As I circled the driveway in front of the former Jewish Catskill Hotel, that was in the process of becoming an ashram, there in front of the then dilapidated building, stood a big white thirty foot long school bus with a FOR SALE sign in the window. After staying for an intensive, become swatted with a feather by Baba Muktananda and having tears roll down my face, I found that I could have the bus which had all the seats removed and had been a meditation sanctuary for Baba. I realized that it was perfect to trundle my furniture across the country and bought it for two thousand dollars.

After we shook our way actoss the country in the old bus, my furniture and five of Babas disciples, I put an AD into the Movement Newspaper in Los Angeles. The bus couldn't sit on Sunset Boulevard under my window forever and Ralph Graber answered the AD. It was he who introduced me to Joya.

It was with Joya Ma that I had the 'spiritual', some called 'religious' Kundalini explosion in my body. I still wandered around wondering what to do with it, as my life disintegtated into chaos. I lost stuff. Things were stolen. Tenants sold my furniture to pay for the rent. I took more classes, meditated intensively and had the Robert Oppenheimer dream.

Then I began to realize that what I wanted to know came out of a different context. The womens movement was beginning to expose us to a parallel, if neglected reality. It came out of a prehistoric time when there was mother centrality.

I again poured over the books, but a linguistic gap seemed to exist around six thousand years ago. There were intimations of planetary cataclysms, of humanoid and human dispersal, of Africa as the source of humanity, of arguments among linguists about the single source of language.

I began to focus in a different direction. If there were great cataclysmic disperals then what did those ancient people carry with them when they had to leave in a hurry? There were no apparent pot sherds, no fragments from that ancient time. At the time that I was searching only small pieces of bone had been discovered.

Then I had one of my AHA moments. If there had been great cataclysms, earthquakes, and volcanic eruptions then our ancient ancestors had to make a quick exit. They may not have been able to gather up their belongings. They may have had to flee with only their tattoos and the sounds of language that they shared. It was to those ancient sounds of language that I had to turn to, to find a way back into what I began to perceive as humanitys almost hidden mother centered prehistory.

It became a thirty year obsession. Some things I had become aware of while studying linguistics at Columbia University, that the (AH) sound was very important. I began to pour over multiple language dictionaries writing down all the syllables that I could find based on the (Ah) sound; ma, la, ba, ra, ka. I filled a lot of notebooks but the answers eleuded me. Then I thought that repetition might give me the answer; mama, lala, baba, kaka. The emerging dyads began to look familiar. Then I mixed the syllables up; mala, taka, rama, hara. The familiarity expanded. There seemed to be something hidden in those ancient shapes and sounds in those linguistic configurations.

Then I remembered that when I was a very small child in Poland, my Alphabet book contained letters that seemed to walk to the right across the page and looked like they were alive. Where did those capital letters come from? What fed into the creation of their SHAPES? I turned to the letters that had been found in the Middle Eastern alphabets. There were more clues, but something seemed to be missing. There seemed to be a linguistic gap between what I had been uncovering and the contemporary capital letters of our Western Alphabet.

Then one of those magical AHA moments happened again. I had been working on the word human. Who was the ancient human being? The hum in HUMan stopped me. Was the human being the creature that hummed? Why would the creature hum? Then I realized that the primary duty of a mother is to provide not only protection, but safe and edible food for her children. As human mothers commenced to chew and savor their food, the only sound that they could make when their mouth was engaged in masticating the morsels was the sound of humming. With the humming sound the ancient mother indicated to her children, mmm it is good to eat. The shape of the letter and the sound that it came to represent, was the shape of the top lip on the mothers face. The magical letter that was the first to surface was the letter M. It not only stood for the humming sound that emanated from the mouth of the mother, telling her offspring that the food was edible, but also defined her as the Ma. Other letters began to find their way out of that ancient motherly visage.

It was becoming clear to me that most of the capital letters of the Western Alphabet evolved out of the SHAPE of the organs and the SOUNDS that they created, out of the mothers face. That was one of the first indicators. Pushing the cart of heresy uphill, I became aware that original mother centered humanity worshipped the body of Mother Earth. It had been the universal ancient faith that subsequent males called Paganism.

All the processes, qualities and functions that the individual mothers possessed were shared with their overwhelming context, the awesome body of Mother Earth. All mothers were considered to be surrogates in the creation of smaller replicas of themselves. They also shared the evolving SOUNDS that emerged as human communication into expanding words and then even more expanding concepts.

The avalanche of linguistic possibilities began to pour over me. I began to realize that so many of the detours that I took along the way, were only the embroidery of a fabric that was weaving its way through my life.

My left handedness and the forced switch to my right hand forced me to use the linear left hemisphere of my brain. Taking logic as one of my philosophy courses at Hunter College forced me into a single focused way of thinking which my art and music oriented mind resisted. Taking linguistics and phonetics at Columbia University laid a ground work for the words that were beginning to take on a different meaning for me.

One of the first clues surfaced with puns across languages with the dyad hara. In Hebrew the word hara had a double meaning. One dealt with the 'pregnant belly'. The other dealt with 'mountain'. Having come to the United States just before the beginning of the Second World War, I was aware of the Japanese hara-kiri, based on loss of honor and the practice of ritual disembowelment. The Hebrew hara out of Israel and the Japanese hara far in the South Pacific, both dealt with the 'belly'. How was that possible?

Another set of words surfaced about that same time and they were puns within a language. In Polish both rana as 'wound' and rana as 'dawn' meant something. The phrase 'wound of dawn' filtered itself through my mind. One dealt with the 'wound' as a break in a specific body. The other dealt with the body of Mother Earth and the emergence of the sun in the Eastern sky out of the break on Her hoirizontal rim. I knew that I was onto something.

I poured over books on mythology and the trials of ancient heroes. What were they chasing around the world? What were they trying to find? Women didn't seem to be involved in that quest. Then as the mythology, the language, the stuff of my life, the Kundalini experience, began to share the same cubicle in my mind, it took a while but it began to make sense. The answers began to pour over me to such a degree that I had to create rules of discovery to organize those ancient sounds. The ancient words themselves, out of female centrality and human heritage held the main keys to the understanding of my Kundalini experience.

When I embarked on the journey, I never knew where it would take me. It took me into corners of human experience that I never anticipated and never even read about.

Those answers as knowlwdge based on wish fulfillment dealt with the questions that I had been asking about how women became peripheral to the managing of their lives and the life of the planet. There was another side to this adventure and it was more personal.

Joya Ma, through her awesome powers, lifted the sadness from me and erased much of my anguish.Using what Werner had taught us about 'choice' and how 'we created it all' gave me a new perspective on human behavior in a mans business world. I learned how to step back and become less reactive. The peace that I had never experienced began to fill the cells of my body. Through meditation and the control of the breath, I learned to pull up the Kundalini energy within my body and cover myself with ecstatic goosepimples as my mind rose into the state of a stoned silence.

During my eighties I became a relatively cheerful old lady ready to do any battle that was necessary. My free and open spirit became an example for others. I knew that what I had wanted to know, was given to me. Some of the offerings may have been convoluted but ultimately they formed some kind of a mystical pattern. As one of my philosophy professors quoted. I think that he was quoting Benedictus Spinoza.

'We cannot know about infinity with our finite minds'.

The question of wish fulfillment as it works on the individual level must also spread its wings to embrace all of humanity.

Since the size of our brains have been the same for approximately two hundred thousand years and we have yearned to know what happens when we die, someone, somewhere must have come across the answer. I'm not talking about reincarnation, resurrection or even immortality, they all have their roots in religious Father based belief systems and some have been debunked. With the change of balance between the two hemispheres of the brain, and the massive growth of the left hemisphere, we have lost the freedom that may have given us the answer. The search goes on.

THE PERFECT STORM
The STAMPEDE of the NATIVES

G lobal warming, over population, over evolution of the left hemisphere of the human brain due to single focus of linear speech and writing, shift from left handedness of the mothers to the right handedness of the fathers, from the physical body of Mother Earth to the 'hidden' mind of a Father God in the sky is upon us.

The result of the shift into male centrality and the primacy of the left hemisphere of the brain has created a sea of problems. It couldn't have come at a worse time. There is a double whammy that faces the human race. One is the cyclical change in climactic patterns that is bringing us climate change, an obfuscating word for global warming.

The other is the shift into the linear, male dominated left hemisphere of the brain that deals with single linear focus, image housed fear, lack of cooperation, competition, selfishness, greed, more is better, abuse, the primacy of the thrust into power and control, a total lack of responsibility on all levels.

The universal use of carbon based fossil fuels feeds into climatic change and works in lock step with the male dominated governments and Alpha male planetary hierarchy based on narcissistic egomania and a single source of control and power.

There is no future for the planet, the helpless people and animals on it, without a massive change in the brain of the human male. Somehow the balance with the severed right hemisphere of the mothers has to be reactivated. We are living at the time of the perfect storm with; global warming, male greed, the use of fossil fuels, over population due to male need to prove their masculinity, loss of forest cover due to human need for expansion, loss of animal specie due to trophy hunting, poaching and land clearing, keeping women in servitude as brood sows, destruction of the air with carbon dioxide pollution, destruction of the oceans with change in their temperature and salinity, depletion of fish stocks, butchering of helpless animals leading to oceanic manure pollution, manipulation of the genetic code in food for higher profits, cloning, sequestered disease pathogens and nuclear proiferation. The list goes on. It is a horrific abomination for old men to sit on billions of dollars when children all over the world are left to starve. Everything that is native and natural to Mother Earth has been put into a panic stricken flight.

The STAMPEDE of the NATIVES is upon us.

It would be a cardinal sin for the human race to spill over into space. Dare we spread our hunger based anger and violent male based seed into the far reaches of the universe? As a process it deals with the bigger creature eating the smaller creature and so on. The violence inherent in that process should stay contained.

As I rushed headlong into my mature years, the thought that kept rising its insistant head was 'there is something wrong with us as a specie'. I thought that it may have been that we were over-evolved in the area of sensory input. That is why we were so skewered. Then it began to dawn on me that we were not the 'Naked Ape' as Desmond Morris proclaimed. We are the CRAZY APE, bent on our own self destruction. The WHY inherent in that quest was replaced by the HOW of it, as it all rolled out of the planetary cornucopian shell.

The answer to why is always a lie.

It is the HOW of it that sHOWs us the way.

COSMOS (KASAMASA) The cosmos contains in its linguistic folds the (KASA) of the mothers coos (KASA), the (SAMA) as 'she alone' in Polish, and the (SA), as either Her creative 'blood' or the 'spiral spin' of the galaxy. The cosmos is a mother based construct.

ATOM (HATAMA) The atom also contains the (MA) of the Mother at Her tip, top (TA), passing through the belly of space (HA) above Her. It seems like a curious coincidence that the structure of the atom is based on SEVEN orbital shells that spin around the relatively stable nucleus or core. On the first orbital shell there are two electrons; helium and hydrogen, both exist at the sun. It always seemed to me that the electrons carried the male essence of change and the core nucleus was the mother core of stability, as the rutting male circled the female in heat, as the planet circled the blazing sun, so the male electron circled the maternal essence at the center of the atom.

It is on the second orbital shell of eight electrons that the possibility for life on Mother Earth begins. The basic process of survival is that the larger creature eats the smaller creature and so on, EAT AND BE EATEN of the first chacra of the Tantrists. As Mother Earth ATE the sun at twilight, the reflected shape of the suns descent off Her surFACE into the briny deep gave us the number EIGHT (8).

It is on the second orbital shell of eight electrons that the adaptive possibility of life can take place. As the atomic structure adds more spins of electrons within its orbital shell, it only creates the possibility of more convoluted evolutional experiments.

CELL DIVISION On its most basic level, the mother cell splits in half creating two identical daughter cells. They, as maturing mother cells do the same thing. They too split in half. That splitting of the female based cells could go on forever. The expanding universe comes into view. But there was a problem. They were doing their splitting on the body of Mother Earth. Their planetary nest was not stable. Climactic changes occurred. Within their identical splitting there was no room for adaptive change. Change was needed to adapt to the environmental chaos that occurred systematically and periodically on the body of Mother Earth.

The first orbital shell of helium and hydrogen of the sun was not enough to create and to sustain life on the circling planet.

The second orbital shell was needed to create and maintain the process of life that carried with it the eight electrons of adaptive change representing the male essence. The male essence carried by the emerging electrons, no longer singularly at the sun, attached itself to the mother based cell. The mother cell kept dividing into identical daughters but carried within it the possibility of adaptive male change. The letter X (KS) (KASA) of the split buttocks criss crossing at the coos (KASA) also surfaces with the phrase, 'X marks the spot'. What is the 'spot' that is being dealt with? It is the bloody estral spotting at the area of the female buttocks where the criss crossing takes place announcing with its red discharge that could be read by the ever ready male that the female is also ready to become a mother.

The Runic Alphabet surfaces with an angle at the internal top of the letter X. It's as if they are indicating through the use of the symbolic letter X, the addition of the male essence into the female creative mix. The angle looks like an erect penis contained within the letter X which can stand for the ten lunar months of gestation within the mothers body to which the erect penis had been added as a creative source. In Latin the letter X stands for ten.

ESTRUS Females responded to the push into reproduction with the movement into puberty and the flow of blood spotting their flanks. The seasonal, solar based estral flow in most female species changed in the human female. She became responsive not to the seasonal cycles of the sun, but the more closely spaced cycles of the moon. Spots on her flanks no longer announced that she was ready, only that she was menstruating. Confusion and rape followed.

TESTOSTERONE Males carrying the seeds of adaptive change responded to the push into puberty with violence and unrelenting mating. They had two jobs to accomplish since the set up of life on the planet dealt with hierarchy. To mate with the estral females the wishful thinkers had to vanquish the reigning Alpha male. This established the roots of war, violence, and endless confrontations between the males. To keep the females in line they also had to establish a territory which would provide food for the subsequent off spring. This led to another set on confrontations. In the male the violence inherent in male power plays and the corralling of females into territorial harems became established in a single specific area of the brain.

The male, to win his place in the alpha male line up had to TEST his strength. During the time of female centrality when the role of males in paternity was unknown, it was believed that the TESTES were external inTESTINES that somehow had been pushed out of the baby boy at birth. One can only wonder at what the ancient mothers did to make the boy more like a girl with her inTESTINES hidden inside. Mythologies the world over are awash with tales of male mutilation. TESTOSTERONE and its violent sexual antecedents came with the male genetic package dealing with change. Then there is TESTy.

BI-PEDAL LOCOMOTION Many changes occurred along the planets evolutionary way. There were disasters that obliterated most living creatures. Adaptive change made it possible for the remaining remnants of life to change and to adapt.

For humanity the next major evolutionary change was standing up straight, walking on the hind legs, and the freeing of the hands. This led to most of the disastrous dislocations that humanity faces today.

For the male, standing up straight created a major shift from the nose of smelling to the eye of seeing. The female in heat with her ruddy spotted flanks that marked the spot, could not be counted on for receptivity to mating.

Major sexual changes occurred in the female. She no longer birthed babies seasonally or periodically, but year round. Menstrual estral blood on her flanks did not indicate that she was receptive. Confusion filled the human reproductive scene. Rape followed as the ever ready male based on his evolving eye of seeing ignored whether she was receptive or not and mounted her anyway. There was universal sexual violence.

Male role in paternity was unknown.

There was another set of problems for the female due to bi-pedal locomotion. Her upright pelvis did not keep up with the shift into bi-pedalism and stayed relatively narrow making it difficult for her to give birth. She had to labor long and hard and pant like a dog in the last stages of labor to help push the large headed baby out of her body. To that end she also used her free hands in masturbation. It not only helped to deliver the baby but led to the awakening of the Kundalini energy carrying with it the gifts of mysticism and the multiple orgasmic spasms that came to define the birth process for most ancient mothers. This whole process did not leave the baby out of the picture. To push its way out of the birth canal, the fetus had to be born smaller and smaller, less and less finished for the large head to push its way through. It even evolved a way to collapse the head and make it narrower so that it could squeeze through more easily. The baby emerged partially finished and helpless needing total care from the mother.

It also emerged conscious of its helpless condition. The initial human panic deals with the realization that human babies are stuck in a body that is totally helpless. They understand that they are at the mercy of the face that is staring down at them. <u>They begin to lay tracks of habitual behavior through the filter of their helplessness.</u>

Since those tracks remain with them for the rest of their lives as mysterious habits, it begins to make sense how human beings are often locked into infantile behavior patterns.

RAPE Changing and confusing sexual cues from the female led to universal rape. To protect themselves and their vulnerable children mothers huddled in clans following the herbivore herds to the verdant savannahs and castrated their first born sons to act as protectors to their subsequent children. This created a class of eunuchs, the avuncular uncles who cared for and protected the familial clan. They also stood at the sides of the mother hailing and welcoming the sun at dawn and wailing at the Western wall at the suns demise and its descent into the waters of the dark night. Younger sons when they reached puverty were pushed out of the familial herd to act as the peripheral band of brothers, the gangs that harassed the matriarchial clans.

HUMAN SPEECH Very early in human evolution, humans began to separate specific aspects from their ground of being. They bagan to name things. The process began with the mothers sharing with their children aspects of survival. To that end they began to give names to objects which were safe and which ones were dangerous, which could be eaten safely and which ones should be spat out. Thus began the journey of single focused orientation that laid its tracks in the left hemisphere of the brain. It is the hemisphere that attached itself to the mother cell to create the process of change and carried the male essence. As words grew into language, the single focus in the left hemisphere also grew. It began to outstrip the right hemisphere of the brain that still dealt with the struggling mother to daughter essence. Whether it has been the thinning of the corpus collosum in the male brain, or just the actual expansion of neuronic pathways in the left hemisphere of the brain, the answer may bear fruit with future discoveries.
The job of the male is to inseminate the female and to create a baby to carry his seed. To that end males have to fight every other male to corral the females and to fight for territory in order to keep them. The left hemisphere dealing with the male sessence contains in it the most basic aspects of survival in which violence plays a major role. No matter how it plays out the male has to win, he has to become the Alpha male. There are no restrictions in that game. Compassion, love and relationships are not necessary. All that is needed is the single focus of beating the adversary and mounting the females.

RIGHT HANDEDNESS It was not only the naming of things one after another, that set the linear left hemisphere of the brain into a thrust into the future. It was writing itself that shifted from the primacy of the left handed mothers to the primacy of the right handed fathers. To WRITE, became the RIGHT thing to do as the RIGHT hand governed by the left hemisphere of the brain ascended into its powerful contemporary destructive state. There is no sense of responsbility when you are in a linear trajectory, you don't return to the mess that you may have left behind. It is the mothers who being governed by circular cycles, are left with the burden of male sexuality and all are left with the abuse, exploitation and the demolition of Mother Earth.

EUNUCH AVUNCULAR UNCLES As the ancient mothers tried to make all human babies into potential mothers through mutilation, they came to realize that their first born castrated sons could act as protectors to their subsequent growing families. They also realized that their castrated first born sons acquired knowledge, once they discarded their male essence, which opened them up to the gifts of shamanism.

MYSTICISM In the human mother, the roots of the mystical experience lay in the large headed baby pushing its way down and out of the mothers narrow pelvis. To push the large head of the struggling infant the mother not only had to push and strain, but she had to pant like a dog in the last stages of labor. Her high fast panting breath acting like a bellows, fanned the Kundalini energy which had been been lying in wait for just such an experience and it shot up through her body bathing her with a cosmic orgasm. The same experience based are the panting breath surfaces in long distance runners and opera singers.

In the castrated male a similar process could be experienced through mutilation or through the internalization of the female energy before birth, in male homosexuality. Both clutches of males, the castrated first born son and the male homosexual became not only the shamans but as a growing priesthood assisted the mothers dealing with the rising and the setting of the sun. In time they became the contemporary power bases which exist in modern religions to this day. The ancient trials of men running around the world searching for their destiny is a parable of them too obtaining the miracle of the Kundalini breath exploding within them. To that end they not only came up with a variety of rituals but found drugs, spirits, rocking back and forth, twirling, drumming all in the name of experiencing the elusive birthing breath of the mother.

NEANDERTHAL There exists a wrinkle in prehistory that cannot be overlooked. At the time that linear focused language was evolving its way through the left hemisphere of the brain there existed two human creatures on the planet. One was the Homo Sapien to whom we ascribe our evolutionary human prehistory. The other was the Neanderthal who seemed to have disappeared. They lived in similar areas for thousands of years. What did Homo Sapien, our evolutionary ancestors do when they saw anything move. They stalked, killed and ate it.

Ironically the Neanderthal had a larger brain size than the Homo Sapien. But they also had shorter legs and were stockier. They could not outrun the Homo Sapien. Some say that the Neanderthal became extinct. Not so. They live among us today with the gifts of his larger brain poking its way to the surface in openness, compassion, kindness, trance, shamanisn, extra sensory perception, psychic phenomena, prophecy, healing, animal whisperers, that exist in the other area of human experience and that has been so suppressed by our left hemispheric linear, 'rational' brain.

It also may be that it was the Neanderthal, with their larger but balanced brains that laid the foundation for human language and the castration of their first born sons to protect the human family from the marauding Homo Sapien, our violent ancestor.

Human survival is based on the recognition of the gorilla that sits in the center of our brains. It is the curse of the Alpha male and his dark side, his inherent power and control driven violence. We can no longer tippy toe around the reality of it and raise our eyes heavenward seeking for the peace that never comes. There are also women in whom the left hemisphere has become dominant. They exist without compassion and compete as well as men.

To survive the PERFECT STORM of global warming and the overevolution of the left hemisphere of the human brain sequestering male violence, human survival has to be based on the restoration of balance between the two hemispheres of the brain. We now exist in the chaotic epoch of STAMPEDE OF THE NATIVES as all creatures, and Mother Earth Herself have been put into a panic stricken flight.

As I was working on the tail end of STAMPEDE OF THE NATIVES in the spring of 2012, Ma Jaya died. Her loss created an empty space in the fabric of time and space that could never be filled. I had wanted to dedicate the book to her for it was she who blasted the opening in me for the answers to the questions that I had been asking to pour through. She had put me in the direction that the horse was going and gave me a flood of ecstatic goosepimples to accompany me on the journey.

There is an ancient whimsical tale. We stumble around in our lives constantly asking for answers to questions that often don't seem to have an answer. Then somehow the gears of questing mesh with the gears carrying the answer and the AHA moment floods us with goosepimples.To KNOW is to have a physical experience in the NOW. To KNOW is not an an idea in the brain. The brain is fickle. To KNOW is to have an experience of truth in the body. The body never lies. Whenever goosepimples erupt across the skin they carry with them the blessings of truth.

Ancient mothers loved the animals around them. They used them as metaphors and gloried in their specific qualities. The snake, because of its specific shape became a guide of the sun through ths intestines under the skin of Mother Earth. They searched for a creature who would specifically represent the truthful answer to their questions.

When the AHA moment hit them with an ANSWER to a question that dogged their footsteps, erupting on their skins with the goosepimples of truth, they turned to a creature whose skin was covered with goosepimples and was perceived to live in the crucible of truth at all times. The lowly goose spread its wings to embrace the symbolic metaphor that emerged as the physical manifestayion for the eruption of truth across its body as the ANSWER in the NOW. The most salient and specific characteristic of a goose is that it has a permanent eruption of goosepimples across its skin. In Latin the name for the goose is ANSER.

The Kundalini energy is neutral.

It is the mainspring of existence as the solar wind pushing its way up to the surface of Mother Earth to create life. When fear traps it into the three lower chacras of survival, sex and power, it can bring forth humanitys predatory monsters. When it rises to the heart chacra and above, it brings with it an open heart, freedom from illusion and transformation.

In human beings as the life force, it lies coiled at the bottom of the spine. Contemporary human beings can go through their whole lives without tapping into it. Others have it born in them as joy and clairvoyance. While still others like myself around a guru, Ma Jaya Sati Bhagavati, have the Kundalini energy awakened in them. On the wings of ecstasy, doors open to hidden vistas. Questions are answered. Peace replaces chaos. The bifurcated human brain starts to heal and strengthen the bridge between the two hemispheres. God the single parent may be dead, but God the ever patient mother is alive and waiting to be heard. HERESY you might answer. It is only HER SAY. It is the ancient mother within that is knocking at our doors. HER SAY is only partially the life of reason. It is also the hidden life of joy, love and ecstasy. That is what She is trying to share with us. We have to balance the two.We have gone too far into the left hemisphere where ecstasy has no home. Individually we have to RE PAIR ourselves. We have to PAIR up the two sides of the brain to create a balance. We have to let Her back in, or we'll lose our children to drugs and those of us who don't turn to liquor to shut down the unrelenting voice over brain will drown in a sea of DES PAIR.

After Ma Jaya died, I despaired over her loss. The many dreams that peppered my internal landscape came to my aid again. When I was a young immigrant girl trying to find my place in a strange new land, a new guttural language and a new alien culture, I had a series of recurrent dreams. One dealt with being downtown in Manhattan at night on Canal Street looking for the right bus that would take me back home. My car was somewhere around the bus station or across the bridge in Jersey but I wasn't sure where it was. As I stumbled around lost in my despair, I became more and more anguished that I would never find my way home.

The other recurrent dream dealt with my lost pocketbook. In that forever missing pocketbook were my keys, my drivers license, my chacks. My whole identity resided in that lost pocket book. As I woke up I tried to figure out where I had seen it last. There were dreams in which I saw it in a strange house that I couldn't get into. Other times it sat on the front stairs of a church or a theatre.

The dreams gave me clues to my search.

When we came to this country we landed in Hoboken, New Jersey when at the age of nine I first felt the loss of my beloved homeland. Part of my identity remained back in the swaying wheat fields and pine scented forests of Poland. Even my name changed. The new pronounciation didn't seem to have anything to do with me as I cringed behind my school desk. The lost car stranded somewhere in Jersey dealt with the loss of movement, with the loss of freedom, with that expansive sense of belonging to that which I had lost.

Finding the right bus to take me home from Canal Street had other implications. Why Canal Street? As I began to ferret out my alienation, I became aware of the helpless panic stricken birthing experience that we all go through. We are conscious at that primary thrust into an external reality for which we have no frame of reference. Immediately we begin to lay down tracks of perception that become ruts eastablishing the habitual canals of our life. We begin to create what we perceive to be our reality. Tracks, ruts, canals perform the same function. They carry into the future what we perceive to be our reality created through a filter of infantile panic.

I realized that my dream of Canal Street in Manhattan was

telling me that the infantile, panic stricken tracks or canals that I had laid down as my habitual reality had to be re-examined. At the time I had tried all the therapeutic systems that were available to me. None of them worked. It wasn't until at the feet of Ma Jaya Sati Bhagavati that the skein of infantile habit began to unravel.

A few months after Ma died another dream filtered itself through my still questing brain. I was back in Rockland County, walking along the path that led to the jetty that stuck out into the Hudson River in Piermont. It was a path that I often took when I actually lived there. I loved the river and the Palisades that flanked its western side. As I absentmindedly trudged my way forward I saw in the distance, across a very smooth pavement a white police car blocking the road. Closer to me, on my left side there were a few males and they too blocked my journey forward. One large ominous looking man in black with very even features told me that I coudn't pass. I moved my way past him and he didn't seem to stop me. Then I realized that I had left my large brown pocketbook on the left side of the road behind me. As I picked it up the weight of it plunged my arm down. Opening it I saw that a large boulder fully occupied it. The boulder was the size of an extended basketball and was very heavy. I heaved it out and closing my now empty pocketbook I proceeded to the jetty that sat in front of me at the curving cove of the Hudson River.

The dream filled me with the realization that I had become a relatively empty vessel, ie pocketbook. With Mas magical ministrations I had been able to rid myself of the boulder of alienation that I had been carrying all of my life. At the age of eighty three I was given a new lease on my remaining destiny. Now that my pocketbook, ie identity was empty, I had the choice that I could go in any direction. I could even try a new name. Without Ma as my guide it may be a difficult remaining journey, but why not?

It was Ma who during the many Saturday darshans that she shared with us, often proclaimed as she demolished one of us for our thickness that 'she would eat it', but that we would have to 'eat it' ourselves the next time. I often wondered what she meant by that. Then slowly it came to me. The word karma (KARAMA) deals with the accumulated negative debris of our lives. The debris that as habit sabotages our every move. In Polish a similar sounding word karmic (KARAMA-) means 'to be fed'. 'to eat'. Jumping scross the linguistic border in German 'to eat' is 'essen'. How far is that from the Hebraic cult of Essenes that existed at the time of Christ. His teaching dealt with the values that exist in the right hemisphere of the human brain, the values associated with the mothers. It was in the experience of the body that Christ was dealing with. The Gnostics dealt with the Greek 'gnosis' that dealt originally with the 'nose that knows' but linguistically more recently with 'knowledge.' To know is to be in the now. To be in the now is to have an experience of ecstatic truth in the body. To know is not an idea in the mind. The mind is fickle. Christ dealt with the experience in the body, not in the mind. You had to have a Kundalini experience out of the physical body of Mother Earth to know God. You didn't need rabbis, priests or mullahs. That is what Ishwari was trying to tell me. Ma Sati Bhagavati shared with us that we had to 'eat our negativity' out of the German word essen, 'to eat', out of the Essene credo of direct contact exemplified by Enoch (HANAKA), out of Christ's teaching of love thy neighbor. We have to watch the ways our minds work. We have to begin to know ourselves without the sumperimposition of illusion. We have to make our way to the inner vision of the third eye in the sixth chacra. What awaits us there is the magical possibility of ecstasy and joy filled survival.

RULES FOR ORIGINAL SOUND DISCOVERY (ROSD).

These rules can be used in any language, ancient or contemporary.

RULE ONE; MONOGENESIS is the single source of language out of Africa, there are no border lines between languages, as there are no country boundries on a planetary globe.

RULE TWO; Study the SHAPES and SOUNDS of the capital letters of the Western Alphabet and their origin.

RULE THREE; Search for the actual individual consonantial SOUNDS and their source, in both contemporary and ancient languages.

RULE FOUR; Deal with the SOUND of the CONSONANTS, not in the way words are written (phantom-fantom) (know-now).

RULE FIVE; Find names of native phenomena, especially out of Africa (Mara River), (wadi), (Baobab tree), (lew, lion in Polish) (hara-pregnant belly or mountain in Hebrew) (Okovongo River Dalta), oko=eye in Polish.

RULE SIX; PHONOLOGICAL CORRESPONDENCE, look for SOUNDS that replace each other; c-s, s-z, k-g-h, t-d, b-p-v.

RULE SEVEN; ANLAUT, the first SOUND as a consonant often establishes the meaning in a word (m of mother) (1 of lengua= tongue in Latin).

RULE EIGHT; ANASTROPHE, PALENDROME, reflection or inversion, read forwards and backwards in a word or cluster (magma) (Ganga- river India) (rama/mara) (hattah= Persian even).

RULE NINE; Replace the existing vowel SOUNDS with the A(ah) SOUND behind all consonants; hed (HADA)=echo in Hebrew).

RULE TEN; Place the H (huh) SOUND before words beginning with vowels; (erb=herb).

RULE ELEVEN; The letter S standing for' it is', is an EMPHATIC. Remove it from words beginning with the S SOUND (show (IS HOW) (sweat (IS WET) (slime (IS LIME) (skin (IS KIN).

RULE TWELVE; Find A (ah) based single syllables, they are the most ancient SOUND clusters, ma, ka, na, la, ba, ra

RULE THIRTEEN; Find DYADS (double syllables) based on A(ah) SOUND using the same consonant; (baba, mama, dada, kaka, lala).

RULE FOURTEEN; Find DYADS based on A(ah) SOUND=different consonant; mata, rama, casa, lara, naka, hana, lava).

RULE FIFTEEN; Repetition of words;(Hanna hanna Anatolian mother Goddess) (chin chin Chinese kiss).

RULE SIXTEEN; Find OVERLAPPING DYADS (two syllables) future (FATARA) fata and tara, and OVERLAPPING TRYADS (three syllables)= migration (MAGARATA) (maga, gara, rata)

RULE SEVENTEEN; HONONYMS, puns within a language (reign, rain in English), (rana both dawn and wound in Polish).

RULE EIGHTEEN; HOMOPHONES, puns across languages = masika = heavy rain in Swahili (sika-she urinates in Polish).

RULE NINETEEN; Check METAPLASM or transposition of letters in a word; Hebrew (HABARA), Arab (HARABA), saint (IS HANATA), satan (IS HATANA), human (HAMANA), enemy (HANAMA). exit-exi(s)t, word-woi(l)d, orgasm-orga(ni)sm

RULE TWENTY; BUZZ or DEROGATORY words for female body parts and functions (coos, cunt, bitch, slut, tuat, tart, butt, curse, snatch, pudenta, pupa, whore, puta, nookie, clyde, prostitute, kurva). etc

RULE TWENTY- ONE; Names of myths and Goddesses, (Creation myths, Separation myths, Maat, Tara, Lara, Artemis).

RULE TWENTY -TWO; Real creatures that set METAPHORIC examples (lions, elephants, snakes, cats, baboons, bees, ants, butterflies, moths, birds, storks, geese).

RULE TWENTY-THREE; SYMBOLS; Uncover original meanings locked in symbols (Yin Yang, Star of David, Tibetan wheel, cross, swastika, the ankh, 666, bindu).

RULE TWENTY-FOUR; NUMBERS discover their original ancient meanings, (one (HANA) the sun (IS HANA) (seven= shape of the solar fall of the edge) (eight=Mother Earth ate the reflected sun as it descended down into the western waters).

RULE TWENTY-FIVE; vowels

MA JAYA SATI BHAGAVATI AND GANGA PRIYA

ABOUT THE AUTHOR

Barbara Redzisz Hammerstein aka Basia, born in Warsaw, Poland as a small child came to the United States in 1938. She attended Washington Irving High School in New York City graduating as head of the Arista Honor Society with medals for her accomplishments in art and service to the school. While singing in Broadway shows she worked on her Bachelors degree in Philosophy at Hunter College, and subsequently at Columbia University for her Masters degree in Theatre Arts and Communication. She worked as a coat and suit model in the Garment Center and was a Copa Girl at La Copacabana nightclub in New York City.

Her theatrical career spanned the 'Golden Age of the Musical Theatre' in the fifties and early sixties. Some of the shows in which she sang included; 'Top Banana' with Phil Silvers and Jack

Albertson, 'Two's Company' a revue with Bette Davis, 'Can Can' with Gwen Verdon, 'Music Man' with Barbara Cook and Robert Preston and 'Fiorello' with Tom Bosley.

She met and married James Hammerstein, the son of Oscar Hammerstein the Second, had a son, divorced and became the ubiquitous single parent. She recounts that rather incredible story in her first book 'CINDERELLA AFTER THE BALL'.

During her stay in New York, as her son attended the Ethical Culture School, she hosted her own radio show 'Out in the Open' on FM station WRVR which subsequently led to her own spot interviewing authors on early cable Channel C. Her roster of guests included Maya Angelou, Anais Nin and Isaac Asimov among others. During a massive and toxic air inversion in New York City in 1967 she joined Citizens for Clean Air and after organizing an awards fund raising dinner at the Waldorf Astoria Hotel that included Nelson Rockefeller, John Lindsey that was hosted not only by Henry Morgan, but by Joan Rivers. As a result of the success of the dinner in 1968 she was elected Chairman of the Board of Citizens for Clean Air.

Continuing her love of Mother Earth, after moving to Rockland County she not only became an avid gardener but joined a series of environmental organizations becoming a board member of the Rockland County Conservation Association, acquiring a Master Gardeners certificate and organizing the Champion Tree survey, expanding to become the Garden Club of Nyack member and director of the Shade Tree Commission of the Town of Orangetown.

During her stay in California she not only took EST but became a staff member in the organization. Her interest peaked, she set out to explore the 'spiritual' world spending time with Baba Muktenanda, Krishna Murti, the Dalai Lama, Hilda Charlton and Ma Jaya Sati Bhagavati at whose feet and in whose powerful presence she became heir to a Kundalini experience.

Her published books include 'IN SEARCH OF LOST ROOTS' that deals with her search for her lost but not forgotten family in Poland and 'HE BE A RODRENT', dealing with an elusive adversary demolishing her garden.

She is also working on another book that deals with the origins of language and how the SHAPES of the capital letters of the Western Alphabet and the SOUNDS with which they are associated are like a Rosetta stone to our ancient prehistoric mother centered heritage. The book will be called 'THE SHAPE OF SOUND', which she has been researching for the past twenty-five years.

CPSIA information can be obtained at www.ICGtesting.com
Printed in the USA
LVOW13s2027061013

355619LV00002B/10/P